Women's Liberation and the Dialectics of Revolution

Reaching for the Future

Women's Liberation and the Dialectics of Revolution

Reaching for the Future

Raya Dunayevskaya

AAKAR

Women's Liberation and the Dialectics of Revolution
Raya Dunayevskaya

© Raya Dunayevskaya Memorial Foundation
© Aakar Books for South Asia 2015

First Published in India 2015
Reprinted 2019

ISBN 978-93-5002-304-4

Published with the permission from
Raya Dunayevskaya Memorial Foundation.

All rights reserved. No part of this book may be reproduced or transmitted, in any form or by any means, without the prior permission of the publisher.

Published by
AAKAR BOOKS
28 E Pocket IV, Mayur Vihar Phase I
Delhi 110 091, India
www.aakarbooks.com

Printed at
Sapra Brothers, Noida

Table of Contents

Acknowledgments — viii
Preface to Wayne State University Press Edition — ix
Introduction and Overview — 1

Part I. Women, Labor and the Black Dimension — 17
  Chapter 1: The Women's Liberation Movement as Reason and as Revolutionary Force (1969–70) — 19
  Chapter 2: The Miners' Wives (1950) — 29
  Chapter 3: Two Excerpts from an Unpublished Essay (1953) — 31
    I: On Women in the Post-War World, and the Old Radicals — 31
    II: On the Abolitionists and their Relation to the Black Dimension — 35
  Chapter 4: Revolution and Counterrevolution in South Africa (1960) — 39
  Chapter 5: African Women Demand "Freedom Now!" (1962) — 43
  Chapter 6: Women's Liberation, in Fact and in Philosophy (1973) — 45
  Chapter 7: The Black Dimension in Women's Liberation (1975–76) — 49
  Chapter 8: The Trail from Marx's Philosophy of Revolution to Today's Women's Liberation Movements (1983) — 53

Part II. Revolutionaries All — 63
  Chapter 9: Iran: Unfoldment of, and Contradictions in, Revolution (1979) — 65
  Chapter 10: In Memoriam: Natalia Sedova Trotsky Role of Women in Revolution (1962) — 71

Chapter 11:	Women as Thinkers and as Revolutionaries (1975–76)	79
Chapter 12:	Two Contributions by Olga Domanski	91
	I: A Summary of Six Lectures for International Women's Year (1975)	91
	II: Women's Liberation in Search of a Theory: The Summary of a Decade (1980)	101
Chapter 13:	New Passions and New Forces: The Black Dimension, The Anti-Vietnam War Youth, Rank-and-File Labor, Women's Liberation (from *Philosophy and Revolution*, 1973)	111

Part III. Sexism, Politics and Revolution — Japan, Portugal, Poland, China, Latin America, the U.S. — Is There an Organizational Answer? 119

Chapter 14:	The New Left in Japan (1966)	121
Chapter 15:	Will the Revolution in Portugal Advance? (1976)	127
Chapter 16:	The Revolutionary Activity of Polish Women: Report by Polish Feminist in Exile (1982)	135
Chapter 17:	Alienation and Revolution: A Hong Kong Interview (1966)	141
Chapter 18:	Sexism, Politics and Revolution in Post-Mao China	149
	I: Chiang Ch'ing, Hua Kuo-feng in Post-Mao China (1977)	149
	II: China's "Gang of Four" Trial Charade (1981)	154
Chapter 19:	International Women's Year: Where to Now? (1977)	159
Chapter 20:	The Latin American Unfinished Revolutions	163
	I: Excerpts from a "Political-Philosophic Letter" (1978) and Exchange of Correspondence with Silvio Frondizi (1963)	163
	II: Excerpts from Article by Mexican Feminist, Marta Lamas (1979)	172
	III: Exchange with Peruvian Feminists (1981, 1982)	173

Table of Contents

Part IV. The Trail to the 1980s:
  The Missing Link — Philosophy — in the Relationship of Revolution to Organization 175

Section I. Reality and Philosophy 177
  Chapter 21: Radio Interview on the Family, Love Relationships and the New Society (1984) 179
  Chapter 22: The *Grundrisse* and Women's Liberation (1974) 183
  Chapter 23: Marx's "New Humanism" and the Dialectics of Women's Liberation in Primitive and Modern Societies (1983) 189

Section II. The Challenge from Today's Global Crises 205
  Chapter 24: Marx's and Engels' Studies Contrasted: Relationship of Philosophy and Revolution to Women's Liberation (1979) 207
  Chapter 25: Selected Letters on the Process of Writing *Rosa Luxemburg, Women's Liberation, and Marx's Philosophy of Revolution* (1978-81) 227
  Chapter 26: On *Rosa Luxemburg, Women's Liberation, and Marx's Philosophy of Revolution* (1981) 257
  Chapter 27: Answers to Questions Raised During the Marx Centenary Lecture Tour on the Book (1983) 267

Bibliography of Works Cited 273
Index 281

Acknowledgments

I wish to thank Humanities Press — whose late Director, Dr. Simon Silverman, undertook the publication of all four of my major theoretical works — for allowing me to quote so generously from *Marxism and Freedom, Philosophy and Revolution,* and *Rosa Luxemburg, Women's Liberation, and Marx's Philosophy of Revolution* in this new book. I am especially grateful to Judith Camlin for the meticulous care she exercised in her work as production manager, and for her creative suggestions. I must also thank Richard Huett for his helpful commentary, and Michael Flug for having created a rigorous Index to reflect the philosophic categories of this book.

The essays and letters are reproduced here exactly as they were written over the 35 years this book encompasses, including the numbered footnotes that appear at the end of the essays. Any footnotes added now have been placed at the bottom of the page, and noted with an asterisk.

R.D.

Preface to Wayne State University Press Edition

Women's Liberation and the Dialectics of Revolution: Reaching for the Future is the last completed major work of Raya Dunayevskaya, the founder of the philosophy of Marxist-Humanism, the first edition having been published only two years before her sudden death in 1987. In her 1986 review of this work for the *Women's Review of Books*, the poet and theorist Adrienne Rich described Dunayevskaya as one of the longest continuously active woman revolutionaries of the 20th century whose thought and activity "matters to our understanding of what and where the movement for women's liberation has been and might go."

> Hers is not the prose of a disembodied intellectual. She argues; she challenges; she urges on; she expostulates; her essays have the spontaneity of an extemporaneous speech . . . you can hear her thinking aloud. She has a prevailing sense of ideas as flesh and blood, of the individual thinking, limited by her or his individuality yet carrying on a conversation in the world. The thought of the philosopher is a product of what she or he has lived through.

This collection of 35 years of Dunayevskaya's essays on women reveals how she saw the dialectics of revolution worked out in one single dimension—"Woman as Reason and Revolutionary Force"—globally and throughout history. Dunayevskaya considered this book to be an extension of her 1982 study, *Rosa Luxemburg, Women's Liberation, and Marx's Philosophy of Revolution*, the third volume of what came to be known as her "trilogy of revolution," the three philosophic works that represent the most comprehensive development of her body of ideas.

The first work in that trilogy was published in 1958 as *Marxism and Freedom, from 1776 until Today*, a work in which Dunayevskaya both reestablished the American roots of Marxism and returned Marx's philosophy to its original form, which Marx called "a thoroughgoing Naturalism, or Humanism." The second volume in her trilogy was her 1973 *Philosophy and Revolution, from Hegel to Sartre and from Marx to Mao*, which she structured on the need for revolutionary theory to be rooted in the Hegelian dialectic, as Marx's philosophy had been. She stressed especially the dimension most overlooked by revolutionaries—the "Absolute," which contained Hegel's fullest projection of his concept of "absolute negativity." She saw this as what Marx translated as "revolution in permanence." With this as her ground, when she saw a new kind of revolutionary woman emerge out of the Left in the 1970s, refusing to put off for the day "after the revolution" the question of the male chauvinism which the Left had to face "before, during, in, and after the revolution," that new Women's Liberation Movement became an impulse for the third of the trilogy, *Rosa Luxemburg, Women's Liberation, and Marx's Philosophy of Revolution*. It was out of this study that she created her category of "post-Marx Marxism as a pejorative" to describe all those who failed to grasp and recreate the fullness of Marx's new continent of thought.

Together with this "trilogy," the richness of the extensive writings that make up her full body of ideas[1] manifest Dunayevskaya's contention that the only biography that has importance is the "biography of an idea." Dunayevskaya had been born in the Ukraine in 1910 and brought to the U.S. as a child by her family. One can see the idea of Marxist-Humanism "in embryo" from the 1920s when, still a teenager, she became active in the Black movement in the U.S. (The Black dimension remained crucial to her work throughout her life, as the reader will see throughout this book.) The idea of Marxist-Humanism can further be seen "in embryo" through the 1930s when, near the end of that decade, she served as Leon Trotsky's Russian Secretary during his exile in Mexico, breaking with him at the outset of World War II to work out in the 1940s her theory that Russia was a state-capitalist society, but continuing her relationship with Trotsky's wife and comrade, Natalia. (Her "In Memoriam" to Natalia is included in Part II of this work.) The idea "in embryo" can be seen most clearly on the threshold of the birth of Marxist-Humanism in her work with miners and their wives in the coal fields of West Virginia during the 1949–50 first strike against automation. (That story appears in Part I of this book.)

The actual birth of Marxist-Humanism, however, came only in 1953 when Dunayevskaya was searching for a totally new kind of revolt to uproot the growing oppression in both East and West. She achieved a philosophic breakthrough on the meaning of Hegel's "Absolute Idea" for the present era of freedom struggles in seeing it as comprising the unity of both "the movement from practice that is itself a form of theory" and "the movement from theory that is itself a form of philosophy and revolution."[2] In her Introduction and Overview to the 35 years of essays collected here, Dunayevskaya situates the work for today by first pointing to the "movement from practice that is itself a form of theory" as what characterized the whole post-World War II world, and then presenting the new Women's Liberation Movement as a crucial manifestation of just such a movement.

That *Women's Liberation and the Dialectics of Revolution* is even more important to a new generation of feminists in the 1990s than when this book first appeared a decade ago is due to the deepening of the retrogression the Women's Liberation Movement has suffered over this decade—not only from the forces of reaction without, but from the contradictions within the movement. What had first drawn Rich to Dunayevskaya's work and a rethinking of the relationship of Women's Liberation to Marxism was the need to confront those contradictions, in particular the tendencies toward an "inner emigration." ("I'm talking not just about lesbian separatism but about versions of female oppression which neglect both female agency and female diversity," Rich wrote.) Her questioning resonated with the profound philosophic discussion Dunayevskaya initiated, in her Introduction and Overview to this book, of the "private enclaves" that had to be overcome for the Women's Liberation Movement to continue working out the dialectic to full freedom and a world of totally new human relations.

The Black feminist writer and theorist Gloria Joseph has likewise welcomed Dunayevskaya's discussion of the contradictions confronting feminists today. In a sharp critique of all those "leading feminist scholars" who "have excluded working-class women and Black women from their elite 'private enclave,'" what Joseph singled out was Dunayevskaya's powerful discussion of Sojourner Truth's phrase "shortminded," which she invented to criticize the great Black Abolitionist leader, Frederick Douglass, for not including women in the struggle for enfranchisement after the Civil War. What Dunayevskaya saw in Sojourner Truth's phrase, Joseph stressed, was "a concept, one that had become a new language of thought against any who would impose a limitation to freedom." Any who today, she concluded, "put limitations on who the movement is for and (ignore) who remains exploited in the process of others being liberated," is similarly "short-minded."[3]

Dunayevskaya wrote her Introduction and Overview to *Women's Liberation and the Dialectics of Revolution* after she had organized these 32 pieces written over 35 years into four parts, not chronologically but as what could show the various stages of the dialectics of revolution. In the 1980s, in the face of the profound worldwide retrogression which Dunayevskaya called a "Changed World," just as this book was coming off the press, she embarked on yet a new study of the relation of dialectics to organization, which she had tentatively titled "Dialectics of Organization and Philosophy: the 'party' and forms of organization born out of spontaneity."

Dunayevskaya did not live to see the collapse in 1989–91 of the state-capitalism that had called itself Communism in Russia and East Europe, nor the nearly complete collapse of the Left, including the anti-Stalinist Left, that followed those events. Yet her entire body of work speaks profoundly to these events because from the very beginning of her development of Marxist-Humanism Dunayevskaya's life had been devoted to liberating Marx's Marxism from the theoretical and organizational systems attributed to him. Margaret Randall, who has written widely on Cuba and Nicaragua, is among those who were brought to seriously "rethink Marxism" after these events. Her 1992 book, *Gathering Rage: The Failure of 20th Century Revolutions to Develop a Feminist Agenda*, is especially illuminating in finding in Dunayevskaya's work the "point of departure for those of us who seek answers in the multiple intersections of class, race, gender, and sexual orientation." Throughout Dunayevskaya's life and work, Randall stresses, "women's liberation was an unnegotiable concern."

It was Raya Dunayevskaya's unique re-creation of the Hegelian-Marxian dialectic "as new beginning" that allowed her to anticipate, as well, many of the current debates over particularity, difference and multiculturalism long before postmodern theories came to the fore in the late 1980s. By incorporating these issues within a unique dialectical perspective, she not only avoided the relativizing, demobilizing tendencies of postmodernism but was enabled to reach far beyond earlier versions of the dialectic.

The second part of the title of this collection: *Reaching for the Future* is what speaks the most directly to today's new generation of "women's liberationists," whose task it becomes to continue working out the dialectic to full freedom. No one has said it better than Meridel LeSueur, the powerful woman writer from the Midwest, best known for her proletarian writings of the 1930s and her classic history of *North Star Country*, whose work for women's liberation has continued well into her 90s. When she heard of the plans for a new edition of *Women's Liberation and the Dialectics of Revolution* she wrote: "There is a wonderful spirit in this book, and it is badly needed in this time of questioning and new problems." She later framed this thought in one insistent sentence: "We need the new moment, we need it badly."

Olga Domanski, December 1995

Notes

1. This body of ideas is preserved in "The Raya Dunayevskaya Collection: Marxist-Humanism, a Half-Century of its World Development" at the Wayne State University Archives of Labor and Urban Affairs, in Detroit, Mich. It now encompasses over 15,000 pages with additional volumes in preparation.

2. In 1987 Dunayevskaya called two Letters on Hegel's Absolutes she had written on May 12 and May 20, 1953, "The Philosophic Moment of Marxist-Humanism." They were reproduced in 1989 together with her last presentation on "Dialectics of Organization and Philosophy" under the title *The Philosophic Moment of Marxist-Humanism* by News and Letters in Chicago.

3. See Gloria Joseph's letter in the June 1990 issue of *News & Letters*, the Marxist-Humanist journal that has continued since its founding by Dunayevskaya in 1955 as a "unique combination of worker and intellectual."

Introduction and Overview

Women's Liberation and the Dialectics of Revolution: Reaching for the Future
A 35-Year Collection of Essays—Historic, Philosophic, Global

What distinguishes the newness and uniqueness of Women's Liberation in our age is the very nature of our epoch, which signified, at one and the same time, a new stage of production—Automation—*and* a new stage of cognition. The fact that the movement from practice was itself a form of theory was manifested in the Miners' General Strike of 1949-50,[1] during which the miners battling Automation were focusing not on wages but on a totally new question about the *kind* of labor man should do, asking why there was such a big gap between thinking and doing. It was also seen in the new kind of activities on the part of the miners' wives, although, in the immediate post-World War II world, Women's Liberation was only an Idea whose time had come and not yet a recognized Movement.

Our age of Women's Liberation is distinguished from all others—whether that be the ancient pre-capitalist societies when women like the Iroquois had some freedoms greater than women in the technologically advanced industrial societies; or the 19th century when women, although they named one of their papers *The Revolution*,[2] concentrated on the elemental right to the vote; or whether it be the early 20th century when revolutionary women Marxists fought alongside the men against the whole capitalist system but never raised the question of male chauvinism, though they were subjected to its brunt.

The movement from practice that is itself a form of theory which marks our age burst forth fully on June 17, 1953 in East Berlin in the first mass strike ever against Russian totalitarianism. That political strike was directed both against the state-capitalist rulers calling themselves Communist and against increased work-norms (speed-up). Developing under the slogan: "Bread and Freedom," the revolt spread

1

to Poland and to Hungary. There the dissidents dug out from the dusty archives Marx's Humanist Essays on "Alienated Labor," "Private Property and Communism," and his "Critique of the Hegelian Dialectic"—which had been penned when Marx broke with private capitalism as well as with what he called "vulgar communism."

These revolts did not stop in the 1950s and were not only against state-capitalism calling itself Communism. Quite the contrary—the post-World War II world witnessed the birth of national liberation revolts against Western imperialism in Asia, in the Middle East, in Africa. Out of these emerged a whole new Third World.

The essays collected here cover the whole 35-year span since this movement from practice arose. They are not presented here in a chronological order. Rather, each of the four Parts into which the essays have been divided comprises the whole three decades; thus, each includes the totality. Part I, "Women, Labor and the Black Dimension," begins with an article written in 1969, when "Woman as Reason as well as Revolutionary Force" was first created as a category. It ends with a talk given in the Marx Centenary year, 1983, to a Third World Women's Conference, after having returned to a 1950 article on "The Miners' Wives."

I had singled out the wives of the miners on strike as I was reporting from the field because I had felt strongly that *new* forces of revolution were emerging—not only in labor, but in women and youth who were not in production. "Women in the Post-War World and the Old Radicals," an excerpt from an unpublished essay written in 1953, discusses women both in and not in production, while another excerpt from that same essay, "The Abolitionists and Their Relationship to the Black Dimension," focuses on the crucial nature of the Black dimension—crucial because, as far back as slavery days, it was the Black revolt that gave impulse to the creation of a whole new dimension to the American character—the birth of Abolitionism.

Naturally, I do not limit the essays either to the past or to the U.S. It is our age and the whole world that preoccupies me. It was in the 1960s that, in both independent and *apartheid* Africa, women, inspired by the Montgomery Bus Boycott, rose up in new revolts there; it was likewise in the 1960s that Black women helped to shape the new Women's Liberation Movement in the U.S.; and it was in the 1960s that I travelled to both West Europe and West Africa, to Hong Kong (as near as an American could get to China at that time), and to Japan. Some of my writings from these trips are included both in Part I and in Part III.

Each of the Parts that follow "Women, Labor and the Black Dimension"—whether it concerns a concrete organizational form or a seemingly abstract, philosophic category—discloses a passion for a total uprooting of this exploitative, racist, sexist society, stretching from the anti-Vietnam War movement and the beginnings of a New Left within socialism to the present search for a philosophy of revolution to meet the challenge of the ongoing revolutions of our day. Take education and youth. The new Black dimension in the South and its Freedom Schools stimulated so new a look at the educational system in elite universities in the North that the Free Speech Movement was born at Berkeley.

The point is that every one of the historic periods recorded here discloses the existence of both a new revolutionary force and a new consciousness—Reason itself—no matter how different the situation or the country in which the events unravel, and no matter how hidden from history, past or in-the-making, it has remained.

The Southern Black dimension saw women Freedom Riders encountering a most unique organization in Mississippi called "Woman Power Unlimited."[3] As the movement of the '60s developed, the dissatisfaction of the women activists with the male leaders—in the Black revolt and in the anti-Vietnam War movement—led to new tensions within the New Left itself, resulting in the development of Women's Liberation not only as an Idea but as a Movement. Which is why today's Women's Liberation Movement, as I put it in *Rosa Luxemburg, Women's Liberation, and Marx's Philosophy of Revolution*, declared:

> *Don't tell us about discrimination everywhere else; and don't tell us it comes only from class oppression; look at yourselves.*
>
> *Don't tell us that "full" freedom can come only the "day after" the revolution; our questions must be faced the* day before. *Furthermore, words are not sufficient; let's see you* practice *it.*
>
> *None of your "theories" will do.* You will have to learn to hear us. You will have to understand what you hear. It's like learning a new language. You will have to learn that you are not the font of all wisdom—or of revolution. You will have to understand that our bodies belong to us and to no one else—and that includes lovers, husbands, and yes, fathers.
>
> *Our bodies have heads, and they, too, belong to us and us alone. And while we are reclaiming our bodies and our heads, we will also reclaim the night. No one except ourselves, as women, will get our freedom. And for that we need full autonomy.*
>
> *We will not open an escape route for you by pointing to the middle-class nature of Betty Friedan's* The Feminine Mystique. *Outside of the fact that the trivialization of housework is also demeaning to the "well-paid"*

housewife, we haven't seen you involved in the struggle of the domestic workers. Our movement didn't begin with The Feminine Mystique *in 1963. In 1961 we were on the Freedom Ride buses with you, got beat up and thrown in jail, and found that the Black women in Mississippi had organized "Woman Power Unlimited."*

Stop telling us, even through the voices of women (of the old left), how great the German Socialist Women's Movement was. We know how many working women's groups Clara Zetkin organized and that it was a real mass movement. We know how great the circulation of Gleichheit *was, and that we have nothing comparable to it. We demand, nevertheless, to be heard, not only because your implication seems to be that we had better hold our tongues, but because her superiority in organizing women on class lines left hidden many aspects of the "Woman Question," most of all how very deep the uprooting of the old must be. And we also know that none of them, Zetkin and Luxemburg included, had brought out the male chauvinism in the party. They had followed the men in considering that nothing must be done to break up the "unity" of the party by diverting to "strictly personal, strictly feminist" matters rather than be lumped with the bourgeois women.*

Now let us ask you: Is it accidental that the male leaders in the SPD so easily plunged into those malodorous, male-chauvinist remarks when Luxemburg broke with Kautsky and Bebel? And could it be accidental that the male Marxists of this day, with and without female support, first resisted the establishment of an autonomous women's movement and now try very much to narrow it by forever bringing out the priority of the party, the party, the party? There is the rub.

Too many revolutions have soured, so we must start anew on very different ground, beginning right here and now. Under no circumstances will we let you hide your male-chauvinist behavior under the shibboleth "the social revolution comes first." That has always served as excuse for your "leadership," for your continuing to make all decisions, write all leaflets, pamphlets, and tracts, while all we do is crank the mimeo machine.

Finally, the most important thing we must all learn to hear are the voices of the Third World. The real Afro-Asian, Latin American struggles— especially of women—are not heard in the rhetoric at the Tri-Continental Congresses, but in the simple words of people like the Black woman who spelled out what freedom meant to her: "I'm not thoroughly convinced that Black Liberation, the way it's being spelled out, will really and truly mean my liberation. I'm not so sure when it comes time 'to put down my gun' that I won't have a broom shoved in my hands, as so many of my Cuban sisters have."

Part II, "Revolutionaries All," turns to the impact on the East of the first Russian Revolution, 1905–07. In Persia (today's Iran) not only did the impact last through 1911, but it became the reference point for the 1979 Iranian Revolution. I here include excerpts from a Political-

Introduction and Overview

Philosophic Letter I wrote as that revolution unfolded. To this day not only has the role of women in the early Persian Revolution been glossed over, but even when the activity of the women in the Russian Revolution has been recorded (and in his *History of the Russian Revolution* Trotsky did write a moving chapter on the "Five Days" that shook Tsarism in February 1917), it is the courage and not the Reason of the women that stands out. Indeed, Reason is nearly totally denied as Trotsky holds that the women really didn't know what they were doing in the February revolution, and that it was only in November, when the Bolsheviks were pre-dominant, that theory was equal to the practice and that power was won.

The truth is that what initiated the actual overthrow of Tsarism was the action of the women in February. Further, the truth is that in February all the revolutionaries—Bolsheviks, Mensheviks, Social Revolutionaries—were advising against that action on International Women's Day.[4] The women dismissed their advice. Marching during wartime against the Tsar, as well as against their factory conditions, produced such massive, spontaneous support, not only from other working women but from housewives and women on the streets, that it finally impelled the male politicos to join them, and the revolution fully unfolded. That was fact and philosophy—but it didn't make the politicos look at the activity of the women as Reason.

Because I held that masses in motion, women as well as men, are the ones who "make" revolutions, transform reality, I had no need to denigrate the so-called role of women. On the contrary, I singled out when they, and they alone, initiated the actual revolution, as witness the milkmaids in what became the Paris Commune. (See footnote, p. 79) In my "In Memoriam: Natalia Sedova Trotsky," I take up the whole question of "The Role of Women in Revolution."

One of the unique features of our age is that the attitude to the activity and thought of women is different today from what it had been in other ages. In the 1970s, when Women's Liberation had moved from an Idea whose time had come to a Movement, I gave a series of lectures at the University Center for Adult Education of Wayne State University and the University of Michigan in Detroit. These were delivered without any written text, and were summarized by my colleague, Olga Domanski. I include in Part II both that summation and her essay on "Women's Liberation in Search of a Theory: Summary of a Decade."

The Part concludes with excerpts from "New Passions and New Forces," the final chapter of my work, *Philosophy and Revolution: From*

Hegel to Sartre and from Marx to Mao. This final chapter reconnects with the first chapter of that work, where I note: "It was as if Hegel's Absolute Method as a simultaneously subjective-objective mediation had taken on flesh. Both in life and in cognition, 'Subjectivity'—live men and women—tried shaping history via a totally new relationship of practice to theory" (p. 42).

Gramsci expressed that thought most succinctly in his essay, "Problems of Marxism": "The philosophy of praxis is consciousness full of contradictions in which the philosopher himself, understood both individually and as an entire social group, not merely grasps the contradictions, but posits himself as an element of the contradictions and elevates this element to a principle of knowledge and therefore of action."

Part III centers on "Sexism, Politics and Revolution—Japan; Portugal; Poland; China; Latin America; the U.S.—Is There an Organizational Answer?" In grappling with Women's Liberation internationally, I found that, no matter how different the group or what the country, one organizational question seemed to prevail: Could a new organizational form be the answer to woman's never-ending oppression, inequality and alienation, at work, in the home, and in the supposedly neutral cultural field?

Marx's new continent of thought and of revolution, grounded in the concept of "revolution in permanence," may seem unconnected to the organizational question. And the whole question of organization as non-elitist and demanding the practice of new relations between men and women was not connected by the Women's Liberationists to Marx's philosophy of "revolution in permanence" as ground for organization. Nevertheless, for the male Left to see the women's demand for new organizational relations as only a question of small vs. larger organization and of decentralization vs. centralization, to consider this only a desire for being "anarchistic" or for talking of "personal" rather than political matters, rather than seeing in it the question of new beginnings, exposes more than the pragmatism of our age. It discloses not only the male chauvinism inherent in the Left but their insensitivity to the key question of Marx's concept of the dialectics of revolution itself—which Marx made inseparable from his concept of the principles of organization, with his *Critique of the Gotha Program*.

The essence of an organizing Idea (with a capital I)—that is to say, the philosophy of revolution—is that the uprooting needed cannot divide theory from practice nor philosophy from organization.[5] There can be no new society short of abolishing the division of mental and manual labor, thereby creating the conditions needed for the self-development of a whole person.

It isn't only Women's Liberationists or today's Left who do not see a connection between Marx's philosophy of revolution and his view of organization. This has characterized the whole post-Marx Marxist world. The greatest illumination of that is the attitude of the revolutionaries in the Russian Revolution of 1905-07. The phrase, "revolution in permanence," was so much in the air then that Trotsky's analysis of the 1905 St. Petersburg Soviet was dubbed by others "the permanent revolution," and Trotsky accepted it. It was the period when the solidarity of Marxists in Japan and in Russia was firmly established as the Japanese Marxist Sen Katayama shook the hand of the Russian Marxist Plekhanov at the International Congress during the 1904-05 Russo-Japanese War. Why then did "revolution in permanence" not sink in as strategy for revolution as well as ground for organization, even when, by 1917, 1905-07 was seen as having been the "dress rehearsal" for 1917?

Consider, too, the New Left in Japan in our age—specifically the section of Zengakuren, which had broken with the Communist Party because they considered Russia a state-capitalist society and which had gone back to the beginning of Marx's Marxism, when he had named his philosophy a "new Humanism." This group was the first to translate and publish, in Japanese, Marx's 1844 Economic-Philosophic Manuscripts, in which the Man/Woman relationship is so central. Yet not only did they disregard that point in Marx's Essays, but they acted as if the concept of Alienated Labor meant only class relations. Their insensitivity to Marx's concepts of the Man/Woman relationship persisted even after a woman became the first to die during the historic snake-dances that kept Eisenhower from landing in Japan in 1960.

When I got to Japan in 1966, I was shocked to find that not only were there no women in the leadership, but women did not take the floor in the meetings the New Left had sponsored for me. It was that fact among many others which I raised in my critique to them for not creating room for the new force of Women's Liberation. While this debate is not included in the report of my trip to Japan which appears in this Part, I have appended to it the discussion of that question I felt compelled to raise in my talk to WRAP (Women's Radical Action Project) in 1969.

The whole question of objectivity *and presence* of the Women's Liberation Movement is so crucial a mark of our age that, whatever the country, and whether there was a recognized autonomous movement or whether the voices were silent, there is absolutely no doubt that deep opposition to sexism exists.

We can see it in the Portuguese Revolution where, even before the mass revolt against fascism burst forth, a book called *The Three Marias* gave notice of an opposition which the authorities thought they could stifle by imprisoning its three authors. So powerful was the protest pouring forth from the Women's Liberation Movement internationally, that not only did the authors gain their freedom but an autonomous women's movement became integral to the revolution itself. Despite this fact, Isabel do Carmo—who headed the revolutionary group, PRP/BR (Revolutionary Party of the Proletariat/Revolutionary Brigades), which had raised the question of *apartidarismo* (non-partyism) for the first time within the Marxist movement—dismissed the autonomous Women's Liberation Movement as purely petty-bourgeois—that is to say, non-revolutionary. But the women who, during her own imprisonment, came to her defense so impressed her that she said: "I'm beginning to think our whole struggle, the struggle of the Revolutionary People's Party, was really a fight carried on by women."[6] That extreme a declaration when you are talking of the revolution as a whole—and being mindful that the Portuguese Revolution really started in Africa—is as wrong as her previous denial of the WLM; but the objectivity of the women's movement as a new revolutionary force and Reason is undeniable.

Still another form of this newness is seen in Poland. I include here, therefore, a report I received from a young Polish exile on the women who were so crucial in the creation of that new world stage of Polish revolt—*Solidarnosc*.[7] Part III also shows two very different attitudes on the part of two women revolutionaries in China to the relationship of philosophy and revolution. One is the autocrat, Jiang Qing; the other is a Chinese refugee I call Jade, whom I interviewed in Hong Kong on the eve of the Cultural Revolution.[8] At the same time, I critique the attitude of the American feminist, Roxane Witke, who, far from comprehending the *revolutionary* essence of Women's Liberation, has forgiven Jiang nearly all her crimes.

At that point we return to the United States, specifically the International Women's Year Conference in Houston, Texas in 1977. This conference was especially important because it made manifest the existence of the Third World *within* the U.S. It is that which cast a new illumination on the whole question of Latin America. Part III thus ends with "The Latin American Unfinished Revolutions," whether that be the 1960s (and my correspondence with Silvio Frondizi during that decade is included here); or whether it be the 1970s (and I include both my Political-Philosophic Letter after a tour where the relationship of Eritrea and Cuba was raised, and my exchange with the Mexican feminists); or whether it be the 1980s and my dialogue with the Peruvian feminists.

It became clear to me that the question: "Can there be an organizational answer?" could not be answered without dealing with the whole question of philosophy, the missing link not only for the pragmatists but for all of post-Marx Marxism. It is to that question that I turn in the final Part of this collection.

Part IV—"The Trail to the 1980s: The Missing Link—Philosophy—in the Relationship of Revolution to Organization"—attempts to gather together all threads, both those of our age of myriad crises and those of Marx's day, especially the last decade of Marx's life as he reached for the future and left a trail to the 1980s. The first of the Part's two sections—"Reality and Philosophy"—begins with an interview with Katherine Davenport, "On the Family, Love Relationships and the New Society," which was aired on radio station WBAI in New York on International Women's Day, 1984. I consider it significant because there is no doubt that the Women's Liberation Movement has imparted a new intensity and a very different, new direction to an old question.

Today's reality—the totality of the crises, economic and political, national and international—confront us with so terrifying a possibility of a nuclear holocaust and create so total an impasse that all too many are looking for an escape, which has reduced philosophy to a religion and the homilies of the family. It was that type of reductionism that Marx attacked when he threw down the gauntlet to bourgeois society with his *Communist Manifesto*:

> On what foundation is the present family, the bourgeois family, based? On capital, on private gain. In its completely developed form this family exists only among the bourgeoisie. But this state of things finds its complement in the practical absence of the family among the proletarians, and in public prostitution. The bourgeois family will vanish as a matter of course when its complement vanishes, and both will vanish with the vanishing of capital...
>
> The bourgeois claptrap about the family and education, about the hallowed co-relation of parent and child, becomes all the more disgusting, the more, by the action of modern industry, all family ties among the proletarians are torn asunder, and their children transformed into simply articles of commerce and instruments of labor.

The second essay in this section was my response to a challenge to deliver, as a single lecture, an analysis of "The *Grundrisse* and Women's Liberation." This 1974 lecture was transcribed and published that year in the *Detroit Women's Press*. I accepted the challenge because Women's Liberation is an illumination of Marx's vision of human development which he articulated as "an absolute movement of becoming" in the *Grundrisse*. In truth, from his very first break with capitalist society in 1843, when he wrote his Economic-Philosophic Manuscripts and declared labor to be the universal class, Marx extended the concept of Alienation to the Man/Woman relationship and to all life under capitalism. This is why he concluded that the system needed to be totally uprooted—that is to say, needed nothing short of a "revolution in permanence." Clearly, that little word, dialectic, which comprised a critique of "all that is"—that is, the "negation of the negation"— opened a whole new continent of thought and of revolution.

Thus, his 1843-44 Humanist Essays did not stop at calling for the overthrow of the system. Instead, he once more articulated the dialectics of revolution, the "revolution in permanence," in his concept of historic transcendence even after communism had been achieved. "But communism, as such, is not the goal of human development, the form of human society," he wrote in "Private Property and Communism." And he rearticulated it in his "Critique of the Hegelian Dialectic" this way: ". . . communism is humanism mediated by the transcendence of private property. Only by the transcendence of this mediation . . . does there arise *positive* Humanism, beginning from itself."

This is what he expressed in 1857-58 in his manuscripts on "Economics" (which we know as the *Grundrisse*[9]) as "the absolute movement of becoming." In a word, far from being all on economics and a departure from philosophy, these manuscripts proved all over again that Marx's new encounter with Hegel's *Logic* and his acceptance of "absolute movement of becoming" was a deepening of his transformation of the Hegelian dialectic from a revolution *in philosophy* into a philosophy *of revolution*.

When, in that 1857 *Grundrisse*, Marx first projected the Asiatic Mode of Production as so fundamental a path of human development that he added it as a fourth form to the three forms he had previously identified—slavery, feudalism, capitalism—he was keeping his mind's eye on the possible future pathways to a new society while studying the historic form of human development. Indeed, he never diverted from that view of "absolute movement of becoming." To make sure that his fundamental fourth form would not be glossed over just because he decided not to publish those manuscripts on "Economics," he included the concept in the Preface to his 1859 *Critique of Political Economy*. To this day, that paragraph remains the most oft-quoted definition of Historical Materialism.

The crucial decade of the 1970s—when for the first time there was finally an opportunity to view Marx's oeuvres *as a totality*, with the publication of his *Ethnological Notebooks*, his final major writings—was the decade when Women's Liberation had moved from an Idea whose time had come to a Movement. What the *Ethnological Notebooks* revealed was how radically different Marx's views were on the dialectics of Women's Liberation from those of Engels' *Origin of the Family, Private Property and the State*, which Engels had published as a "bequest" from Marx. While the third essay in this section concentrates on the "Dialectics of Women's Liberation in Primitive and Modern Societies," the final section concentrates on the *Ethnological Notebooks* as a challenge to non-Marxists as well as to all post-Marx Marxists.

What prevails in that final section on "The Challenge from Today's Global Crises" is the need to overcome this stifling nuclear reality; indeed, it motivated the entire collection. The "why" of so many aborted revolutions has led dissidents, even in this pragmatic land, to search for the missing link of philosophy to revolution as well as to new forms of organization. Thus, today's Women's Liberationists began their discussion of dialectics and forms of organization through a criticism of the male Left. I had been feeling that the whole post-World War II generation had been raising totally new questions ever since the end of that war had solved none of the myriad crises brought on by the Depression and the rise of fascism which had led to the war.

Put another way, new forces of revolution were challenging the theoreticians to come up with nothing short of a new form of cognition, a new way of life. Instead, they were being saddled with new political tyrannies, new forms of mass destruction, a new stage of production, and a total way of nuclear terror and death.

The first essay in this final section on the "Relationship of Philosophy to Revolution," which contrasts Marx's and Engels's studies, had originally been conceived as the first chapter in a new work I was projecting on Women's Liberation. I intended to deal, on the one hand, with new forms of organization, and, on the other, to critique Women's Liberationists for disregarding Rosa Luxemburg, the great woman revolutionary from whom we today could learn a great deal on the dialectics of revolution and the spontaneity of the masses which involved a new approach to organization. In the process of my research,

I found that Marx's heretofore unknown *Ethnological Notebooks* disclosed a deep gulf between Marx and his closest collaborator, Engels, whose unilinear view has nothing in common with Marx's multilinear view of human development. All too many of today's Women's Liberationists have rejected "Marxism" as if Engels' *Origin of the Family* was Marx's view, without ever digging into *Marx's* Marxism. I felt this to be a challenge to all post-Marx Marxists as well as to non-Marxists. My analysis of Marx's *Ethnological Notebooks*, appearing here, was the first draft chapter written for *Rosa Luxemburg, Women's Liberation, and Marx's Philosophy of Revolution*.

Because this analysis has proved to be the most controversial part of that book, it is necessary to stress the process by which Marx came to his *Ethnological Notebooks*. Post-Marx Marxists have treated Marx's Marxism either as a dogma or as a mere description of his age with no ramifications for ours. None of the conclusions that Marx drew, however, no matter how well-founded, seriously researched, or profoundly projected, were ever stated as a *given* conclusion, never to be reviewed—as is obvious from his letter answering the Populist critic, Mikhailovsky, on that most fundamental principle of the accumulation of capital, which climaxes Marx's description of the "law of motion of capitalism" as leading to its doom. Marx denied that this description of what held true for Western Europe had been analyzed as a Universal. He insisted that, indeed, technologically backward lands (such as Russia) could follow a different path, and even have the revolution ahead of the West. Nor was this something written only in a letter to an editor, that was never sent. He developed it also in four long unpublished letters to Vera Zasulitch.

In those letters he cites the fact that "an American writer" who was no revolutionary or historical materialist (he was referring to Lewis Henry Morgan) had written a most exciting book which disclosed all sorts of new findings about pre-capitalist society, the Iroquois especially. He was at that time working on what we now know as the *Ethnological Notebooks*—and Morgan's *Ancient Society* was the central point, but Marx's notes included a great many other anthropological studies, by Maine, Lubbock, and others. Clearly, it was those studies, when set in the context of his philosophy of revolution and human development, that led to the conclusion that revolution could come first in a backward land, *provided* the historic conditions were ripe and the revolution related itself to the rest of the world. Indeed, this was proclaimed openly in nothing less than the 1882 Introduction to the Russian edition of the *Communist Manifesto*.

In this author's mind an entirely different element relates to the question of the attitude the author has to what others think of the problem that is preoccupying her. It is not only academics or like-minded colleagues, in my mind, who should be brought into the process of working out the ideas of a book. Rather, ideas have to be submitted to the scrutiny of workers, intellectuals, women, youth—that is to say, the forces of revolution—both as one develops a book and after it reaches completion. This was done with every one of my major theoretical works. The final section of the last Part of this collection presents letters written during the process of writing *Rosa Luxemburg, Women's Liberation, and Marx's Philosophy of Revolution*. It likewise presents the first lecture given (on Dec. 13, 1981) when the book was completed.

After the book was published I embarked on a national lecture tour during the Marx centenary year, 1983, and there was confronted with new questions on the relationship of philosophy to reality and to revolution. The final selection included here consists of my answers to the new questions posed. What seemed to me to be crucial was the missing link of philosophy in relationship to revolutions both in theory and in fact. That is what is meant by the dialectics of revolution. Indeed, it appeared to me that this is what is missing in all those who have been writing on the new moments in Marx's last decade *not* as a continuity of Marx's whole philosophy of revolution, but as if they were a break in Marx's development. It is no accident that they do not relate any of the "new moments" which they discuss to the new forces of revolution, especially Women's Liberation.

It is imperative to look anew at other historic turning points and in that way to grasp how the practicality of philosophy can be seen when objective crises are so total as to bring on actual world wars. It was precisely at such critical points that two such disparate historic figures as Sartre, the professional philosopher, and Lenin, the revolutionary practitioner, each felt the need to turn to philosophy—Lenin at the outbreak of World War I and Sartre on the eve of World War II.

In his *What is Literature?* Sartre wrote: "Metaphysics is not a sterile discussion about abstract notions which have nothing to do with experience. It is a living effort to embrace from within the human condition in its totality."[10] Unfortunately, when it came to *practice*, Sartre tailended the Communist Party instead of adhering to Marx's definition that: "The practice of philosophy is itself theoretical. It is a critique that measures the Individual existence by the Essence, the particular by the Idea."[11]

When Lenin was faced with the extremes of the Second International's betrayal and collapse at the outbreak of World War I and turned to Hegel's *Science of Logic*, he hailed that dialectic work of abstract notions for including a chapter on "Life"—and including it in the final part of the Doctrine of Notion at that. Lenin wrote, in his *Philosophic Notebooks*: "The idea of including L i f e in logic is comprehensible—and brilliant—from the standpoint of the process of the reflection of the objective world in the (at first individual) consciousness of man and of the testing of this consciousness (reflection) through practice..." (Lenin's *Collected Works*, Vol. 38, p. 202).

Lenin praised the whole section of the *Science of Logic* on "The Idea" as containing "the very best of the dialectic," and dug deeper into the chapter on "Life," writing down: "Schmerz ist 'eine wirkliche Existenz' des Widerspruchs* in the living individual." Lenin stops to note especially what Hegel emphasized on "*process*," "kind," "intersubjectivity," "introreflection," and "totality" as the chapter on "Life" was moving to "transcendence" and "transition." Hegel ended Chapter I and introduced Chapter II on "The Idea of Cognition": "The Idea, which ... transcended its particularity which constituted the living generations ..." (*Science of Logic*, p. 415).

Lenin spent even more time on the chapter, "The Idea of Cognition," where he singled out: "Man's cognition not only reflects the objective world, but creates it," calling attention to the fact that Hegel himself, instead of proceeding with the word, "Notion," suddenly used the word, "Subject." Lenin finally "translated" the whole concept of the "actuality" of oneself and the "*non-actuality*" of the world" as: "i.e. the world does not satisfy man and man decides to change it by his activity."

No one, of course, was more creative than Marx, who had discovered a whole new continent of thought as he grappled with his "Critique of the Hegelian Dialectic," where, as we have showed, he transformed Hegel's revolution *in philosophy* into a philosophy *of revolution*. The task is to unchain the dialectic.

This, this precisely, stamps the uniqueness, the originality, the continuity in Marx's development of the dialectic. We can see his Promethean vision in the last decade of his life as he projected the possibility of a social revolution coming first in a technologically underdeveloped country before the so-called advanced economies. This was the same period when he also wrote the *Critique of the Gotha Program*—a sharp critique of the organizational form of a proposed new Party, the proposed merger of those who considered themselves

*Pain is 'actual existence' of contradiction

Marxists with the Lassalleans. That *Critique* was a theoretical differentiation between Marxism and Lassalleanism, which he extended also against the practical points they would engage in. Marx dismissed these five points of action as nothing but "bourgeois twaddle."

As will be evident throughout this book (which covers 35 years of writings on a single subject, Women's Liberation) the sharp differentiation between Marx's Marxism and post-Marx Marxism is not limited to that one question. A deep gulf existed between Marx's multilinear view of all human development and Engels' unilinear view. Which is why this single subject—Women's Liberation, whether viewed as it relates to philosophy or to form of organization—is inseparable from the dialectics of revolution. Both of these questions were raised anew during my 1983 lecture tour. Specifically, I was questioned about what appeared contradictory to some in my audience, when I had written (on p. 109 of *Rosa Luxemburg, Women's Liberation, and Marx's Philosophy of Revolution*) that social revolution comes first "*provided* it is not—indeed revolutions cannot be—without Women's Liberation or behind women's backs, or by using them only as helpmates." I therefore elaborated that concept as follows:

> History proves a very different truth, whether we look at February 1917, where the women were the ones who *initiated* the revolution; whether we turn further back to the Persian Revolution of 1906–11, where the women created the very first women's soviet; or whether we look to our own age in the 1970s in Portugal, where Isabel do Carmo raised the totally new concept of *apartidarismo*. It is precisely because women's liberationists are both revolutionary force *and* Reason that they are crucial. If we are to achieve success in the new revolutions, we have to see that the uprooting of the old is total from the start.

The Absolute Method allows for no "private enclaves"—i.e., exceptions to the principle of Marx's Dialectics, whether on the theoretical or the organizational questions. As Marx insisted from the very beginning, nothing can be a private enclave: neither any part of life, nor organization, nor even science. In his Economic-Philosophic Manuscripts he proclaimed that: "To have one basis for life and another for science is *a priori* a lie."

The truth of this statement has never been more immediate and urgent than in our nuclear world, over which hangs nothing short of the threat to the very survival of civilization as we have known it.

— Raya Dunayevskaya
Chicago, Illinois
September 17, 1984

NOTES

1. See especially the listing of my philosophic correspondence during this period, which appears as an Appendix to *A 1980s View: The Coal Miners' General Strike of 1949-50 and the Birth of Marxist-Humanism*, by Andy Phillips and Raya Dunayevskaya (Chicago: News & Letters, 1984), where the entire struggle has been recorded.
2. *The Revolution* was the name of the journal issued by Susan B. Anthony and Elizabeth Cady Stanton, the motto of which read: "Men, their rights and nothing more; women, their rights and nothing less."
3. On their return North, these Freedom Riders recorded this experience in *Freedom Riders Speak for Themselves* (Detroit: News & Letters, 1961).
4. March 8 was February 25 in the old Russian calendar.
5. I deal with the relationship of philosophy to organization as Marx developed it in his *Critique of the Gotha Program* in detail in Chapter XI, "The Philosopher of Permanent Revolution Creates New Ground for Organization," of *Rosa Luxemburg, Women's Liberation and Marx's Philosophy of Revolution* (New Jersey: Humanities Press, 1982).
6. See *New York Times*, Feb. 24, 1984.
7. For the dissident Russian women's movement, see *Women and Russia*, edited by Tatyana Mamonova (Boston: Beacon Press, 1984).
8. My analysis of this movement, when it arose, can be found in my work, *Philosophy and Revolution* (New York: Dell, 1973; New Jersey: Humanities Press, 1982), pp. 176-9. For a more recent opposition, see *The Revolution is Dead, Long Live the Revolution* (Hong Kong: The 70s, 1976), which includes an important essay by the woman theoretician, Yu Shuet.
9. *Grundrisse* was the title designated by the Marx-Engels Institute in Moscow when they finally got around to publishing these 1857-58 manuscripts in 1939-41. Marx had simply titled them "Economics."
10. *What is Literature?* trans. by Bernard Frechtman (New York: Washington Square, 1966), p. 153.
11. See Marx-Engels, *Collected Works*, vol. 1 (New York: International Pub., 1975), p. 85.

PART I
Women, Labor and the Black Dimension

CHAPTER 1

The Women's Liberation Movement as Reason and as Revolutionary Force*

Deep in the Siberian mine,
Keep your patience proud;
The bitter toil shall not be lost,
The rebel thought unbowed . . .
The heavy-hanging chains will fall,
The walls will crumble at a word;
And Freedom greet you in the light,
And brothers give you back the sword.

As unrelated as this poem by Pushkin about the Decembrist revolt of 1825 may seem to be to the Women's Liberation Movement of our day, the very fact that, in 1953, the political prisoners in the forced labor camps in Vorkuta used it as their freedom song illustrates both the universality and the individuality of liberation struggles. Clearly, the poem celebrated not only a fight against Tsarism. What the 20th century Freedom Fighters aspired to, in fighting also against Communism, was not a return to the old, but a reaching out for a totally new dimension.

It was this aspiration, not only for a particular type of freedom, but for total liberation, that enunciated a new stage of the consciousness of freedom. It is in this sense that the American woman has suddenly

---

*This lecture, given to the Ethical Culture Society, Philadelphia, April 26, 1970, incorporated points made in earlier talks with the Women's Radical Action Project (WRAP), University of Chicago, April 1969, and with a group from the Women's Liberation Coalition of Michigan, Detroit, July 1970. The essay was translated into Farsi by Iranian feminists and issued, together with other writings of Raya Dunayevskaya on Women's Liberation, for International Women's Day, March 8, 1980. It was translated into Spanish and issued in the pamphlet *La Mujer como razón y fuerza revolucionaria* by the Peruvian feminist group ALIMUPER, March 1982.

begun speaking of her enslavement. All the talk about the American women as "the freest in the world" has not, and will not, stop their feeling chained, their concept of liberation as something a great deal more than simply not being a chattel slave, and having the vote. Their point is that *so long as* they are *objects* (even where that means an object of love), they are not truly free. They refuse to stand up and shout "hurrah" for such type of "love." They demand to be whole human beings.

Ever since the myth of Eve giving Adam the apple was created, women have been presented as devils or as angels, but definitely not as human beings. Only one philosopher, Hegel, related the myth not to sin, but to knowledge. No doubt the concept of knowledge is an improvement on the concept of sin, but that hardly takes issue with why woman is blamed for the expulsion from Paradise. In literature, we seem to have been found guilty ever since. The portrayal of women in our day as either dumb blondes or devils keeps up to date the male chauvinist myth.

Let us begin with Greece, not only as the birthplace of Western Civilization, but the birthplace of the tragic drama. Take the *Oresteia*, the greatest trilogy in dramatic literature. Until fairly recently, I seem to have seen nothing male chauvinistic about Athena's speech. I am sure I am not the only one. The pursuit of the furies, after Orestes murdered his mother for having murdered his father, is so unrelenting that the audience is happy when Athena pronounces him not guilty:

> *So for Orestes shall this vote be cast.*
> *No mother gave me birth, and in all things*
> *Save marriage I, my father's child indeed,*
> *With all my heart commend the masculine.*
> *Wherefore I shall not hold of higher worth*
> *A woman who was killed because she killed*
> *Her wedded lord and master of her home.*
> *Upon an equal vote Orestes wins.*

LITERATURE AND HISTORY: THE BLACK DIMENSION

All history being contemporary history, we cannot help but look at the same drama with eyes of today, with the consciousness of today's Women's Liberation Movement. This time, when I watched the drama—in Ypsilanti where we tried to recreate the Greek tragedies and comedies in a (more or less) genuine Greek theatre with a Greek director and Judith Anderson as Clytemnestra—I was saying to myself: Well, what do you know, here is Athena telling us that since she sprang full-grown from the forehead of Zeus, it seems that a mother is nothing but a receptacle for the seed of the man and that, therefore, Orestes has not really committed the greatest crime on earth in murdering his mother. Though the words are spoken by a woman, it is a typically male chauvinistic speech. What I am trying to say is that this awareness is what the Women's Liberation Movement of today has brought to today's feminism.

Whether we are talking of the women characters in Greek tragedy—Clytemnestra, Medea, Electra—or whether we look at Shakespeare's Lady Macbeth or that horrible creature in *King Lear*—Goneril—or we come down to the 20th century, be it Eugene O'Neill's *Mourning Becomes Electra* or Jean-Paul Sartre's *The Flies*, dramatists seem to be doing nothing but updating these characters. The whole point is that literature, even at its greatest, reflects the male-dominated society under which we live, which, in turn, affects all of us, women included. We will not escape male chauvinistic speeches coming out of our mouths until we tear this alienated society up by its roots.

As against the myths of either prehistory or literature, the history of the struggles of women for freedom show women in a very different light. This is especially clear in the U.S., where the Black dimension became a catalyst for liberation long before the Women's Liberation Movement of today. It arose during the Abolitionist movement, when the Sojourner Truths and the Harriet Tubmans were speakers, "generals," leaders, while the white women were, still, mainly the ones who arranged the picnics, raised the money, and in every way were subordinate to the male Abolitionist leaders. When the white middle-class women saw the Black women being and acting as leaders of the Underground Railway, the white women decided to be more than handmaidens. The suffragist movement arose out of the Abolitionist Movement.

For some peculiar reason, at their very first convention in 1848, the women still felt a man should function as chairman of their meetings. They soon found out that, though the Abolitionist Movement was by far the most advanced movement of the time, it nevertheless held many prejudices on the question of women. The men Abolitionists, who were giving their lives to end slavery, nevertheless refused to chair the meeting of the women. The only one who consented was Frederick Douglass. (In fairness to the founder of Abolitionism, it should be said that when the Anti-Slavery Conference in England refused to seat the American women delegates, forcing them to sit in the balcony, William Lloyd Garrison, who was supposed to give the main speech to the Conference, refused to do so. He sat with the women in the gallery, as a protest.)

So long as they were related to both the Black and proletarian women, the suffragists, even though they were middle-class women, went very far in fighting for more than just rights for themselves. But after the abolition of slavery, Susan B. Anthony and Lucretia Mott and all the middle-class women who continued the long bitter fight nevertheless showed a narrowing of the struggle along class lines. When they finally did get the vote, it was far removed from what the proletarian women needed and were doing. This separation along class lines has not stopped, so that today we must face those degrading TV commercials that try to sell us the idea that the hard-fought battle for equality has been met by our right to wear mini-skirts (at least until fashion dictators tell us otherwise) and having "our own" brand of cigarettes!

As against the past, all of the past, including some of the revolutionary past and the women who made it in a man's world, today's Women's Liberation Movement not only refuses to stop short of total freedom, but refuses to wait for "the day after" the revolution to obtain it. On the contrary, today's Women's Liberationist will be part of that historic process of making freedom real for all.

THE NEWNESS OF TODAY'S WOMEN'S LIBERATION MOVEMENT

The uniqueness of the Women's Liberation Movement is seen also in this, that even the women in the revolutionary movement are saying: "We are not waiting for tomorrow to get our freedom. We're beginning the struggle today. We are not leaving it to the men comrades to gain freedom 'for' us. We're struggling for it ourselves. We refuse to subordinate it to another movement; the Women's Liberation Movement itself is a revolutionary force toward total liberation for all. The very emergence of an independent Women's Liberation Movement is proof of the validity of its independent existence. That wasn't created from above; it wasn't built by men, not even by male revolutionaries; it won't fold up so that a political party, as some 'general will,' should be preeminent."

And I should add that, in distinction to my generation whose aim was to be "just like men" (since they seemed to be having all the privileges), the new generation of feminists do not wish to be "just like men." The young women feel that men, too, are alienated beings, and they want to be whole human beings. Having seen revolutions as great as the Russian Revolution go sour, and the Chinese Revolution—or Cuban, for that matter—remain incompleted, they have added to their sense of world revolution that it be not only against the old exploitative system, but aim *for* a totally new society on truly human foundations.

Put differently, they do not consider the relationship of woman to man to be a "private matter" either before or the day of or the day after the revolution. Precisely because it had been dealt with as a private matter, it was easy to play the game of waiting till "the day after." If we are to begin that liberation struggle today—and that's what the women have begun in the past few years—the relationship of man to woman cannot be treated as a private matter, as if it were only a question of husband and wife, or mother and child, or single girl and parents. That is only one more way to make women feel isolated and helpless. Once there is a Women's Liberation Movement, the whole atmosphere of the country changes, so that even where it is a question of establishing personal relations with sweetheart or husband, with father or brother, you don't feel alone any longer, just as you don't feel alone when you fight for the right to abortion.

Collectivity and individuality have become inseparable not merely because after you have had your fight at home, you can come to the Women's Liberation meeting and hear of others' struggles, but because of the heightened consciousness which makes you see, be it man or woman, that he or she "is only individualized through the process of history."[1]

I am sorry to criticize the organization before which I'm speaking—I do appreciate your inviting me to speak on Women's Liberation. But it shocked me to hear that you still use the word "auxiliary"—Women's Auxiliary of the Ethical Culture Society. Women are not "auxiliaries." As you saw, the historical origin of the Women's Liberation Movement, even when it centered around getting the vote, was born in opposition to being mere auxiliaries to the Abolitionist Movement. Today, as we shall see later, it is far, far beyond the political struggles for vote or property rights. When I spoke to the Women's Liberation group at the University of Chicago, they presented me with statistics about how few women are professors, the restrictions on promotions, etc., etc. Women workers are presenting their demands. It is clear that the struggle will not stop until there will be total liberation.

What is involved now is a whole new philosophy. Where Hegel had moved the myth of Adam and Eve from the theology of sin to the sphere of knowledge, Marx looked at history as a development of labor, and, *therefore*, of the need of a totally new way of life, a philosophy of liberation he called the new Humanism. In his early Humanist essays, he kept reiterating that so long as we talk only about different property forms, we will never get to new human relations, least of all the relationship of man to woman. Private property, Marx insisted, has made us so stupid that we think only of possessions. We are constantly substituting a "to have" for a "to be." But the abolition of private property would not, alone, bring about a new society, as the vulgar communists thought; this, Marx insisted, only "negates the personality of man," not to mention the most fundamental of all relations, that of man to woman.

It is this type of totally new relations that many in the Women's Liberation Movement are aspiring to. There are many different varieties of groups, from the so-called grandmother of them all—the National Organization for Women (NOW), which is directed to the professional women—*through* Women's Radical Action Project (WRAP) which was concerned not merely with the status of women in academia but with actual class struggles (especially those that regard women hospital workers and their demand for a nursery for working mothers), *to* the Women's Liberation Coalition of Michigan that retains the decentralized small group nuclei. I am mostly concerned with those in Detroit who have issued the pamphlet *Notes on Women's Liberation: We Speak in Many Voices*—which has Black and white and Chicana, both proletarian and student—who do not separate "culture" from a total philosophy. The many voices include the apolitical as well as the Marxist-Humanist, but the latter are a minority, *deliberately* a minority among the many voices. I would like to read to you two of the pieces by Black women contributors. One, Ethel Dunbar, criticizes the white woman:

> Men have run this world out by organizing it into a hate-society. Today that is why white women can't sit down to discuss with Black women about women's problems. White men have taught them for so long that they are better than Black women, that it keeps coming out all the time. I was at a discussion several weeks ago on the question of women's rights ... where one white woman, an old politico, said she had just left a caucus in her union which had been discussing the problems of women in the shop. The question came up of white women fighting for higher pay, because even Black men were getting higher wages than white women. Being a Black woman, it made me angry to have it put that way, because it sounded as though white women thought they should make *more* than Black men. Black men do hard, hard work. And there is something wrong with that whole way of thinking ... White women have to make sure that they do not let white men mix up their thinking.

The other Black worker was concerned, instead, with the fact that Black women workers "are so busy with other fights around the job and racial discrimination, and they feel these are more important to do first. But really they should all go along together, because they are all in the same vein. I am fighting for someone who is a woman as well as Black; to me it is the same fight. . . . I am divorced and it's hard to be alone. But I have enough to do without taking on any more projects, and men are projects."

To try to deny that men are "projects," to feel so self-conscious about women being "apolitical" (and because of that "backward") that you think preoccupation with male chauvinism is to the detriment of "socialist politics" leads, of necessity, to degrading the very concept of revolutionary socialism to a variety of reformism, "a radical feminism commensurate with the reformists' political sophistication and efficacy."[2] In conclusion, therefore, I wish to turn to a criticism of the "Left," old and new, and to do so from the vantage point of Marx's Humanism.

MARX'S HUMANISM AND TODAY'S MARXISTS

It is not only the young Marx who had demonstrated the decrepit state of capitalism, through both an analysis of the exploitation of labor and of the five senses in the alienated state that exploitative society imposes on them: "In place of all the physical and spiritual senses, there is the sense of possession, which is the alienation of all these senses." Fragmentation of the individual would continue, the mature Marx of the *Grundrisse* states, so long as we do not reunite man as doer and man as thinker. Indeed, insofar as the enslavement of women is concerned, it occurred within *communal* society itself before the institution of slavery. Furthermore, the free, unpaid labor of wife and child continued *after* the abolition of chattel slavery.

Marx's whole point is that nothing, nothing short of a new "thoroughgoing Naturalism or Humanism," that is to say, the self-development of men and women (and, for that matter, children, for we all live and suffer from living in what Marx called the "pre-history" of humanity), the reconstitution of being as a laboring, thinking, passionate, whole *human* being signifies a *new* society. Thus the abolition of private capitalism is but the "first negation." This too must be transcended for "only by the transcendence of this mediation [communism] . . . does there arise *positive* Humanism, beginning from itself."[3]

As we have shown, this is not only the young Marx (1844), but the Marx of the *Grundrisse* (1857). Indeed, it is Marx at his highest point of activity (theoretically, in *Capital*; practically and politically, in the Paris Commune) and all the way until his death in 1883. The fetishism that Marx lifts off from the commodity form is not only for purposes of showing that what appears in the market as an equal exchange of things is, in reality, an exploitative relationship of capital to labor at the point of production. It is also, and above all, to demonstrate that "the fantastic appearance" is true. This is what human relations have become in class society; labor has become reified, made into a thing as if labor were no more than an extension of the machine. Therefore the old must be overthrown, root and branch—its "ideology" (false consciousness) as well as its exploitation.

Today's radicals are insensitive to the distrust the rebels entertain toward them because they cannot conceive that the Women's Liberation Movement has a point when it considers the politicos as no more than still another group that wishes to transform them into mere auxiliaries of *other* movements. Whether they are asked merely to form a "Committee to Support the Socialist Workers Party Candidates," or they are invited "to build a labor party," their disgust is the same. They are sure they are *being used*, when someone like Claire Moriarty rushes to the wrong conclusions that "Just as the 'Negro problem' is in reality a white problem, chauvinism should be the concern of men."

The truth is the exact opposite. While socialists were busy proclaiming the impossibility for Negroes to solve the "Negro problem" "by themselves," the Blacks proceeded to create their own independent mass movement. It is not labor or "socialism" which acted as catalyst for both the anti-war movement and, indeed, gave birth to a whole new generation of revolutionaries, but the Black revolution which was both catalyst and reason, *and continues to be that ceaseless movement today*. To hold that the women rebels are now to consider male chauvinism "the concern of men" may sound as thunderous as Simone de Beauvoir's *The Second Sex* (it is she who proclaimed it early and loudest), and may produce a few more women who have made it in a man's world. But the *movement* was created, not by her, but by these "apolitical" women who took matters into their own hands.

The whole attitude of today's "Marxists" to Women's Liberation is not helping but endangering the movement *just when* it is trying to overcome its own empiricism and distrust of ideologues and is beginning to search for theory, for a total philosophy that is a way of life in search of other life forces of liberation who would look to be whole men as they look to be whole women. Communists, Socialists, Trotskyists, Maoists, and even Fidelistas cannot, after all, hide the fact that, despite the countless revolutionary women, and many martyrs, there has been one, only one, woman who has served not only as revolutionary muscle but revolutionary theoretician—Rosa Luxemburg.

We need theoreticians who can face today's problems. It is true that women theoreticians can be "created" neither via isolation from men nor by spending all their time denouncing male chauvinism. But why be so fearful of "excesses" on the question of fighting male chauvinism, and why be so eager a beaver in getting women "to participate" in the working out of "political strategy" that you are led to plunge into asinine assertion? Thus Claire Moriarty writes so glowingly of technology that it would appear it has indeed "eliminated" nothing short of the "inconvenience of pregnancy"!!! Naturally she didn't mean the absurdity that loose phrasing makes it sound. But how could she have slipped into such bizarre expressions?

The answer lies deep in the recesses of the concept of the backwardness of the apolitical women. So weighted down is she by this elitist concept that she is led inexorably to vulgarize Marx's greatest discovery: Historical Materialism. She so sharply separates the ideal from the material that she can write: "Given our position as historical materialists, we understand that changes in consciousness do not precede but accompany institutional change, hence, it is relatively fruitless for women to attempt to combat male chauvinism."

There, the cat finally is out of the bag. Along with the concept of the backwardness of the apolitical women is the concept of the immobility of the males from their dominant position. Poor Marx! Added to all the vulgarization the bourgeoisie attributes to his discovery of historical materialism, we now have an independent socialist blaming that historic discovery for making it "relatively fruitless for women to attempt to combat male chauvinism"!

Material conditions, it is true, determine consciousness, not vice versa, as we look at a historical stretch of the development of mankind through history. History is process, is dialectics. Every unit is invested with its opposite. The future is inherent in the present. The forces opposed to the existing society not only fight it, but gain the consciousness both about the significance of their fight and an intimation of a direction toward that future. Otherwise Marx would never have been able to work out a philosophy of revolution; we would have remained the one-dimensional men and women Herbert Marcuse thinks we are.

The dialectic, even in the bourgeois idealist Hegel's concept, was a great voyage of discovery for all because it let us see the antagonistic duality of opposing forces living in the same nation, country, world. Hegel's genius saw that the very process of laboring produced, in the slave, a "mind of his own." Marx expressed this more concretely and comprehensively when he said the very alienation of the laborer produces "a quest for universality." If that were not so, humanity might as well wait for the moon to visit earth! Compare the confining walls built by today's Marxists with the vision of Marx who could describe wealth in the future in the *Grundrisse*:

> ... when the narrow bourgeois form has been peeled away, what is wealth, if not the universality of needs, capacities, enjoyments, productive powers, etc. of individuals, produced in universal exchange? What, if not the full development of human control over the forces of nature—those of his own nature as well as those of so-called "nature"? What, if not the absolute elaboration of his creative dispositions, without any preconditions other than antecedent historical evolution which makes the totality of this evolution—i.e., the evolution of all human powers as such, unmeasured by any *previously established* yardstick— an end in itself? What is this, if not a situation where man does not reproduce himself in any determined form, but produces his totality? Where he does not seek to remain something formed by the past, but is in the absolute movement of becoming?

No doubt we will not fully overcome male chauvinism so long as class society exists. But we can and will break up its monolithism. We can and will witness the development of women themselves not only as force but as reason. We can and will be a catalyst not only for our development as all-round human beings, but also for that of men. The first step in that direction is to meet the challenge as it appears, everywhere it appears, any time it rears its head, under no matter what disguises. The first act of liberation is to demand back our own heads.

NOTES

1. Karl Marx, *Pre-Capitalist Economic Formations* (London: Lawrence and Wishart, 1964; New York: International Publishers, 1965), p. 96. This is the first translation and publication in English of part of Marx's *Grundrisse*. It contains the passages both on individualization through history and Marx's view of woman in primitive communism, which differ sharply from Engels'. See especially pages 85, 91, 96.
2. Most of the quotes that follow are from Claire Moriarty's article in *New Politics*, Spring 1970, titled "On Women's Liberation." However, I'm actually taking issue with the whole Left, old and new—Stalinists, Maoists, Trotskyists, independent socialists. It just happens that Claire Moriarty has expressed these politicos' views best.
3. Marx's now famous *Economic-Philosophic Manuscripts, 1844*, have undergone many English translations. I'm quoting from my own translation of "Critique of the Hegelian Dialectic," which appeared as Appendix A in the first edition of my work *Marxism and Freedom* (New York: Bookman, 1958).
4. *Pre-Capitalist Economic Formations*, pp. 84–85.

CHAPTER 2

The Miners' Wives*

A trip to northern West Virginia, seat of some of the most militant mass picketing of the just-concluded mine strike, reveals that the miners' wives played an important role. This is one of the many facets of the successful mine struggle that the local press dealt with sketchily and the national capitalist press not at all. The most that could be gleaned from the big dailies was that the wives were "taking" the long fight and empty food baskets because they had no choice. In truth, however, the role they played was not a passive but an active one. Here are but a few incidents.

It seems that the union had permitted pumpers and a few other maintenance men to work for the Pursglove Coal Co. during the strike. The women took a different attitude. They threw up two picket lines, one blocking the road and the other the bridge leading to the tipple. They let only the foremen through. This action on the part of 50 women who took matters into their own hands not only stopped the maintenance men but quickly led the company to "reconsider" its decision to try to have maintenance men.

In Charleston, W. Va., the women joined the picket line of their men. The snobbery of the owner's son particularly aroused their anger. The women pickets stripped his shirt and jabbed hatpins into his shoulders. The "roughing up" of the scion of wealth led to arrests but did not stop the women from continuing with their picketing.

The women also took an active role on the question of miners' relief. While the miners appealed to other labor bodies, the wives went door to door in their own and surrounding communities, and then they

---

*An article published under the name of "F. Forest" in *The Militant*, in 1950. For a full discussion of the 1949–50 miners strike, see *A 1980's View: The Coal Miners' General Strike of 1949-50 and the Birth of Marxist-Humanism in the U.S.* by Andy Phillips and Raya Dunayevskaya (Chicago: News & Letters, 1984).

helped decorate the hall, meet delegations of UAW and other workers who had displayed their labor solidarity by contributing to miners' relief, and aided in the distribution of the food to the most needy families.

Precisely because the role of the women was an active one, it was inevitable that it should lead to organization. In Beckley, W. Va., the women decided to back up their husbands in the fight for a contract by organizing themselves into a Women's Auxiliary. They formed this organization "to help miners at all times, particularly during strikes." Mrs. Haynes Hayworth, wife of the treasurer of the UMWA local at Amigo, and organizer of this women's auxiliary, was asked what the wives would do if their husbands decided to go back to work without a contract.

"Then," she answered quickly, "they'd have to do the housework too. They will have to build fires, cook their own food, wash their own clothes, clean the house and hire baby sitters to take care of the children while they are in the mines."

But there was never any question at all—except in the minds of capitalist reporters—of the miners returning to work without a contract. The miners themselves not only fought against the coal barons; they also welcomed the action of their wives. One miner said: "Our wives are right. We can't work on empty stomachs. And we won't work without a contract."

These actions on the part of the women will be sure to leave their mark on the community as a whole.

CHAPTER 3

Two Excerpts From An Unpublished Essay*

I

On Women in the Post-War World, and the Old Radicals

During the war, women by the millions left the kitchen for the factory. The physiognomy of the labor force changed very considerably, and with it, the relationships in the home. But this is by no means a completed battle. The revolt of the women, which began during the war, did not end with the end of the war. Quite the contrary, it has intensified. It is a daily, an hourly struggle in which the woman wants to establish *new* relations with her husband, with the children, with other women, and other men.

From all this, the radical parties were as isolated as they are from the mass movement in general. But the new imprint that the women were making in society as a whole could not leave the parties unaffected, and the struggle burst out there when the men began to return from the war and resume their old posts, even as it did in bourgeois society. But it was so wrapped up in Marxist jargon that it was not always easy to see

---

*Two excerpts from an unpublished rough draft of an essay written in January-February 1953. See *The Raya Dunayevskaya Collection: Marxist-Humanism, Its Origins and Development in the U.S., 1941 to Today*, Vol. III. (Detroit: Wayne State University Archives of Labor History and Urban Affairs. Available on microfilm.) The reference to "our tendency" is to the State-Capitalist Tendency in the American Trotskyist movement in the 1940s, led by C.L.R. James and Raya Dunayevskaya, whose position was that Russia was no longer a workers' state, but a state-capitalist society. The tendency, also known as the Johnson-Forest Tendency, from the movement names of James (Johnson) and Dunayevskaya (Forest), broke with Trotskyism in 1951. To see how the question of Abolitionism was developed after the breakup of the State-Capitalist Tendency, see "Toward a New Unity of Theory and Practice in the Abolitionist and Marxist Tradition" in *Marxism and Freedom—from 1776 Until Today* (first edition, New York: Bookman, 1958; fifth edition, Humanities Press, Harvester Press, 1982), pp. 276-287.

that between the party and bourgeois society there was no basic distinction on this very basic question.

To get a concept of the smaller battle in the party, it is best to see it in society as a whole first. The mass movement into the factories was looked upon with suspicion by men in the same manner as the first movement of the Negroes into industry, before the CIO: would they bring their working conditions and standards down? And just as the Negroes proved to be loyal fellow workers, so did the women. Only the women looked at the men with suspicion, too: will these try to dominate them in the factory as their husbands, fathers, brothers do in the home? *They were determined that no such thing should happen.*

When the women as human beings proved to have a *class* loyalty, the men loosened up sufficiently in their relations to note that in fact something new had happened on the American scene: not only the women in factories, but even white collar women, telephone workers and such, took to the picket line and mass worker approach. They said of the awakening of these new strata in the population: "I didn't know they had it in them."

They also didn't know that the women workers would "have it in them" to come home and wish to establish new relations there, too. There the men stopped. The woman was still expected to do all the housework and take care of the children, and stay at home while the men went out to play poker. The women, however, took their new role in production seriously; they gained a new dignity and a new concept of what their relations to their fellowmen and fellowwomen should be, and they refused to submit to the subordinate role in which they had been placed in the home before they got their factory jobs. So where they could not work out the new relations, they took to breaking up the homes, even where it meant the woman would become the sole support also of her children.

The politicians thought all that was needed to re-establish the stability of the home was to give the women a few posts in the government, business, the army, and point with pride to the expanding American economy and all the gadgets for the kitchen to make life easier for "the little woman."

Not so the women. They categorically refused to remain an appendage to the men. They wished to have not only sexual but human relations with them. They were out searching for a *total reorganization of society*. In that search, some women also came to the radical parties. These radical parties failed to recognize this new concrete revolutionary force in society, but that force recognized *them*, for it had set up new standards by which to judge this so-called revolutionary movement.

In that same period, at the end of the war, a fight broke out in the Workers Party over their failure to grow. They looked not to the type of propaganda they had put out which was governed by their view that the American masses were "backward." No, they looked only at the *people* who had carried out the line and, since these happened to have been women who had replaced the men in all posts where needed, it was against them that the fight had started.

For the first time our tendency, which had never paid any attention to struggles between members for posts, was to begin to pay attention to this one. For it was clear that this was not an *individual* question, but here a *social* problem was involved.

We came to the defense of the woman who had occupied the post of city organizer which was now being contested: "What is this bourgeois nonsense of the men returning to their posts as if the women who had done all the work during the war years were not genuine political leaders, but just substitutes?" But this new element was buried in the *old political* terms: "it is your political line, not the person executing it, which brought about this mess, and stultified the party's growth."

Our own use of old political terms, instead of seeing the entirely new element—that the Woman Question, in and of itself, was playing a new role, not alone outside, but inside the organization—left us unaware of the significance that women, in increasing numbers, were workers. One woman in particular had a special problem, since she had a 12-year-old child and no husband. But we paid no special attention to this problem as if, to the extent that it was not just a personal but a social problem, it was in any case unsolvable under capitalism. That is the monstrous trap that awaits all who do not see the new in a situation, and we ourselves almost fell into it.

What prevented us from so doing in this case was our ranks, and especially the women. First, one thing was clear. There was a new type of response to certain historic incidents which would stress "the affinity of the struggle of Negroes and women in America." The new women members in our tendency would listen, for example, to the relationship between the Women's Rights Movement and the Abolitionists, to the fact that Frederick Douglass was the only one, even among the Abolitionists, who was willing to chair the women's meeting, as if this was something that occurred not in the last century, but something that in one form or another they were encountering right now daily, at the bench and in the home.

These historic questions assumed that contemporary coloration because of the urgency of their present revolt. What was pushing itself outward was the intensity and totality of the approach. By continuing her revolt daily at her home, the women were giving a new dimension to politics. She was by-passing the specialized organization of women and looking for a new, a total way out. This our own women were sensing by their association with their shopmates and the proletarian housewives in their neighborhoods.

It was from these new social types among the masses outside that our women were getting new impulses. They were finding their best friends, moreover, not among the so-called revolutionaries on the inside, but amongst their shopmates on the outside. If this had brought them into conflict with the petty-bourgeois women in the Workers Party, it reached even a greater intensity when they began talking to the women in the Socialist Workers Party, which our tendency rejoined in 1947, when it looked as if they were at least retaining their revolutionary perspective on the American scene.

Our rank and file women first came into conflict with the women in the SWP because some occupied the same subordinate position that women did in bourgeois society: they worked to support their men, who were "leaders" in the party. They were equally hostile, however, to the women leaders in the party who looked to them like the career women in the bourgeois world. These weren't the new social types they were meeting on the outside, who added a new dimension to the American character by their present revolt. Not at all. They were women with a "mission"—to lead other women. The struggle was one of the rank and file against the leaders, male and female.

The first incident came about as follows. Our ranks had been talking to their shopmates and to the neighborhood women, and from them they began to get tales of revolt, described rather broadly above, but very vividly and concretely by these women from the outside. One young woman of our tendency stated that the Woman Question was not something merely historic, and she for one was not interested in the development of matriarchal societies, but instead would like very much to talk about the women of today, the revolt that is still going on.

When she was permitted to present her little talk, the male intellectuals listened, amused, while their outstanding woman leader stated that the only real solution was for women not to be women. This was the very woman who, in electioneering, wore tight skirts, with a slit on the side, and advised our woman comrade, who was her junior in campaigning: "You've got to use sex."

The mannishness of these SWP women, on the one hand, and their mawkishness, on the other hand, was too much, not only for the women in our tendency, but the rank and file women in the SWP also began to rebel. It was impossible, they said, to bring around proletarian women and have their leaders appear as nothing but "exceptional women." There was nowhere a concept of the question being a *social* question . . .

II

On the Abolitionists and their Relation to the Black Dimension

. . . We break our story to go back over 100 years and show the roots of true Bolshevism in the Abolition Movement. This, the most amazing development of our country's history and the most outstanding example of what Marxist history knows as Bolshevism, was born in America 83 years before its birth in Russia. Being American, it was no accident that it centered around white and Negro relations. It was the question of slavery which brooked no compromises either on the part of the Bourbons who established a hateful totalitarian society or among the Abolitionists who sought to establish entirely new human relations. When we have finished telling this story, the question of white and Negro relations in the Marxist movement right here will have an objective, and thoroughly American, point of reference. It is only under those circumstances that our own history and strivings will be fully understood, for each country must solve its own problems.

One hundred and twenty years ago the Negro slave was the laboring class of this country. American prosperity depended on Southern cotton. Southern cotton depended on the slave's labor. Of all the things wrong in this young country, slavery was the most *concrete*. The slave lived under the whip. He moved in the chained coffle. When fleeing he was pursued by dogs. When caught he would lose an ear or a nose to mark him as a runaway.

More than cotton and cruelty, the bondage of slavery produced the most intimate bond of the human kind. Here was the closest contact with other slave laborers, knowing one another, trusting each other, strengthening each other. Slave revolt was inevitable. For the master to keep his slaves from fleeing was impossible. When the slave came North he brought the war with him. Now it was on a larger stage. Those whites who helped the slave flee and protected him at his destination took on the same human qualities as the Negro himself.

Garrison, Phillips, and others were talented white intellectuals: speakers, writers, and propagandists. Abolition organization began when these surrounded themselves with the bitterly militant ex-slaves. It was they who decided the difference between one organization and the next.

The first issue was whether the Negro was an American. The Colonizationist Society said, No. The free Negro was an African and should be returned there. The Negro slave was a Southerner and should be kept hard at work there. Garrison destroyed the colonizationists for all time, both in the United States and in England.

The second issue was whether there ought to be immediate freedom for all slaves. Some said time will take care of it. Garrison said *men* will take care of it. The gradualists said the slaveholders ought to be reformed. "It is the reformers who have to be reformed," was Garrison's reply. His strength was that he always brought the question home, while everyone else put it out of sight—in Africa, the Southland, or the millenium.

Anti-slavery was an ever growing war. New layers of the population were entering into it all the time. Some began to insist that anti-slavery was the business of a specialized group of people: the churchmen, the charity giver, the social worker. Garrison drew together the different fragments of the anti-slavery movement on the central principle that the whole nation was involved in anti-slavery, however unaware of it. This was not in his head. He proceeded to publish a paper, *Liberator*, which became famous all over the United States. For the ex-slaves, the *Liberator* was the means by which they spoke to each other and to the whole country. The slavemaster recognized in the *Liberator* the *spirit* of the slaves all around them who were not allowed to read or write.

Everyone recognized that abolition had finally come home from England, from Liberia, from missionary and Bible tract societies. It was the beginning of an American movement.

Others debated issues in the anti-slavery movement. The ex-slaves did not have to debate anybody. They voted not with their hands but as an immovable body. "They have risen in their hopes and feelings to the perfect stature of men; in this city [Boston], every one of them is as tall as a giant." Again, Garrison writes that an opponent " . . . is trying to influence our colored friends . . . but he finds them true as steel, and therefore angrily tells them that he believes that if Garrison should go to hell, they would go with him."

This constantly moving relationship between the ex-slaves, who were the base always, and the other layers of the movement, is the sole secret of their success. This unusual—and typically American— movement had no trade union posts, no government patronage, no party favors to offer anybody. People *grew* in this movement at a time when growth was the greatest hunger of the country as a whole. Inside this movement, the different elements of the population were brought closest together, making for the sharpest clashes and the speediest developments. Since Garrison's specialty was fighting slavery close to home, the climax came when white women brought anti-slavery right into their homes. It began simply on the masthead of the *Liberator*. A woodcut showed a kneeling slave woman. It was entitled, "Am I not a woman and a sister?" The slavemaster claimed he was protecting Southern womanhood. The Abolitionist claimed that slavery had turned the South into one huge brothel. The most intimate human function of childbirth had become planned public breeding of slave laborers. The *Liberator* opened the question up for the Northern women to decide for themselves. They looked into their own lives. Here too, industry had made sexual relations and childbirth the mere reproduction of factory workers. These women tied their lives to that of the slave and enlisted completely behind Garrison.

Once more this new relation broke up old patterns. Abolition had revolutionized relations between the slave and his master, Negro and white, and now between men and women. The movement broke in half. The World Anti-Slavery Convention which forbade women's participation saw the conservatives on the floor pleading with the abstaining Garrison in the balcony to come down. He never did. During the Civil War, upper-class British anti-slavery fell apart and deserted the North, leaving this field clear for the British workers. It took twenty years to show the class issue involved.

It was Wendell Phillips' wife-to-be who recruited him to the movement. "Don't shilly shally, Wendell." she told him. He never did. He scored in deadly style on every political target. He finished up the flag-waving, spread eagle style of speaking for all time. When he spoke to thousands, it was as if he was sitting at each man's elbow holding a personal conversation. When drowned out by a screaming audience, he spoke to the newspaper reporters below him until he obtained quiet. The most social medium possible was the one for him. He believed that the man who jumped up to speak from the back row created often more interest and excitement than the platform speaker. He believed that the theatres brought out more of men's true feelings than the churches or colleges. He lived the greatest part of his life on his feet in the midst of his audience, and they loved him for it. He was not an exceptional man but an American of a new type produced by a new social power. "Let no one despise the Negro any more—*he* has given us Wendell Phillips," said one listener. Of all the anti-slavery speakers, he was the most popular with workers and trade unionists.

The best selling book of the 19th century, next to the Bible, was a book written about a Negro slave by a white woman. Anti-slavery was the Bible of the 19th century. As a book, *Uncle Tom's Cabin* isn't very much and as a play even less. It was read and played countless times because it was the meeting point of two layers of the population who had never met before. The American people were reading and acting out their own lives with the greatest passion and feeling. A stunned Harriet Beecher Stowe could only proclaim that "God wrote it." With the help of a hundred years, we can more rightfully claim that it was produced by the concretely new relations inside the anti-slavery movement.

Abolition was the new dimension in the American character. In a society falling to pieces from slavery on one side and industry on the other, the integrated, willful personalities of Garrison, Douglass, Phillips, and Brown were *the* form of revival and reorganization of the American and his world. Only revolutionists know the quality of American individualism.

Garrison began the *Liberator* with these fateful words: "I will be as harsh as truth—as uncompromising as justice—I will not equivocate—I will not excuse—I will not retreat a single inch—and I will be heard!" Those who thought they were listening to one man's boasting were mistaken. It was the particular stamp of the movement towards the American Civil War: one man speaking and everyone recognizing through him the nature of their times and their own true nature.

"I wish to say, furthermore, that you had better, all you people at the South, prepare yourselves for a settlement of that question, that must come up for settlement sooner than you are prepared for it. The sooner you are prepared for it the better. You may dispose of me very easily . . . but this question is still to be settled . . . the end of that is not yet." This was John Brown speaking in 1859. Everyone was listening now. In 1861 came the greatest civil war mankind has ever known . . .

CHAPTER 4

Revolution and Counterrevolution in South Africa*

"Izwe Lethu" (Our Land), shouted thousands of Africans as they burned their "passes" and marched to the police stations, asking to be arrested for thus having violated the fascist type of internal passports imposed upon them by the white rulers.

In response to Act One of this bloodless revolution for human rights, the counterrevolution burst forth in an orgy of violence, machine-gunning the unarmed mass of humanity—men, women, and children. The Revolution mourned its dead by a mass funeral and staying away from work. The counterrevolutionary *apartheid* (segregationist) Africa followed up its inhuman violence with vicious baton charges into African crowds, declaring a state of emergency, and outlawing any political organization, mainly Black, but Black or white, that dared challenge the savage white supremacy.

The Revolution—the struggle for freedom—though it comprises the overwhelming majority, 15 million against 3 million whites, must face, unarmed, the white rulers who are armed to the teeth with everything from bull whips to machine guns, and from the armed forces to jet planes, not to mention prisons, the legislature, factories, mines, farms, ships, and concentration camps.

This is the face of "civilized" white rule in South Africa as the economy of the country came to a standstill when Black labor stopped to mourn its dead.

87% of the industrial labor force and 92% of the agricultural labor force is African. Since without this Black labor force white oppression could not last, the mailed fist is not reserved for military attacks. When in 1946, 75,000 miners dared to strike, the strike was bloodily suppressed. For demanding the "extortionate" wage of 10 shillings ($1.40)

*From *News & Letters*, April 1960

per 8-hour shift, workers were forced down. "They sat in the tunnels and refused to come up until police drove them to the surface 'stope by stope and level by level'," as the white *Rand Daily Mail* described it.

According to official figures, 69% of Black families had a combined income below even what white Africa admits is the *minimum* for life and health. The result has been that 50% of all Africans never reach the working age of 16; infant mortality rate is estimated at 200–300 per 1,000. But what are pot bellies and rickets and babies dead in corners to white "God-fearing Christians"? Life is cheap when its skin is Black!

Only 40% of urban white Africans are wage workers, and these are mainly skilled (85%) or semi-skilled (12%). While there is nothing extraordinary about the *monthly* wage of white workers—£65 ($182), it is *five-fold* that of the Black worker's monthly wage of £13 ($36.40). Moreover, the white workers' unions are recognized while those of the Africans are not. At the same time, the Black worker is forbidden to strike, and the dividing line between a strike and a dispute is so vague that the police just move in when there is any sort of stoppage and put down the dispute even where management would be willing to come to terms. Refusal to work is punishable with $1,400 fine or 5 years in prison or both!

The revolt of Black labor has been as continuous as it has been brave nevertheless. And the illegal strikes jumped, after they were forbidden, from 33 in 1954 to 73 in 1955. When South Africans were involved in the great bus boycott of 1957, hundreds of thousands walked 20 miles to work and trudged another 20 miles back to their segregated townships for three solid months until they won the fight against the rise in fares.

The Government of Dr. Verwoerd (the Hitler of South Africa) issued the following statement: "It is quite clear that this is not so much an economic matter; it is a political movement."

There is no doubt that the economic, political, social struggle for freedom is indivisible. So is the tyranny of white oppression total— totally depraved. *Every* African male in the cities can expect to be arrested at least once a year for some petty offense or other.

The indignity of the pass puts yet extra power in the hands of white "labor officials" (Government men). If it shows that one is a "trouble maker," he can be sent off in silence to a "farm compound" which is actually a forced labor camp where the white-African big farmers get their cheap labor. The notorious eastern Transvaal area "hires" convicts and others for 2 shillings (25¢) a day.

Nothing has changed since the 1947 disclosures when it was shown that African laborers dressed in sacks were clawing out potatoes with their bare hands. They work under the hot sun and the sjambok and spend their nights in stuffy windowless barns with fierce watchdogs outside to cut off escape.

When in 1952 pass-carrying extended to African women, the resistance of the women burst forth in the Zecrust and Sekhurhuneland uprisings, as well as street demonstrations in Johannesburg. Thus both in the cities and in the "Reserves" the revolt is continuous.

Just as arms are denied the native African, so is the representation in parliament. With the 1950 so-called Suppression of Communism Act and the Criminal Law Amendment Act of February 1953, the white rulers have indeed destroyed *all* legal activity by political or industrial organizations that are not dedicated to white supremacy. The one organization left to them was the African National Congress under the leadership of Chief Albert Luthuli. Recently the left wing of that split off, named itself Pan-Africanism, and elected Robert Mangaliso Sobukwe as its president. It is he who called for the demonstration in opposition to the pass-carrying. These two leaders, along with 300 other Africans, have been arrested, as well as even the mildest of white liberals who opposed total, brutal white supremacy. All political organizations except those of the ruling class have been outlawed.

The African National Congress and the Pan-Africanist Congress immediately announced that they would go underground but would not give up the fight for freedom.

Whatever orgy of violence the white rulers will now indulge in, South Africa will never again be the same. The tiny minority of whites who have opposed this inhuman, insane, savage rule of the white supremacists long ago saw that if the Africans are not allowed to live like human beings, it is the inhuman regime, not the human beings that will have to go. It is only a question of when and how.

As Ronald M. Segal, the editor of the journal *Africa South*, whose passport had been seized some months back, wrote in an editorial entitled "Revolution Is Now": "In a society where revolt walks always in the shadow of massacre . . . change and revolution have become finally inseparable."

CHAPTER 5

*African Women Demand "Freedom Now!"**

Yesterday I had my first experience in the Protectorate, where meetings are called without a moment's notice, to be attended by hundreds, complete with political speeches, singing, dancing, and drums.

The most exciting one of all took place at Brikama where 800 people gathered to hear the speaker of the People's Progressive Party. The PPP is the opposition party here which is modeling itself on Pan-Africanism and bases itself on the Mandinkas.

The women were the most dramatic and inspiring of all the participants. Most are illiterate, and yet they are the most intelligent, the most revolutionary, and with the greatest integrity (not to mention the fact that they are very beautiful in features, in their carriage, with their long golden earrings and with some golden jewelry on their foreheads).

The extension of fraternal greetings to Americans, especially Negro Americans, "and women like ourselves," was spontaneous, and spoken simply and movingly.

The Chairman of the Women's section said: "I am very happy that you came here all the way from America to visit this village and see what we are trying to do for our country. The women are eager to improve their lot. They will get more out of independence than the men. Women are more sensible than men, and no one can corrupt them. They know what is good for them and do not listen to bribery because they have integrity." The speaker was a young Mandinka.

Following her was a speaker for the elder women, who received a tremendous ovation from the open air meeting with her slogan, *"Freedom Now!"*

After welcoming me and saying she was speaking for the women

---

*A report from the Protectorate, Brikama, The Gambia, published in *News & Letters*, May 1962. Other reports by Dunayevskaya on her 1962 Africa trip were published in *Africa Today*, July and December 1962, and *Presence Africaine* #48, 1963.

elders, she said, "The struggle is to remove ourselves now from the condition of slavery toward freedom. For this struggle we must display integrity. Otherwise before we get ourselves out of slavery we would again be brought into another."

She then turned to me personally and said, "I speak to you as one woman to another. You have made something out of yourself in the world, writing books and coming to see us here. We women too are struggling for something; we see a future in this party, the PPP, which we have promised to support because it is fighting for freedom which we should have had long ago. We want freedom NOW!"

Since *"Freedom Now"* is also the slogan of the Freedom Riders and since I was also able to add what an impact the role of the African women in the African freedom struggles has made on the American workers, some of whom have even named their children in honor of these, I did not at all feel like a stranger but a Gambia Mandinka on the freedom road.

CHAPTER 6

Women's Liberation, in Fact and in Philosophy*

Our second women's movement has to realize both the continuity and discontinuity from the first women's movement. The greatness of history is that in it you see your own age in a totally new light and begin to know what to single out. For example, the greatest thing is the Black Dimension. The first women's movement arose from the antislavery movement. They were a different world from the slave society they were fighting against not only because so many of the Abolitionists were slaves who had followed the North Star to freedom, but because the entire relationship among the Abolitionists, their whole idea of freedom, was so different.

Take such a simple thing as one's name... Way back in the early part of the 19th century, when one Black woman was asked her name she said, Sojourner Truth... She wanted the idea of freedom and travelling all over the world—"the world is my country." That kind of identification of national and international means that the name she created was not just a name.

Or take the white, middle-class women who were also an important part of the Abolitionist movement... They began to question why they shouldn't also be free. When the suffrage movement arose from within the Abolitionist movement, it was on the basis of what [the white women] had seen women, Black women, could be—revolutionary force and Reason...

The second stage of the first women's rights movement was a very sad stage. Once the Civil War was over and the 14th Amendment was finally passed, women still had no suffrage or other legal rights. The weakness in the dialectics of liberation at this point however, was its

---

*Excerpts from an abbreviated summary of a speech delivered at the University of California-Los Angeles' Women's Week, April 1973

isolation from the Blacks and from the new kinds of struggles being fought by the working women who were going into the factories.

Susan B. Anthony had a paper called *Revolution*, and the motto under it read: "Men, their rights and nothing more: Women, their rights and nothing less." You would think that with such a vision and a philosophic view, they would have realized that isolating themselves from the Black and labor dimensions meant they were cutting their own throats. Lucy Stone was worse and became an actual racist. She said she was not asking for freedom for the "dregs of society." She made such class and racial distinctions about who deserves freedom that, no matter how brave the women were, it not only took all the way from 1868 to 1920 to get the vote, but when they got it, it didn't mean anything.

When an Idea's time has come, there are just as many contradictions and challenges as when the Idea was first thought of. In this country it is the Black Dimension, the Black masses as vanguard, that is the crucial element. It is because it isn't just an Idea, but a movement. It's going to act, to try to make the Idea of freedom become real. And it is the kind of philosophy we have that will determine if we constantly check ourselves to see what has to be opened up, and enable us to see ourselves not as the fragmented people class society makes of us.

Otherwise you wind up with less than freedom. You may not be limited to just making sandwiches, you may even be able to enter the arts. Isn't that great? The trouble is that you're not changing society at its roots, at its exploitative, male-dominated roots. For those who think it's enough to be for women's rights, to go out for any and all careers, and to keep away from a revolutionary organization, means that they not only exclude themselves from the most serious, total work of reorganizing society, but cut themselves off from the working women, who are the source of the very theory they need.

What we've been looking at in studying the first women's movement was what was happening objectively in the world, objectively in this country. When we come down to our own age we have to ask what was happening objectively again, that suddenly the quiescent '50s, when the youth were supposed to be the "beat generation," burst out into the revolt of the '60s . . .

In the '60s we're once again back to the Black Dimension. People laughed uproariously at *Marxism and Freedom*, which had just been published the year after the Montgomery Bus Boycott, because I said that that Bus Boycott of 1956 was an entirely new stage that was related to the new stage in the Workers' Councils of Hungary, where they had got rid of capitalism but wanted to be free from Communism, too, because it was just another form of state-capitalism. It became a world phenomenon, and a national phenomenon in 1960 when the Black youth in Greensboro, North Carolina refused to move until they were served at the lunch counters.

The white students who were supposed to have been the beat generation went South—they thought they were going to do something for the Civil Rights Movement of the Blacks. But when they got there they found that the Blacks who were asking them to set up schools had an idea of education that they had never dreamed of. Our education is factory-made, completely administered, designed to prepare those who will oppress others. But the Freedom Schools were asking totally different questions: they wanted an education so they could find out how to get rid of the Bull Connors for good. The white students suddenly realized that instead of helping the Blacks like social workers, they were learning a totally new dimension themselves. They came back North and realized that it wasn't only the worker who is alienated, but the comfortable, middle-class whites going to a "great university" like Berkeley were just numbers put into a computer.

It was in February of 1965, when L.B. Johnson first rained the bombs on Hanoi that, instead of having just a Civil Rights Movement, or a Free Speech Movement, we suddenly had the birth of an entirely new generation of revolutionaries who were questioning everything in this society. The one thing, unfortunately, they still didn't question was philosophy. They were all very proud of their pragmatism—but it didn't help them too much.

It was at this point that the women began saying: "Now this is strange. I'm part of this great movement, and yet I'm cranking the mimeo machine instead of writing the leaflets." Nobody could accuse them of not being revolutionary. They were questioning whether something wasn't wrong with a movement that supposedly believes in a new society and yet practices the same division of labor as the one we live in. Not only that. Nobody could accuse them of being against Blacks. But when it came to the woman question, there was Stokely Carmichael saying "The only position for women is prone." The women's questioning brought us to an entirely new stage.

We were moving to the highpoint of 1968, and it was a highpoint internationally. In this country the anti-Vietnam War movement was still growing. And for the first time in an advanced country like France we had a near-revolution. It started as a student movement, but they suddenly realized why Marx said the proletariat was the force for revolution. When you have 10,000 students in Paris on strike it looks very great, but if you have 10 million workers putting down their tools and stopping production, it is a very different situation.

Why did we get only a near-revolution out of all this? Those who were concerned with where the philosophy was were likely to be told, whether by Mario Savio or Cohn-Bendit, "We will pick it up en route." All they picked up was an aborted revolution . . .

SDS (Students for a Democratic Society) wound up in completely mindless activism. The women who had just begun the Women's Liberation Movement wound up "following their men" in all of the splits and factions. But it isn't quite true they were just following their men. It was worse. They voted for the same resolutions the men did because that is what they really believed.

In a word, once you do not have a total philosophy of liberation, once you do not see that the dialectics of liberation are forces *and* reason, then there is no place to go but the male-dominated, pragmatic, so-called revolutionary groups that thought they could pick up philosophy "en route."

We have to realize that even though we have an independent movement; even though we are not in isolation from the men or from the children, for that matter; even though we are not isolated from the other movements, it takes a great deal more than just activity. It takes the kind of unity of objective and subjective where you suddenly see that you cannot have a successful revolution without having the underlying philosophy that is the liberation of humanity . . .

CHAPTER 7

The Black Dimension in Women's Liberation*

To grasp the Black Dimension is to learn a new language, the language of thought, Black thought. For many, this new language will be difficult because they are hard of hearing. Hard of hearing because they are not used to this type of thought, a language which is both a struggle for freedom and the thought of freedom.

Take the question of the language of activity in the Underground Railroad where Harriet Tubman was one of the greatest conductors. She didn't just escape from the South. She returned 19 times, and she brought out 300 people—and there is more. In a few books you will find her name and they will acknowledge that she was a conductor and a great one. But do they speak of all the creativity that goes into being a conductor of the Underground Railway, that you become a guerrilla fighter as well as a conductor, that you're a leader of men and women? Just look what it means to know your country, the South, so that you not only bring out Blacks, but are the leader of a battalion of whites . . .

When we move to the period after the Civil War when slavery was abolished we see that even such greats as Frederick Douglass—who had been with the women in their battles before this struggle for the 14th Amendment—now were willing to drop the demand for the inclusion of the vote for the women; and we find that Sojourner Truth and Harriet Tubman separate from Frederick Douglass. They insist on continuing the struggle for women's liberation.

Listen to the poetry of Sojourner Truth's prose: "I am coming from the land of slavery." This is *after* the Civil War was won by the North.

---

*Excerpted from lectures given to Union W.A.G.E. (Women's Alliance to Gain Equality) in San Francisco, Hunter College in New York, De Paul University in Chicago, California State University in Los Angeles, and George Washington University in Washington, D.C., 1975–76

She turns to her own Black people, appealing for continuation of the struggle for women's vote: "I hate to see my Black man being as bad as the white man." Then turning to the greatest of them, who are stepping aside, she says that it is "short-minded" to stop the struggle at getting the vote only for Black men.

In the concentration on the struggle for freedom, the Black dimension in women's liberation extended the whole philosophy of human liberation. Now if we jump to the early 20th century, we find the same thing. A much underrated woman in that sphere is Amy Jacques Garvey. She wasn't just the wife of Marcus Garvey. She both edited the women's page in *Negro World* and edited Garvey's works after he died, giving to them a great name—*Philosophy and Opinions of Marcus Garvey.**

Here she is, writing in 1925: "A race must be saved, a country must be redeemed, and unless you strengthen the leadership of vacillating Negro men, we will remain marking time . . .

"We are tired of hearing Negro men say, 'There is a better day coming', while they do nothing to usher in the day. We are becoming so impatient that we are getting in the front ranks, and serve notice on the world that we [she is talking about Black women] will brush aside the halting, cowardly Negro men, and with prayer on our lips and arms prepared for any fray, we will press on and on until victory is ours . . .

"Mr. Black man, watch your step! Ethiopia's queens will reign again, and her Amazons protect her shores and people. Stengthen your shaking knees, and move forward, or we will displace you . . ."

Or take the African continent where, again, it was not the educated men, but illiterate women who added a new page to history, when, in 1929, the British imperialists in Eastern Nigeria decided to tax the women. They got so furious they went on spontaneous strike—which was, of course, called a "riot." The great Aba riots. It was not only spontaneous, it was against all the advice of everyone, including the educated males. It was not only against British imperialism, but against their own African chiefs, who had not defended them. Above

---

*In 1983 the University of California Press published the first two volumes (1826–August 1919; Aug. 27, 1919–August 1920) of a projected monumental ten-volume survey, edited by Robert A. Hill, under the title, *The Marcus Garvey and Universal Negro Improvement Association Papers*. It is the most scholarly research ever undertaken on Marcus Garvey. (See also Lou Turner's review of this study, in his "Black World" column in *News & Letters*, Jan.-Feb. and March, 1984.)

all, they crossed all tribal lines. And they won, though not until after 40 women were killed and countless others injured . . .

What happened right here in the U.S. in 1960? It is true it was the wonderful North Carolina youth who sat in at a restaurant lunch counter and started the magnificent Black Revolution. But the fact is that, *five years earlier*, one solitary woman, Rosa Parks, a seamstress, refused to give up her seat on a bus and got arrested, and the incident so aroused the youth that the entire Black population behaved in a different manner than they had ever dreamed of. They decided they would all go to the courthouse; they organized their own transportation and boycotted all the buses; they inspired Rev. King to be with them, and they kept all decisions in their own hands by meeting three times a week. The new stage of Black revolt began there.

Right up to our own period we find there is a double rhythm in revolution. The overthrow, what is called the first negation, is saying *No* to what is. But the second negation, the creation of the new, is harder, because you want to have entirely new human relations. In addition to all the great Black women I have mentioned, there is another in the new Women's Liberation Movement, Doris Wright, who raised exactly this question when she said, "I'm not thoroughly convinced that Black Liberation, the way it's being spelled out, will really and truly mean *my* liberation. I'm not sure that when it comes time to 'put down my gun', that I won't have a broom shoved in my hands, as so many of my Cuban sisters have."

She was not putting the question down as a condition—"I will not make a revolution unless you promise." She was posing the question of what happens *after*. That is what we have to answer *before*, in the practice of our own organizations, our own thought and our own activity.

CHAPTER 8

The Trail from Marx's Philosophy of Revolution to Today's Women's Liberation Movements*

I. MARX'S "NEW HUMANISM" SEEN WITH EYES OF TODAY

Let's go adventuring into Marx's discovery of a whole new continent of thought and of revolution that he named "a new Humanism," which, in this Marx centenary year, has left us a trail to the 1980s. It is precisely this that makes me very happy to talk to a conference of Third World women, because the very mention of "Third World" opens the door to both women and men, to all revolutionary forces as Reason.

In the last decade of Marx's life he was still discovering "New Moments"—that is, stages of new human development which we call the Third World. It rounded out that new continent of thought and revolution which he discovered when he first broke with bourgeois society in 1843. In transforming Hegel's *revolution in philosophy* into a *philosophy of revolution*, Marx stressed that he was breaking not only with capitalism as an exploitative social order, but also with what he called "vulgar communism"—that is to say, people who thought that all you needed to do was to abolish private property in order to have a new social order. Marx's point was that a new society was not a matter of form of property, private or state, but of new human relations.

To stress how total was the uprooting needed, in his *1844 Economic-Philosophic Manuscripts* Marx asked the reader to probe not only the class struggle, but also a most fundamental relationship, Man/Woman: "The direct, natural, necessary relationship of man to man is the *relationship of man to woman*." And because that is so alienating an

---

*A lecture delivered during the Marx Centenary to the Conference on "Common Differences: Third World Women and Feminist Perspectives" at the University of Illinois at Urbana-Champaign, April, 1983

experience, where the woman is always subordinate to the man, be it in the home or in the factory, Marx called all societies, including capitalism, the *pre-history of humanity*. In a word, it was not a truly human relationship and pointed to the necessity of uprooting all the existing relations. Marx called for a "revolution in permanence" which would abolish and transcend all exploitative relations and see, in place of either the profit motive of capitalism or the state-form of property in vulgar communism, the self-development of man, woman, and child— with all of humanity in the process of "the absolute movement of becoming."

The dual rhythm of revolution—the overthrow of the old and the creation of the new foundations—is what Marx first encountered in the 1848 revolutions throughout Europe. In the U.S. that was the year of the first Woman's Rights Convention, and it is in the dialectic of that movement that we witness the vanguard element of the Black dimension. We can see it most specifically in the very name Sojourner Truth chose for herself. Let me explain.

Today, when Women's Liberation is not just an Idea whose time has come but an actual movement, we naturally think that past history is but "backdrop," and yet if we look at even so simple a question as choosing a name and how we think we have achieved a great revolution by adopting our mother's maiden name instead of our father's name, we have to stop and compare that with what Sojourner Truth did. She said she went to God and told Him she would no longer be a slave, and would certainly not bear the name of her slave-master. She asked what she should call herself, then? His answer was supposed to have been: "Sojourn the world over and tell the truth about American democracy. The Declaration of Independence says all men are free, but obviously they mean only white men, and women don't seem to count at all. Go tell the world the truth." Since that was precisely the answer she was waiting to hear, she called herself from that moment on "Sojourner Truth." Which one of us, in 1983, has chosen a name that expresses our whole philosophy?

It is this type of Reason that discloses that intelligence is related to one's experience and aspiration and is not merely a matter of literacy or illiteracy. It is the drive to freedom that determines one's philosophy and that makes one see what Marx meant by "history and its process." And because Marx saw men and women as shapers of history in a continuing process and did not separate past from present or future, in his very last decade he rediscovered the Man/Woman relationship in the very latest anthropological works then coming out where ancient was revealed as a possible ground for future.

I'm referring to the fact that Lewis Henry Morgan's *Ancient Society* had just been published (1877), and Marx became so enamoured of the greater freedoms that the Iroquois women had than what exists under the so-called advanced capitalist democracy that he began referring to the primitive communism of the American Indians as a more inspiring form of human development than capitalism.

It is only natural that we view history with eyes of today. In the panel on "Women in Revolutionary Movements," half an hour ago, I showed that it was no accident that two of the burning questions of today—women's liberation and color—were also the most exciting in history and in Marx's discovery of what he called "the Asiatic mode of production" and what we call "the Third World." I thereupon quoted women from such different parts of the world as South Africa, East Timor, Guatemala—and, for that matter, Poland.

In South Africa in 1978, Miriam Gafoor, a Capetown student, told a Supreme Court judge: "Apartheid has become an insult to our human dignity. Our whole being rebels against the whole South African experience . . . I am 16 years old and have been locked up, refused food and interrogated . . . We, the youth of South Africa, reject the subservient heritage that has been handed down to us."

In East Timor in 1975, Rosa Muki Bonaparte organized the Popular Organization of Timorese Women as a group within Fretelin. She was the first one murdered when Indonesia invaded East Timor after they had already achieved freedom and ended 446 years of Portuguese rule. She had courageously expounded her philosophy: "The ideology of a system in which women are considered as 'inferior beings' has submitted Timorese women to a double exploitation: a general form which applies without distinction to both men and women, and which manifests itself by forced labor, starvation salaries, racism, etc. . . Another form of a specific character, directed to women in particular."

In 1982, Manuela Saquic, a 17-year-old Ixil Indian from Guatemala, said: "The rich have always treated us Indians as people who are crazy, who can't think. They think of Indians as animals, who don't have the capacity to learn and the capacity to become conscious . . . At first the army persecuted only men. They never paid any attention to the women; they thought we were invisible. But they discovered that the women were organized, too . . . The government is massacring us because we're organizing and rising up . . . We have great hope that we will arrive in power and create a new Guatemala."

When it comes to Poland, however, although it is a woman of today, Anna Walentynowicz, who began the tremendous, ongoing movement Solidarnosc, I prefer to return to history and to Rosa Luxemburg, the

Polish, German, Russian, international revolutionary. That is not only because my latest work, *Rosa Luxemburg, Women's Liberation, and Marx's Philosophy of Revolution*, centers around her, but because it was Luxemburg who had directly related all her thought and activity in the revolutions of 1905 and 1919 to Marx's whole philosophy of revolution, which has laid the trail to the 1980s for us. Like all other Marxists, when the 1905 revolution broke out in Russia and Poland (then part of the Russian empire), she based herself on what Marx had done in the 1848 revolutions. Where she differed from the others was that, where they considered 1905 as the last of the 19th century revolutions, she insisted that it was the first of the new 20th century revolutions. Even she did not fully grasp how right she was in the way it was extended to Persia. It was there, where the revolution continued to 1911, that women organized the very first women's soviet (anjumen) in the world.

II. LUXEMBURG'S FLASH OF GENIUS ON IMPERIALISM

In Luxemburg's case, it was but the beginning of many original theoretical and practical activities in which she recreated Marxism for her own age—on the question of the General Strike as the ground for revolution and on the question of spontaneity as the very form of revolution which demands a new concept of the relationship of revolution to "the party." Not only was she the very first of the Marxists to see a new global development of capitalism—imperialism, at the very start of the 20th century; but it was her persistent, consistent, antimilitarist work that landed her in jail even before the outbreak of World War I and then led to her leadership of the Spartacist Uprising in 1919, when she was murdered.

It was her flash of genius on the question of imperialism that led to her break with Kautsky (who was considered the greatest orthodox Marxist in the world) because the German Social-Democracy in 1910 did nothing to oppose their rulers' sending the gunboat, *Panther*, first to Morocco and then to Southwest Africa (which we today know as Namibia). To this day, her eloquent, revolutionary defense of the Black women and children gunned down in the Kalahari desert by the German General von Trotha not only sends shivers down our backs but makes us feel how unfinished the task remains in overcoming imperialism.

Let us follow her revolutionary legacy, both in the heretofore unknown feminist dimension and in her definition of humanism: "I'm telling you that as soon as I can stick my nose out again," she wrote from prison to Mathilde Wurm, castigating not only those who had capitulated to the war but those who devised theories for the capitulators, "I will hunt and harry your society of frogs with trumpet blasts, whip crackings, and bloodhounds—like Penthesilea I wanted to say, but by God, you people are no Achilles. Have you had enough of a New Year's greeting now? Then see to it that you stay *human* . . . Being human means joyfully throwing your whole life 'on the scales of destiny' when need be, but all the while rejoicing in every sunny day and every beautiful cloud. Ach, I know of no formula to write you for being human . . . ."

Whatever the reason Luxemburg, in her fight with the Social-Democracy's betrayal in voting war credits to the Kaiser, called upon Penthesilea, the Queen of the Amazons, the point is that her unknown feminist dimension manifested itself even there. But the *totality* of Marx's dialectic of revolution, which never separated the philosophy of revolution from actual revolution, was nevertheless missing, even in Rosa Luxemburg.

III. MARX'S 'NEW MOMENTS' AS THE TRAIL TO TODAY

What is needed now is a challenge to post-Marx Marxists. And I mean *revolutionary* post-Marx Marxists. I'm not here concerned with the betrayal of the Second International, which had voted those war credits for the Kaiser and helped behead the German Revolution led by Luxemburg, Liebknecht, and the Spartacists. Nor am I referring to Stalinism; we now have all of the East European revolutions to show even those who didn't before believe that Stalin had transformed the only successful proletarian revolution into its opposite, the state-capitalist, totalitarian society it now is. I'm referring only to those revolutionaries who lived up to the Marxist heritage but did not live up to Marx's philosophy of revolution which never got separated from actual revolution. In his last decade Marx was still discovering all those new moments, seeing them in an elementary form in primitive communal society and hurrying to integrate them into his total philosophy of liberation. The revolutionaries who did not match up to that begin with his closest collaborator, Frederick Engels—who never betrayed; without whose meticulous, hard labor we would never have had Volumes II and III of Marx's *Capital*; and who claimed that his very first work after Marx died, *The Origin of the Family, Private Property and the State*, was a bequest of Marx which he was fulfilling by summarizing what he found in the posthumous notes of Marx.

Was he?

Let's take a look at the four or five paragraphs Engels included in his *Origin of the Family* and the actual *Ethnological Notebooks* of Marx. [Here I showed a copy of the 400 page work published in 1972 which contains Marx's Notebooks transcribed by Lawrence Krader, to which I said we had to add Marx's notes on Kovalevsky, also transcribed by Krader and published in 1975 under the title *The Asiatic Mode of Production*].

When we compare four or five paragraphs with hundreds of pages, we can see that nothing could be further from the truth. Moreover, it was in the *Origin of the Family* that Engels writes of "the world historic defeat of the female sex" that supposedly came with the change from matrilineal to patrilineal society—as if women have not been most active in all the revolutions, especially the Paris Commune, which Marx had singled out as *the* political form in which to work out the economic emancipation of the proletariat. Yet because, compared to the capitalist ideologues, Engels' demand for equality for women was so superior to the *status quo*, all socialists have accepted that work as if it were a joint work of Engels "and Marx."

Let's see what Engels worked out as a so-called bequest of Marx. It is true that Marx was so impressed with Morgan's *Ancient Society* that he asked Engels to get a copy to read at once. It is not true that Marx took everything Morgan had written as if it were a work of historical materialism. On the contrary, as the letter he wrote to Vera Zasulitch shows, while he praises Morgan's work as bringing out something quite new on primitive communism, he calls attention at the same time to the fact that Morgan's work was authorized by the bourgeois U.S. government.

And what about Engels—after not even trying to get the book until Marx died and he found his Notes? He accepted Morgan's work in a very unilinear way—as if all that was needed was to superimpose some modern technological development onto primitive communism, and we would have a "communist society." When he referred to Marx's Notebooks, he left the impression that the few paragraphs he included were all Marx had written. We must repeat: nothing could be further from the truth.

Moreover, Marx was not only making notes from Morgan on ancient society but was summarizing *and commenting upon* all the new anthropological studies, which included works by Phear, Maine, and Lubbock. At the same time that he was stressing the greatness of primitive society, he was also stressing that it was not a question of an outside force, but that right from *within* the primitive communal society there had already arisen elements of difference between the chief and the ranks, in which we could, indeed, see the class struggle and the disintegration of the old society. Which is why he not only let stand the most famous statement of the *Communist Manifesto*—"The history of all hitherto existing society is the history of class struggles"—but added, in the new 1882 Introduction to the Russian edition of the *Manifesto*, that it was not out of the question, since there is more than one path to social revolution, that revolution could come to backward Russia ahead of the technologically advanced West; provided that it became the signal for revolution in the advanced countries, it could be the successful "starting point for communist development."

Although Engels had cosigned that new Introduction to the 1882 edition of the *Manifesto*, after Marx died and he was bringing out a British edition (in 1888), he starred that first historic sentence and in a footnote said that Marx meant all *written* history, because at the time that had been written we didn't know about primitive communism, and therefore the reader should read his *Origin of the Family*. The truth is that Marx had known a great deal, but far from being an evolutionist, or a biologist, or any other type of unilinear analyst, Marx had a multilinear, dialectical view of human development which had led him, from the 1857 *Grundrisse* on, to stop saying that all of human development consisted of three main stages—slavery, feudalism, capitalism. He added a fourth, which he called "Asiatic mode of production" and which was not only a geographic designation but a manifestation of a historically new stage of human development. (Indeed, he even pointed to his own birthplace, Trier, Germany, as having some relation to that element.)

In that last decade of Marx's life, when he turned to all the new anthropological studies and saw so many new moments even on a trip for his health to Algiers where he came back "with his head full of Africa and the Arabs," he was led to reinterpret the penultimate chapter of his greatest theoretical work, *Capital*, the chapter on "Historical Tendency of Capitalist Accumulation." First, he eliminated Part VIII ("The So-Called Primitive Accumulation") as a separate Part (and please note that Marx had called it "so-called") and made it integral to Part VII ("The Accumulation of Capital"). Marx saw no impenetrable wall between the primitive accumulation and the accumulation of capital. On the contrary he now stressed, in his letter on Mihailovsky (1877) that the law of motion of capitalist society he had discerned, the constant increase of machinery at the expense of living workers, was *not* a universal but the development which characterized Western Europe; and that, furthermore, there was no automatic collapse of capitalism. It needed a good, hefty push from the masses. And those living masses were not limited to a single path of development. There were other paths. It was that other path which then got developed in the letter to Zasulitch and was finally articulated in the Introduction to the Russian edition of the *Communist Manifesto* itself, as a possible way for Russia to achieve the revolution ahead of the West.

Feminists of today are right when they separate themselves from Engels' *Origin of the Family* and certainly are right when they refuse to follow the so-called "orthodox" who consider Marx and Engels as one and who stagify the whole question by insisting that we must overthrow capitalism "first" and then, after the revolution, we will be free. Feminists have no right, however, to consider *Origin of the Family* to be a work of Marx. They are absolutely right to deny that male chauvinism is a characteristic only of capitalism. The uniqueness of today's Women's Liberation Movement, indeed, is precisely that it has illuminated the male chauvinism *within* the Left.

When the National Black Feminist Organization was organized in 1973, one of their spokeswomen said:

> We are often asked the ugly question, "Where are your loyalties? To the Black movement or the feminist movement?" It would be nice if we were oppressed as women Monday through Thursday, then oppressed as Blacks the rest of the week. We could combat one or the other on those days—but we have to fight both every day of the week.

Their Statement of Principles said:

> We will encourage the Black community to stop falling into the trap of the white male Left, utilizing women only in terms of domestic or servile needs. We will remind the Black Liberation Movement that there can't be liberation for half a race.

As we can see, it isn't only that Engels' *Origin of the Family* is not a work of Marx, but that the trail Marx did leave for us is by no means as finished as the works he left for publication. What we have in his Notes is a mine of new moments that must first be worked out for our own age.

We are the ones who, through the last three decades, have seen a movement from practice that is itself a form of theory and that is challenging the theoretician to rise to the point of philosophy while we root ourselves in that movement from practice. It is there that all sorts of new forces of revolution as Reason have arisen—from Women's

Liberationists to the whole new generation of anti-war youth and Black revolutionaries. A whole new world, the Third World, has emerged. We have seen East European revolutionaries bring Marx's early Humanist Essays onto the current historic stage because they were fighting Communist totalitarianism, even as the Third World was fighting Western imperialism.

When Marx, in his *Ethnological Notebooks*, refers to the "lousy orientalists," he means the British imperialist ideologues who specialized in so-called "Oriental" work. He called them "blockheaded" British rulers. When he commented on Lubbock's criticism of the "backward" Australian aborigine, Marx turned it completely around and called the aborigine "that intelligent black."

Above all, we can see that Marx—whether he is speaking of the Arabs in Algiers or the American Indians or the Irish women who had more rights before British imperialism took over or the youth fighting the educational system—is ending with further development of what he began with: the revolution in permanence that is needed to uproot all the old and create totally new human relations.

Permit me to conclude, then, with the last two paragraphs from my new work, *Rosa Luxemburg, Women's Liberation, and Marx's Philosophy of Revolution:*

> It isn't because we are any "smarter" that we can see so much more than other post-Marx Marxists. Rather, it is because of the maturity of our age. It is true that other post-Marx Marxists have rested on a truncated Marxism; it is equally true that no other generation could have seen the problematic of our age, much less solve our problems. Only live human beings can recreate the revolutionary dialectic forever anew. And these live human beings must do so in theory as well as in practice. It is not a question only of meeting the challenge from practice, but of being able to meet the challenge from the self-development of the Idea, and of deepening theory to the point where it reaches Marx's concept of the philosophy of "revolution in permanence."
>
> What is needed is a new unifying principle, on Marx's ground of humanism, that truly alters both human thought and human experience. Marx's *Ethnological Notebooks* are a historic happening that proves, one hundred years after he wrote them, that Marx's legacy is no mere heirloom, but a live body of ideas and perspectives that is in need of concretization. Every moment of Marx's development, as well as the totality of his works, spells out the need for "revolution in permanence." This is the absolute challenge to our age.

PART II

PART II
Revolutionaries All

CHAPTER 9

Iran: Unfoldment of, and Contradictions in, Revolution*

A whole host of specters are haunting Khomeini's "Islamic Republic" before it is ever officially established. There is the specter of a full social revolution in the very unfoldment of the Iranian Revolution which, after all, witnessed a series of the greatest, most powerful, and sustained mass mobilizations for months on end before the three days of insurrection. Clearly, February 9–12 had not only driven the Shah and his stooge, Bakhtiar, from the throne, but the manner in which the workers ended their general strike to return to work without returning their guns, as the Ayatollah had commanded, showed that only Chapter 1 of the Revolution had ended. It put a special emphasis to the complaints of his appointed Prime Minister, Bazargan, about lack of production. As the Deputy Prime Minister, Entezam, put it: "Despite the Ayatollah's commands, none of the major industries in the country are functioning because the workers spend all their time holding political meetings."

As if Workers' Councils, Neighborhood Committees, Anjumen, many new forms of spontaneous organization, and youth dominant in all, did not take on the apparition of a dual government, there came, with the celebration of International Women's Day, a mass outpouring of women, bearing the banner, "We made the revolution for freedom, and got unfreedom," which may very well have opened Chapter 2 of the Iranian Revolution. It is true there had been other outbursts of criticism of Khomeini from the Fedayeen. But whereas Khomeini's friend, Arafat of the PLO, persuaded them to call off the march to Khomeini's headquarters[1] and, instead, hold a rally at Teheran University, the Women's Liberationists took to the streets.

---

*Excerpts from a "Political-Philosophic Letter" written March 25, 1979. This Letter was translated into Farsi by Iranian revolutionaries in the spring of 1979. It became part of the Farsi-language pamphlet *Raya Dunayevskaya's Political-Philosophic Letters on Revolution and Counter-Revolution in Iran*, published in late 1981.

No doubt Khomeini was ignorant of the fact that March 8 was International Women's Day, and the Iranian women intended to make their celebration of the past a claim on the present and future when he issued the March 7 order for the women to wear the chador. But his mild retreat—the claim that it was a "duty, not an order"—hardly succeeded in exorcising the new specter. Quite the contrary. Though the Ayatollah criticized the goons who attacked the march, tried to stone the women, and shot three, the women felt that those goons were in fact practicing what the Ayatollah preached as "Islamic law."

For five straight days the women continued their marches, and not only against Khomeini, but against Prime Minister Bazargan, and on March 10 held a 3 hour sit-in at the Ministry of Justice. Nor did they tolerate the mass media's autocratic choice of what they would photograph, whom they would give voice to, whom they would focus on. Instead of letting their protests go unrecorded, the women marched upon the mass media, thus exposing the fact that the censorship there is now almost as total as it was during the Shah's dictatorship. Think how quickly those bourgeois and petty-bourgeois opportunists changed sides. They waited two days after the insurrection started before they came to the radio to announce that they will not oppose the people but be "the voice of the revolution." That was February 11. The very next day they snuck in an adjective; they now called themselves the "voice of the *Islamic* revolution" . . .

THE MAIN ENEMY IS ALWAYS AT HOME

. . . Unfortunately, all those powerful mass mobilizations, and deaths of thousands, which culminated in ending the Shah's and SAVAK's (CIA-trained in torture) despotism and terrorism and exploitation, are but the merest beginnings of anything new, that is to say, worker-controlled. Unfortunately, Khomeini still remains very nearly unchallenged, that is *seriously* unchallenged, as if his intransigence in demanding "Death to the Shah!," which had acted as a unifying force when the weak National Front was still bargaining with the Shah, was, in fact, what had begun *and* deepened the revolution. And, unfortunately, the Left, too, had unfurled no new banner of freedom, and some are willing to settle for much, much less, being part of State Administration, that is, part of the new ruling bureaucracy while shouting "anti-imperialism."

Of course U.S. imperialism is the most gigantic, militaristic, nuclearly-armed Titan in the world. Of course we, as American revolutionaries, must work to see that it never re-establishes itself in Iran or anywhere else. And, of course, we must point to the fact that the rush to the present Middle East treaty was induced precisely by the fear of the consequences of the Iranian Revolution.[2] Nevertheless, we must not permit the indigenous Iranian counter-revolution to hide under the slogan of anti-imperialism, as some in the Left are trying to do by branding not only U.S. imperialism but Kate Millett (who had come to Iran to express her solidarity with the Iranian women revolutionaries) and, indeed, the whole women's revolutionary movement as if they are "agents of imperialism."[3] Nothing could assure the victory of the counter-revolution more than that kind of "anti-imperialism."

Let us, instead, turn to the genuine indigenous roots of a most unique revolution, the very one that is now being so bandied about as if the only point involved in it, great though that was for that year, was the Constitution of 1906. The Revolution lasted from 1906 to 1911. We turn to this period not only for nationalism but internationalism, and not only for the past but the present.

TWO IRANIAN REVOLUTIONS, 1906-11, AND TODAY'S

One look at the 1906 Revolution[4] will reveal its two greatest features that today's Islamic celebrants keep quiet about. One is its inspiration in the Russian Revolution of 1905. Indeed, it was at the height of the Russian Revolution, November-December 1905, that the first general strike broke out in Teheran. While today Iran means oil, in 1905 it was Baku, Russia, that meant oil, and because thousands of Iranian oil workers were in Russia and were inspired by the Russian workers fighting Tsarism, they learned also about a very new form of organization—Soviets. This, then, was what became the form of spontaneous organization in Iran as well.

The uniqueness in Iran was that what had started out, indigenously enough, as a secret organization, became Anjumen (Soviets), a very nearly dual government—local units organized independently of the Shah *and the Majlis* (Parliament) by popular elections, defending their independence on the ground that there was too much bureaucratic corruption in the government. By 1907, these Anjumen were by no means limited to Teheran but functioned also in Tabriz, Enzeli, and not only in the towns, but spread to rural areas. What is ironic is that one—Shuster—who was very far removed from any Anjumen, much less that of women, revealed the historic role of the women by the mere description of what happened: "The Persian women since 1907 had become almost at a bound the most progressive, not to say radical, in the world. That this statement upsets the ideas of centuries makes no difference. It is the fact." (p. 191)

Shuster describes how "out from their walled courtyards and harems marched 300 of that weak sex; with the flush of undying determination in their cheeks, they were clad in their plain black robes with the white nets of their veils dropped over their faces. Many held pistols under their skirts or in the folds of their sleeves." (p. 198)

Shuster concludes: "During the five years following the successful but bloodless revolution in 1906 against the oppressions and cruelty of the Shah, a feverish and at times fierce light shone in the veiled eyes of Persia's women, and in their struggles for liberty and its modern expressions, they broke through some of the most sacred customs which for centuries past had bound their sex in the land of Iran." (p. 192)

It is true—and this uniqueness exists unto today and must under no circumstances be disregarded in coping with the ulemas, mullahs, and ayatollahs—that the religious leaders sided with the revolution, or at least its first stages. As against Russia where—though Father Gapon had triggered the opening of the Revolution when his march to the Tsar's Palace was transformed into Bloody Sunday in January 1905, by the Cossacks firing into the march—the Orthodox Church sided with the Tsar, the religious leaders in Iran went with the Iranian masses both in opposing Russian domination and demanding the Shah grant a Constitution and allow them to establish a Majlis.

But even here we must see the negative features. For the first chapter, the one so celebrated now, the December 1906 Constitution, limited the Shah's power and produced a Majlis. There then followed many spontaneous organizations that worked independently of it. Once the Majlis convened, the religious leaders began moving away from any class struggle. By October 1907, the Amendments the Majlis passed restored many powers to the Shah, especially the supreme command of the armed forces, so that one could hardly call him just a figurehead. In any case, Tsarism, which had been too busy putting down the Russian Revolution to be overly involved in Iran, decided to move against it, and by 1908 the Cossack Regiment bombarded the Majlis and put down the revolution. But here still another unique feature emerges. Whereas the Russian Revolution was totally crushed in 1908, in Iran it reemerged, and the Shah was driven from his throne. It took more Cossack brigades and British imperialism as well as the Shah, after three more years, finally to destroy entirely that revolution.

Now, it is the difference between the December 1906 Constitution and the October 1907 Amendments which points not just to the duality in the Shi'ite leadership in various periods *within* an ongoing revolution. It points as well to today: the March 30 plebiscite staring us in the face.

Khomeini-Bazargan must not succeed just because they will have won so fake an "election." Yet we cannot entertain any illusions. It will be much, much harder for revolutionaries to function. The imminent counterrevolution is being institutionalized . . .

Ayatollah Khomeini's stopping the revolutionary tribunals against the Shah's most powerful and vicious henchmen in the SAVAK and in the government has focused on just how rapidly he is turning the clock back, and by no means only at the expense of the women's freedom. *Those* acts of retrogression are not only dangerous logic. They are acts of outright *counter*revolution. Let us extend our solidarity to the embattled revolutionaries—the new generation of revolutionary students as well as workers; Women's Liberationists as well as national minorities, Kurds especially, fighting for self-determination. Let us extend the activities here to stop the interfering hand of U.S. imperialism hungering for oil and the strategic location for its nuclear global aim.

The struggle continues.

NOTES

1. That this is not the first time Arafat helped stifle an ongoing revolution is seen clearest in Lebanon. See my Political-Philosophic Letter of August 1976, "Lebanon: The Test Not Only of the PLO but the Whole Left."
2. See the Editorial "Egypt-Israel: U.S. Imperialism's Middle East Outpost," *News & Letters*, April 1979.
3. *Le Monde* (March 14, 1979) prints an article, "Left Groups Advise Women Against Continuing Street Demonstrations," by its correspondent in Teheran, Jean Gueyros, that quotes a leader of the Fedayeen condemning the women demonstrators for weakening the Bazargan government, thus letting "the country sink into a civil war which will profit nobody." Evidently that part of the Fedayeen, Maoist-tinged and otherwise, is ready to settle for becoming part of the state!

In Detroit, Women's Liberationists demonstrating in solidarity with the Iranian women had their own experience of being heckled by Iranian students, mostly Maoists, combining their slogans against U.S. imperialism with "Long Live Khomeini." The following week, those Iranian students held a press conference in which, once again, they slandered Kate Millett and had the gall to claim that, though the Iranian women had invited her, she did not represent the Iranian women. Proof? No one stopped her expulsion. Did they ever try to stop a state power and its goons? See the *Detroit Free Press*, March 21, 1979.
4. The most relevant book is *The First Russian Revolution: Its Impact on Asia* by Ivar Spector (Englewood Cliffs, N.J.: Prentice-Hall, 1962). Far from being, as the other books listed, out of context of the Russian Revolution, it is directly related to it, and though the author is a bourgeois academic, he is objective. The book that is an in-person account is *The Strangling of Persia (A Personal Narrative)* by W. Morgan Shuster (New York: Greenwood Press, 1968; copyright 1912); page references in the text are to this edition. Two other works on this period are *The Persian Revolution of 1905–1909* by Edward G. Browne (London: Cambridge University Press, 1910) and *The Shuster Mission and the Persian*

Constitutional Revolution by Robert A. McDaniel (Minneapolis: Bibliotheca Islamica, 1974). The most current books from the Left in English cannot compete with either daily reports or actual revolution. Still they should be consulted for background. See the following works by Fred Halliday: *Arabia Without Sultans* (Middlesex, England: Penguin Books, 1974) and *Iran: Dictatorship and Development* (Middlesex, England: Penguin Books, 1979).

CHAPTER 10

In Memoriam: Natalia Sedova Trotsky
Role of Women in Revolution*

The death of Natalia Sedova Trotsky marks the end of the generation that achieved the greatest, and only successful, proletarian revolution in history—the Russian Revolution in 1917. It has brought into sharp focus that other unique phenomenon—the unusual role of women in the original Russian Marxist movement.

One has only to compare an opportunist like Furtseva, the only woman to reach, for a single year, the Political Bureau of the Russian Communist Party, with a Vera Zasulitch—one of the three founders of the Russian Marxist movement—to see the class abyss that divides one from the other.

I mention Zasulitch rather than the one woman in the world Marxist movement that has made her mark as an original theoretician—Rosa Luxemburg—because, in memoriam of Natalia, I wish to speak of those women who had not gained theoretical leadership and therefore were very nearly disregarded except as faithful wives and mothers.[1] Vera Zasulitch, though a leader, was known for her bravery and emotions rather than for any theoretical contributions, although it was her letter to Karl Marx that had produced his answer on the special role that the *mir* (old Russian agricultural commune existing even in Tsarist days) might play *if* Russia could find a way "to skip" capitalism in her path to industrialization.

Vera Zasulitch was only 16, in 1861, when she was first arrested. She was in and out of jails when she gained prominence for shooting the most hated Tsarist Governor General of St. Petersburg, Trepov, for the flogging of an imprisoned fellow student. The exciting thing was that she had turned her trial into such an exposé of the horrors of Tsarism that even in those days (1878), the jury acquitted her! She was then

*From *News & Letters*, February 1962.

smuggled out to exile, and it is to her place that all who escaped from Tsarism found their way—Martov, Lenin, Trotsky. She was Plekhanov's colleague when he broke with the Populists, attacked terrorism, and founded Russian Marxism.

Natalia told me that even though they were all convinced Marxists, that is to say, believing that only the mass movement can overthrow Tsarism or capitalism, and writing heated articles against terrorism, they would all feel so elated when some particularly hated Tsarist official was shot that they would quietly drink to the daring terrorist who had made that attempt.

When, on January 23, the airwaves from France carried the news of the death of Natalia, there came over me both extreme sadness and yet a warmth and the kind of good feeling that comes from having witnessed intellectual daring, and never-ending revolutionary optimism. For the tragic news of death followed on the heels of the last letter from her addressed to the French press that I received, in which she hit back against the misrepresentations of the French press that had quoted her as saying that Leon Trotsky was allegedly "the spiritual father of Mao Tse-tung."

"These words don't belong to me at all," she fired back, "they were introduced by the writer of the interview ... A great revolutionary like Leon Trotsky could not in any way be the father of Mao Tse-tung who won his position in direct struggle with the Left Opposition (Trotskyist) and consolidated it by the murder and persecution of revolutionaries just as Chiang Kai-shek did ... I don't expect anything from the Russian party nor from its fundamentally anti-communist imitators. All de-Stalinization will prove to be a trap if it doesn't lead to the seizure of power by the proletariat and the dissolution of the police institutions, political, military, and economic, based on the counterrevolution which established Stalinist state-capitalism."[2]

This was the first time that Natalia Trotsky had used the designation of state-capitalism in her reference to *established* Communism, in China or Russia "or all others based on the latter model." Never before had Natalia developed a position beyond that developed by her famous husband. Because of this, I must confess that when, in 1947, I had come to visit her, I still thought that her theoretical development had been willingly stifled because she had subordinated everything in her life to that of Leon Trotsky.

I had asked her about her Diary (to which Trotsky refers and quotes in his *My Life*). She said she had undertaken it only to help Trotsky remember certain events in periods when he was so preoccupied that he couldn't pay attention to them, and that Trotsky had exaggerated the diary's value. I felt that in no case would she publish it if she thought any views she had might differ from those of Trotsky. But both 1951, when she broke with the American Trotskyists, and 1961, when she exposed Khrushchev's de-Stalinization as a fraud "based on the counterrevolution which established Stalinist state-capitalism" proved me wrong.

Natalia Sedova Trotsky first came in contact with the revolutionary movement in Tsarist Russia when she was only 15. When still in her teens she emigrated to Europe to study and there joined the small Russian emigré group around the paper *Iskra*. This modest self-effacing young woman had been assigned to get a room for a new and promising young theoretician who had just escaped from Siberia and whose name she had not been told. It turned out to be Lev Davidovitch Trotsky, and she was asked to make sure that he was not wasting time but preparing for his first lecture in Paris.

This was the only incident of her personal life that Natalia ever told me during the years (1937–38) that I was in Mexico as Trotsky's secretary. She said that she just couldn't get herself to enter Trotsky's room and deliver the message of the need to concentrate on the lecture. She therefore told the older comrade that she thought he was preparing since she had heard him whistling. Her interpretation of the whistle, however, was not accepted and she was sent back to knock on the door and speak to him. She was blushing and walking slowly toward the room when Lev Davidovitch burst out of it, almost knocking her over.

It was love at first sight. She was then almost 21. She remained his lifelong companion. Through the exile from Tsarism, and in Tsarist prisons, through the tidal wave of revolution and in power, in exile from Stalin till the tragic murder parted them.

I shall never forget the only time I ever saw Natalia cry. News came of the death of her son, Leon Sedoff, in Paris. I happened to have been the first to have gotten the tragic news when I answered the phone while we were all at the table eating lunch. I did not dare face anyone with that news. Stalin had persecuted her other son whose whereabouts we didn't know. He had persecuted Trotsky's daughters by his first wife as well as the wife herself until death by suicide or torture. And now this—I just sat through lunch, pretending that it was a wrong number, and at the end of the lunch the secretariat got together to figure out who should break the news to Leon Trotsky and who to

Natalia. We all decided that only Leon Trotsky could be the bearer of such news to Natalia.

They departed to their rooms and in a moment came her scream. We did not see them for eight days. The blow was the harder not only because Leon Sedoff had been their only living child, but also because he had been Trotsky's closest literary and political collaborator. When Trotsky was interned in Norway, gagged, unable to answer the monstrous charges levelled against him in the first (August 1936) Moscow Trials, Sedoff had penned *Le Livre Rouge*,[3] which, by brilliantly exposing the Moscow falsifiers, dealt an irreparable blow to the prestige of the GPU (Russian Secret Police).

In the dark days after the tragic news had reached us, when Leon Trotsky and Natalia were closeted in their room, Trotsky wrote the story of their son's brief life. It was the first time since prerevolutionary days that Trotsky had written by hand.

On the eighth day Leon Trotsky emerged from his room. I was petrified at the sight of him. The neat, meticulous Leon Trotsky had not shaved for a whole week. His face was deeply lined. His eyes were swollen from so much crying. Without uttering a word, he handed me the hand-written manuscript, *Leon Sedoff, Son, Friend, Fighter*, which contained some of Trotsky's most poignant writing. My eyes set first on this statement, "I told Natalia of the death of our son—in the same month of February in which, 32 years ago, she brought to me in jail the news of his birth. Thus ended for us the day of February 16th, the blackest day in our personal lives . . . Together with our boy has died everything that still remained young within us." The pamphlet was dedicated "to the proletarian youth."

The following morning the papers carried the announcement of the Third (March 1938) Moscow Trials, scheduled to open within two short weeks of the death of Leon Sedoff.

One day shortly after this Natalia went for a walk with me in the woods, and there she began to cry quietly and asked me not to let Leon Trotsky know since he more than anyone needed all his strength and our help to answer these fantastic, slanderous charges from the man in the Kremlin who was bent on murdering the one man (Trotsky) who could still lead a revolution against the bureaucracy and restore the Russian, and thereby the international, movement to its Marxist path of liberation.

With the beginning of the Third Moscow Trials we had to forget everything else and concentrate on fighting the fantastic charges. Stalin, backed up by the might of Russian state and military power, had been preparing the stage for these monstrous frame-ups for a full decade. Leon Trotsky had only two hours in which to answer—and that only because the Mexican press would tell him what charges came over the teletype and held the presses open for him to answer.

Two years after the Trials had been exposed not only by Trotsky himself, but by the Commission of Inquiry, headed by the late John Dewey, as the greatest frame-up in history, a GPU agent drove an ice-axe into the head of Leon Trotsky. In the lonely, hectic decade that followed, Natalia also found that she had to separate herself from the Fourth International her husband had founded.

When I had visited Natalia in 1947, she had asked me about my writings. Although I had broken with Trotsky over the class nature of Russia and its defense, she not only treated me as a colleague because of my past association with Trotsky, but was very interested in finding out what were the theoretical reasons for the break. She had me translate for her, word for word, my articles on the Russian revisions of Marx's theory of value.[4]

She refused, however, to take a position on the designation of Russia as state-capitalist. She said that it was implicit in Trotsky's fight against the bureaucracy, that she felt he himself would have reached that position had he lived through to the end of the war and seen the Stalinist exploitation of Eastern Europe. But she insisted that she simply did not know enough theory to venture out on her own when Trotsky had died before coming to such a conclusion.

In 1951, however, she felt she had to speak out against the American Trotskyists for falling into the trap created by Tito's break from Stalin as well as the Korean War. She wrote to the Political Committee of the Socialist Workers Party in unflinching Bolshevik language.*

A decade passed before we saw from her pen her final conclusion that Russia was a state-capitalist society. It came during the 22nd Russian Communist Party Congress where that obedient Stalinist in Stalin's lifetime—Nikita Khrushchev—dared to picture himself as an anti-Stalinist as if his suppression of the Hungarian Revolution of 1956 had not been in the true counterrevolutionary tradition of Stalin. The Trotskyists, not having learned anything from these counterrevolutionary actions, were now tending to accept the ground rules that Mao was laying down on war and revolution.

Again Natalia refused to follow. This time she hit out against both Khrushchev and Mao. She did not limit her attack to an attack of "bureaucracy." She rose to

---

*The full text of her statement was printed together with this *In Memoriam* in the February 1962 *News & Letters*.

her full stature and declared both countries state-capitalist, warning that all "de-Stalinization will prove to be a trap if it doesn't lead to the seizure of power by the proletariat, and the dissolution of the police institutions, political, military, and economic . . ."

Shortly thereafter she fell ill. On January 23 she died. The last words of this frail 81-year-old Bolshevik had all the revolutionary vigor and the optimism of a new, youthful adherent to Marxism. She leaves this generation a great heritage of heroism, independent thought, and devotion to world liberation that gives the appearance of a lack of any personal life. But I shall never forget the one moment of tears when her son died.

I shall remember Natalia in that one moment when she let the tears rain down, but reminded me not to tell Trotsky about it, and not to let it interfere with the needs of the movement—to expose the Moscow Frame-Up Trials. It so clearly expressed the combination of personal tragedy and world-wide concern, the discipline old Bolsheviks imposed on themselves not to let anything interfere with the liberating movement that presses ever forward.

I shall remember Natalia as the great revolutionary whose thoughts were as majestic as her devotion and her daring in speaking out even against those who had led the movement her husband had founded because nothing at all could stay in the way of principles.

I shall remember Natalia as the mother who had brought up her children in the midst of all these hardships to be revolutionaries in their own right, men of character who knew how to stand up to might and not flinch.

I shall remember Natalia for the legacy she has left us of a generation that made a revolution, saw the first workers' state transformed into its opposite—state capitalism—and yet wavered not either in its principledness or its optimism.

I shall always remember the tenderness that shone through the hard-as-flint attitude toward the rulers of the world who are now leading us to a nuclear holocaust.

Death here becomes a beacon to the future—the intercommunication between the ages will continue until a new, liberated world is born.

NOTES

1. To this day the American Trotskyists maintain this type of bourgeois attitude. In the February 5, 1962 issue of *The Militant*, the article that is supposed to praise Natalia's life is, in actuality, derogatory of her role as a revolutionary and as an independent

thinker. Their condescension reaches its most paternalistic hue in a reference to disagreements between them: "But this [period of political disagreements] never altered the respect or affection or material support which the movement tendered her." While they fail to publish her letter breaking with them, they do go out of the way to slander her by innuendos which imply that, if it were not for the wisdom of "the leaders of the SWP" (Socialist Workers Party), Natalia would have fallen into the trap of the House Un-American Activities Committee. Wouldn't it have been more honest if they, at least, had published her last statement denouncing Khrushchev and Mao which showed how totally different her method of fighting Stalinism is from their shadow-boxing!

2. For the full text, see the January 1962 issue of *News & Letters*.

3. It first appeared in Russian as a special issue of the *Opposition Bulletin* (organ of the Russian Bolshevik-Leninists), edited by Sedoff in Paris.

4. "A New Revision of Marxian Economics" in *The American Economic Review*, September 1944 and September 1945.

CHAPTER 11

Women as Thinkers and as Revolutionaries*

Good evening. Let's go adventuring, first in women's activities that have not been recognized as revolutions, such as the first Women's Rights Convention at Seneca Falls, N.Y. in 1848, and the Aba "riots" in Nigeria, 1929, and then take the plunge into three revolutions: Russia, February 1917; Germany, January 1919; and the ongoing revolution in Portugal now. In each case we will become a witness to women's creativity as a liberating force.

MASS CREATIVITY AND THE BLACK DIMENSION

Creativity is so very characteristic of masses in motion that you tell a story of the past and have it sound like something just happening before your eyes.† Or you can describe a happening of today and have it sound as something that will first happen tomorrow. The temptation is also great to start the story of women's creativity neither at its beginning, nor at the end, that is, today, but somewhere in the middle. This is not due to any sort of Existentialist obsession with "extreme situations." Rather it is rooted in the truth that women's struggles have

---

* Excerpted from two lectures: "Today's Women Theorists," given in Detroit, at the Wayne State University-University of Michigan Cultural Center, Sept. 1975; and "Rosa Luxemburg," given at the University of Wisconsin at Madison, May 1976.

† Here is the way I described such a spontaneous action in my *Marxism and Freedom* in 1957, in a section on "The Paris Commune—a Form of Workers' Rule":

On March 18th, the soldiers were ordered by M. Thiers, the head of the reactionary government, to transport the cannon of Paris to Versailles. The milkmaids, who were on the streets before dawn, saw what was afoot and thwarted the treacherous plans of the reactionary government. They surrounded the soldiers and prevented them from carrying out Thiers' orders. Although the men had not yet come into the streets on this early morning and although the women were not armed, they held their own. As in every real peoples' revolution, new strata of the population were awakened. This time it was the women who were to act first. When reveille was sounded, all of Paris was in the streets. Thiers' spies barely escaped with the information that it was impossible to inform on who the leaders of the uprising were, since the *entire* population was involved.

79

created totally new situations, hidden from history and still unrecognized as philosophic ground. What today we call Women's Liberation, as an Idea whose time has come, are movements from practice, from below, that have been accumulating through the ages.

Take the so-called Aba "riots" in Eastern Nigeria in 1929, some 30 years before anyone thought seriously of Africa, much less African women, as a new development of world freedom. It was in that inauspicious year that the market women in Eastern Nigeria were suddenly taxed by the occupying British Empire. This was done with the consent of the African chiefs. The anger of the women, however, was unbounded and therefore, though the men, the educated ones, would not help the illiterate women resist the imposition of the tax, the women decided, themselves, to revolt.

The self-organization of the women established a totally new form of struggle which transcended all tribal divisions—Ibo, Yoruba, Hausa, as well as the smaller tribes. So united, powerful, and violent was the opposition of the women to the edicts, to their own chiefs, as well as to the British imperial rule, that it became impossible to contain the revolt. Shots were fired into the crowd, and only when 40 women lay dead and many more injured was so-called "order" restored. Even then, however, it was achieved only after the tax was revoked, with British rulers claiming that they had been unaware of African "traditions" that the women not be taxed.

The attitude towards women's struggles seems always to play down women's actions as not meriting the description "revolutionary." For that matter, even up to our day, has any historian, or even revolutionary, seen that historic act as ground from which a great leap into freedom as well as leadership was achieved in the 1960s? Nor can the neglect be explained only by the fact that the event occurred in far-off Africa, back at the outbreak of the Great Depression.

Take the Women's Rights Convention in this country in 1848, at Seneca Falls, N.Y., a fact often enough recorded by women historians of today. All underestimate the Black dimension which inspired the white, middle-class, educated women to strike out on their own. Sojourner Truth and sometimes also Harriet Tubman are dutifully mentioned, condescendingly admitting their bravery—and of course their suffering as slaves—but never as Reason which drove the educated to face reality: that the Black women were the orators, generals, and, yes, thinkers, whereas they, the middle-class intellectuals, were but subordinates.

For that matter, have we asked ourselves, as we proudly repeat

Women's Liberation is an Idea whose time has come, such simple questions as: (1) How does it happen that our very names, "freed from patriarchy," do not measure up to Sojourner Truth's, whose whole philosophy of liberation is included in her name? (2) Have we even today, as we inveigh against "male domination," compared that to Sojourner Truth's separation from Frederick Douglass after the Civil War for being "short-minded" because he did not wish to burden the struggle for passage of the 14th Amendment by demanding also the right of women to vote? And (3) Have today's women theorists built on that movement from below, not only as force, but as Reason? Nor have any analyzed it within the context of that year of revolutions, 1848.

Let's take a second look at that year, 1848. Was the first Women's Rights Convention really totally unrelated to the revolutions that covered the length and breadth of Europe? Isn't it a fact, though hardly recorded, that the women of the French Revolution of that year published a daily paper, *La Voix des Femmes* (which is something the women of today have yet to create)?

Other than Marx's genius, what *was* in the air that led to Marx's discovery of a whole new continent of thought? Can we today afford to let the ruling ideology keep us hemmed into American pragmatism? Shouldn't we, as women, at least be aware of the fact that the year Marx first broke with bourgeois society and worked out a philosophy of liberation which he called "a new Humanism"—1843—was also the year when a woman, Flora Tristan, proclaimed the need for an International of men and women that would put an end to the division of mental and manual labor?

Young Flora Tristan died that year in the London plague. In Germany, the young Marx continued to develop a whole body of works, a theory of proletarian revolution, a whole philosophy of human liberation, deeply rooted both in the class struggles *and* in that most fundamental relationship, Man/Woman. Marx helped organize women's movements, not only for better wages, but for totally different conditions of labor; not only for the right to vote, but for full freedom. Eighty full pages on women and child labor went into *Capital*, Vol. I, not only as description and resistance, but, as Marx expressed it when he drew the whole work to a conclusion, "the new passions and new forces" that would produce the "negation of the negation," that is to say, become the "grave diggers" of capitalism, creating a whole new society where "the development of human power is its own end."

Some 100 years after Flora Tristan's declaration for an international organization of working men and women; after Marx's discovery of a whole new continent of thought; after the first Women's Rights Convention, in New York; and after the greatest revolution in Marx's lifetime, the Paris Commune, in which *The Women Incendiaries*[1] surely acted as both force and Reason; isn't it time to work out a philosophy so urgently needed by the Women's Liberation Movement which does not, *does not*, limit the question of women's liberation to an exposé of "the Man" and thereby becomes practically no more than a bystander to Marx's philosophy of liberation on the excuse that it is "male defined,"[2] as Sheila Rowbotham puts it?

Marx practiced what he preached, again both in the class struggle and on the question of women as Reason as well as force. Thus, in the International Workingmen's Association, Madame Law was a member of its leadership, the General Council. Thus, he encouraged Dmitrieva to go to Paris and there establish the women's section of the First International. Along with the French women like the great Louise Michel, Dmitrieva became central to the whole Committee for the Defense of Paris and Care of the Wounded in the Paris Commune. There was no break in Marx's philosophy of liberation from the time the young Marx called his philosophy a "new Humanism," and declared Man/Woman to be the most fundamental human relationship, to the Marx of the Paris Commune when he declared the greatest achievement to be "its own working existence."

Of course, Marx answered the questions of his day, not ours, but can we afford, as Women's Liberationists today, to be without a total philosophy, because the greatest philosophy for uprooting the exploitative old and creating ground for the new was formulated by "a man"?

RUSSIA, FEBRUARY 1917; GERMANY, JANUARY 1919; AND ROSA LUXEMBURG

Now let's turn to the 20th century and see, firstly, what can we learn from women *as masses in motion*, initiating nothing short of the overthrow of that reactionary Russian colossus, Tsarism—the dramatic, creative, empire-shaking five days in February, 1917; and, secondly, let's turn to the 1919 German Revolution and its greatest theoretician, Rosa Luxemburg.

That first day, Feb. 23, in Russia, appeared simple enough as a celebration of International Women's Day by the textile workers in Petrograd. But was it that simple, when they insisted it become a strike, despite a raging world war in which their country was doing very badly? Was it that simple when all revolutionary parties—Bolsheviks, Left Mensheviks, Social Revolutionaries, Anarchists—were telling them that they were courting a massacre, and they shouldn't go out on strike? Was that first day of the revolution, when 50,000 women marched despite all advice against it, a "male-defined" revolution? Was the letter they addressed to the metal workers, which the metal workers honored by joining the strike—and 50,000 grew to 90,000: men and women, housewives as well as factory workers—a proof of the fact that they didn't really "know" what they were doing?

When the Bolsheviks did join the women textile workers and the strike turned into political opposition to the imperialist war and the Cossacks did open fire, it was too late to save the Russian empire. By then the soldiers also joined the masses in revolt, and "spontaneously" the whole rotten empire toppled.

It is true that those five historic days that crumbled the might of Tsarism led, in turn, to the Revolution of Oct. 25, and that certainly was led by the Bolshevik Party. That, however, can no more detract from what the women workers initiated on Feb. 23, than the October Revolution can be blamed for its transformation into opposite under Stalin a decade later.

What had happened in action, what had happened in thought, what had happened in consciousness of the mass participants—all this is ground on which we build today. Or should be. But even if some still insist on playing down women *both* as masses in motion and as leadership, let them consider the German Revolution, January 1919, led by Rosa Luxemburg. None questioned that she was the leader.

From 1898 when she fought the first appearance of reformism in the Marxist movement, through the 1905 Revolution in which she was both a participant and out of which she drew her famous theory of the Mass Strike; from 1910–13 when she broke with Karl Kautsky—four years in advance of Lenin's designation of Kautsky as not only opportunist but betrayer of the proletariat—and when she first developed her anti-imperialist struggles and writings, not only as political militant but carving out her greatest and most original theoretical work, *Accumulation of Capital*, to the 1919 Revolution; she made no division between her theory and her practice.

Take her *Reform or Revolution* against Bernstein, who demanded that "the dialectical scaffolding" be removed from Marx's "materialism." Talking of Bernstein, she wrote:

> When he directs his keenest arrows against our dialectic system, he is really attacking the specific mode of thought employed by the conscious proletariat in its struggle for liberation .... It is an attempt to shatter the intellectual arm with the aid of which the

proletariat, though materially under the yoke of the bourgeoisie, is yet enabled to triumph over the bourgeoisie. For it is our dialectical system that shows to the working class the transitory character of this yoke, proving to the workers the inevitability of their victory, and is already realizing a revolution in the domain of thought.[3]

The next great historic event—the Russian Revolution of 1905—again reveals her as theorist and activist-participant who did not stop at oratory but, with gun in hand, made the proprietor-printer print a workers' leaflet. What she singled out, however, from the great experience, what she made ground for other revolutions, what she created as a theory also for the relationship of spontaneity to party, was *The Mass Strike, the Political Party and the Trade Unions*:

> The revolution is not an open-field maneuver of the proletariat, even if the proletariat with social democracy at its head plays the leading role, but it is a struggle in the middle of incessant movement, the creaking, crumbling and displacement of all social foundations. In short, the element of spontaneity plays such a supreme role in the mass strikes in Russia, not because the Russian proletariat is "unschooled", but because revolutions are not subject to schoolmastering.[4]

It is this concept and this activity and this perspective that led, in 1907, to Luxemburg's joining with Lenin and Trotsky to amend the resolution at the Stuttgart meeting of the International that declared socialist opposition to war and the imperative need to transform it into revolution.

At the time when Luxemburg recognized the non-revolutionary character of Karl Kautsky, when all other Marxists, Lenin included, were still acknowledging him as the greatest theoretician of the Second International, she embarked on the most hectic point of activity outside of a revolution itself.

She felt very strongly that the German Social Democracy had been hardly more than a bystander instead of militant fighter against Germany's imperialist adventures. It was this, and not mere "organizational" questions, which made her return to her original analysis of mass strike which had always meant to her that "the masses will be the active chorus, and the leaders only 'speaking parts', the interpreters of the will of the masses."

Luxemburg was not only involved in lecturing and developing an anti-imperialist struggle over the Morocco crisis which would, in turn, lead to her greatest theoretical work, *Accumulation of Capital*,[5] but she also turned to work on the "Woman Question,"[6] which heretofore she had left entirely to Clara Zetkin, who was editing the greatest German women's magazine, *Die Gleichheit*, from 1891 to 1917.

The magazine's circulation rose from 9,500 in 1903 to 112,000 in 1913. Indeed, by the outbreak of the war, the female membership in the German Social Democracy was no less than 170,000. It is clear that, as great a theoretician as Rosa Luxemburg was, and as great an organizer as Clara Zetkin was, they were not exceptions to the alleged apathy of German women. On the contrary, it would be more correct to say that there wouldn't have been as massive and important a revolution in Germany were there not that many women involved in the revolution. Naturally none could compare with Rosa Luxemburg as theoretician. That is certainly true of genius whether that be woman or man. As one of the very few persons who has written on the subject put it, were it not for the proletarian women, "there might have been no revolution in Germany."[7]

Despite all the misrepresentation of her position on the Russian Revolution, Luxemburg had hailed it as the greatest proletarian revolution ever, insisting that the Russian Bolsheviks alone had dared and dared again. It was exactly for such a daring act that she was preparing herself from her jail cell, from which she was not freed until Nov. 9, 1918, when the German masses in revolt had driven the Kaiser from the throne. Anyone who tried to use her criticism of the Russian Revolution as the German Revolution unfolded got from her the following: Where did you learn the ABCs of revolution? Is it not from the Russians? Who taught you the slogan, "All power to the soldiers, workers, and peasants"? Isn't it the Russians? This is the dialectics of revolution: that is what Spartakus wants; this is the road we are taking now.

Rosa Luxemburg lived only two and a half months after being let out of jail. Two and a half months in which the upsurge of the masses led to the establishment first of the Spartakus League and then the independent Communist Party in Germany. Two and a half months in which to call for all power to the soldiers' and workers' councils. And then the counterrevolution caught up with her, shot her, bashed in her head, and threw her body into the Landwehr Canal.

Does the beheading of the German Revolution—Liebknecht and Jogiches were murdered along with Luxemburg—mean that we're not to learn from a revolution because it was "unsuccessful"?

Has the Women's Liberation Movement nothing to learn from Rosa Luxemburg just because she hasn't written "directly" on the "Woman Question"? Outside the fact that the latter doesn't happen to be true, should not the corpus of her works become the real test of woman as revolutionary and as thinker and as someone who has a great deal to tell us as Women's Liberationists today? Are we to throw all that into the dustbin of history because she had not written on the "Woman Question"?

AN ONGOING REVOLUTION AND TODAY'S WOMEN THEORISTS

The plunge into revolutions is being undertaken because they not only are exciting events of the early 20th century, but also will illuminate the problems of our day. We need to examine, if only briefly, today's ongoing Portuguese Revolution to see the historic continuity of working class women in motion as shapers of history. As far back as two decades ago, when the totally new movement from below began with the outbreak of the East European revolt against Russian totalitarianism, signaling a new world stage of struggle for freedom from under totalitarianism, and no one was paying attention to the fascist regime in Portugal, there were struggles of workers, of women, of peasants.

The first woman to die in Portugal, in the mid-1950s, in the fight for the eight-hour day, was Caterina Eufemia. It is she who was to become the symbol for the women's movement—MDM—that was organized in the underground. For that matter, she became also the symbol for the struggle for women's rights of the new MLM, which was organized by intellectuals and middle-class women, when the "Three Marias"[8] were freed from jail.

The undercurrents of revolt had actually been germinating long before 1974. When no others were paying attention to Portugal as the youth rebellion around the world reached a highpoint in 1968, there was, in fact, an outbreak of revolts in Portugal by students who were fighting not only for academic freedom, but against being drafted for the Portuguese imperialist wars in Africa. The two highpoints that were reached in all these undercurrents of revolt came from within the army in Mozambique, Guinea-Bissau and Angola,[9] and from within Portugal itself.

Within the country itself there was a whole series of wildcats in 1973. Women became especially important in 1973 when a labor shortage sent them into textiles and electronics, directly into the fight against multinationals. It is in textiles and electronics and shipyards where the grass roots workers' movement first erupted, and where none questioned the militancy of women workers. But they were asking not only for a fundamental change in labor conditions, but for different relations at home, as well as raising totally new questions of revolution and new human relations.

With the overthrow of the fascist Caetano regime in April 1974, there were outbreaks of all sorts of wildcats, freeing the revolution itself from the neo-fascist "leadership" of Spinola and creating the foundation also of a new Women's Liberation Movement. Women's participation became critical as three movements—the rebellion within the army, and the wildcats of industrial workers covering the length and breadth of the country, as well as the peasant occupation of the land—coalesced. It was no accident that one of the revolutionary political movements that arose, PRP/BR, was headed by a woman, Isabel do Carmo.

As can be seen, the question of revolutionary creativity is not just that of an individual, not even when she's as great as Rosa Luxemburg, and certainly not that of artists or scientists. Now then, let us see whether the movement from practice was the stuff out of which the women theorists of today, whether they be in the U.S., England, or any other technologically advanced country, built their theories.

With the rise of the Women's Liberation Movement in the mid-1960s, when a whole new generation of revolutionaries was born out of the Black Revolution, the anti-Vietnam War movement, and the world-wide national liberation struggles, we had the rise also of women theorists. The new in the struggles of the mid-1960s, when it came to the Women's Liberation Movement was the women's refusal to wait for the day *after* "the Revolution" for *their* total freedom. They refused to narrow their struggles to a fight for equal wages or, for that matter, any other economic demands. They raised all sorts of new questions, from sexuality to opposition both to patriarchy and the ingrained division between mental and manual labor. For what they aspired to was nothing short of the wholeness of the person.

The women theorists have done considerable work in exposing male chauvinism in history and in the Movement itself. It was certainly of the essence to make such relatively undiscussable subjects as sexuality discussable, not à la Freud, but against Freud. Works like Kate Millett's *Sexual Politics* exposed the male chauvinism of great writers of our day, from D.H. Lawrence to Norman Mailer. Others took issue with all forms of patriarchy. The weak point was that none of them were in any serious way related to working-class women, their activities, their thoughts, their aspirations. The one exception was Sheila Rowbotham's *Women, Resistance and Revolution*.

In dealing with 300 years of women's struggles, in concentrating on labor struggles and revolutions and openly espousing socialism, and in bringing in the question of male chauvinism not as something only capitalistic, but very much pervasive within the Movement itself, she focused on the validity of an independent women's movement. Unfortunately, so preoccupied was she with "the new" that she neither dug deeply into philosophic roots nor so much as mentioned one of the greatest revolutionary theoreticians, Rosa Luxemburg. Whatever the reason—whether it was because Rosa didn't write voluminously on the "Woman Question," or Rosa Luxemburg's works and activities are not, to her mind, relevant to today's women's tasks, or whatever—she thereby actually degraded women's revolutionary role. Indeed, flying in the face of history, she writes as if all revolutions were "male-defined." This only leads her to a vanguardist conclusion that women, even when doing nothing short of initiating a great revolution that toppled Tsarism, lacked "consciousness." That is still one other form of considering women "backward." In a word, no matter how "consciously" one favors an independent women's movement, one doesn't really consider them capable of "getting there"—unless led by a "Vanguard Party." Vanguardism, elitism cannot but impede the Women's Liberation Movement of today from working out a new relationship of spontaneity to organization, theory to practice, philosophy to revolution. It is but one more form of separating thinking from doing, especially as it relates to women as thinkers and as revolutionaries.

Working-class women have a very special reason for their passionate interest in revolutions, not simply because they're exciting events, but because they show working-class women in motion as shapers of history. The dialectical relationship of spontaneity to organization is of the essence to all of us as we face today's crises. It is not only Portugal which is under the whip of counterrevolution that began Nov. 25, 1975. The global struggle for power between capitalist imperialism and state-capitalist societies calling themselves Communist, all nuclearly armed, has put a question mark over the very survival of humanity.

Creativity that can really tear things up at their roots and genuinely start something new, humanly new, can only come from mass creativity. It is only then when it is totally revolutionary, is not hemmed in by the concept and practice of the "Party to lead," and it is only then it can once and for all end aborted and unfinished revolutions.

Be it something as "simple" as the question of women's struggle for equality in the very midst of all the myriad crises, or the deep recession and racism in the U.S., what women are hungering for is working out the relationship of their creativity to a philosophy of liberation. We surely do not need yet one more form of elitism. What we do need is a *unity* of philosophy and revolution. Without it, we will not be able to get out from under the whip of the counterrevolution.

NOTES

1. See *The Women Incendiaries* by Edith Thomas (New York: George Braziller, 1966). This work on the women in the Paris Commune, a must for all Women's Liberationists, is out of print, and so far there has been no paperback edition. It is a most detailed and creative analysis of the revolution of 1871.

2. Sheila Rowbotham, *Women, Resistance and Revolution* (New York: Vintage Books Edition, 1974), p. 11.

3. Rosa Luxemburg, *Reform or Revolution* (New York: Three Arrows Press, 1937), p. 47.

4. Luxemburg's pamphlet on *The Mass Strike* is included in *Rosa Luxemburg Speaks*, Mary-Alice Waters, ed. (New York: Pathfinder Press, 1970), pp. 155–218.

5. I happen to disagree seriously with her theory in *Accumulation of Capital*, because I consider it a deviation from Marx. This cannot, however, detract from the important contribution it made in the struggle against imperialism in her day. See my *State-Capitalism and Marx's Humanism or Philosophy and Revolution* (Detroit: News & Letters, 1967).

6. See Rosa Luxemburg's speech on "Women's Suffrage and Class Struggle" at the Stuttgart Second Social Democratic Women's Rally, May 12, 1912, included in *Selected Political Writings of Rosa Luxemburg*, Dick Howard, ed., (New York: Monthly Review Press, 1971), pp. 216–222.

7. A good beginning on this subject has been made by William A. Pelz in his unpublished thesis, "The Role of Proletarian Women in the German Revolution, 1918–19," presented at the Conference on the History of Women, College of Ste. Catherine, St. Paul, Minn., Oct. 24–25, 1975.

8. The original title of the work for which Maria Isabel Barreno, Maria Teresa Horta, and Maria Velho da Costa were imprisoned was *New Portuguese Letters*, published in 1972. It was published in English as *The Three Marias* (New York: Doubleday & Co., 1974).

9. The leaflets of the FRELIMO in Mozambique, the PAIGC in Guinea-Bissau, and MPLA in Angola may not match the fraternization leaflets that the Bolsheviks wrote in 1917, but they certainly were an entirely new ground for fighting in Portugal, 1974. In urging the Portuguese soldiers to go home and make their own revolution, the national liberation forces were raising questions, including the role of women, that the "advanced" Portuguese had not even heard of. See *The Struggle for Mozambique* by Eduardo Mondlane (Baltimore: Penguin Books, 1969) and *Return to the Source* by Amilcar Cabral (New York: Monthly Review Press, 1973).

CHAPTER 12

Two Contributions by Olga Domanski*

I

A Summary of Six Lectures for International Women's Year

November 6, 1975

Dear Friends:

How can you adequately summarize the series of lectures on "Women as Thinkers and as Revolutionaries" that we have just concluded in Detroit at the University Center for Adult Education, when it had a scope so vast that the participants in the class were sometimes unable to even formulate their questions afterwards because they were "overwhelmed," to use their own words? There is not a single question facing the movement for freedom today—whether it be the relationship between spontaneity and organization, between theory and practice, between philosophy and revolution, between workers and intellectuals, or the relationship between the races, the sexes, or the historic ages—that the lectures did not illuminate.

The running theme throughout the entire series was the dual rhythm of revolution—as it is expressed in the movement from practice to theory AND the movement from theory to practice—seen in the movement of women throughout history. The lectures were thus the kind of extension of *Philosophy and Revolution* that deepened it so greatly that Raya is now considering these as the framework of a whole new

---

*The series of six lectures given by Raya Dunayevskaya in Fall, 1975 for the Wayne State University-University of Michigan University Courses in Adult Education was summarized by Olga Domanski, a member of the National Editorial Board of News & Letters in Detroit. Her own essay, "Women's Liberation in Search of a Theory," was published by *News & Letters*, June, 1980.

book. In fact, she extended an invitation, during the lectures, to others who would wish to work with her on it . . .

First, let's take the question of the fantastic amount of sheer "facts" Raya unearthed in her voluminous reading for the course. (The bibliography for the series is an education in itself—and Raya expanded it greatly at every lecture.) Never was it clearer to me what Hegel means when he describes facts as "emerging out of ground." Think of the way Raya took both the "facts" that have been buried in the countless different books she read, *and* the facts that all of us have heard so often we may think we know them by heart, and presented them in so new a relationship with all the other facts of history and philosophy that something totally new is seen in them.

Take the two lectures on Working Women and on the Black Dimension. Raya traveled in the lecture on *WORKING WOMEN* all the way from 1647 (when the first maid's petition was handed to the British Parliament to demand "liberty every second Tuesday") all the way to our own period of the '50s, '60s and '70s (when she deals with the seamstress Rosa Parks who started the Black Revolution, the electrical worker Angela Terrano who talks about Automation in *Marxism and Freedom*, and the recent developments in the Coalition of Labor Union Women)—all to show how critical it is to grasp what comes from practice and from "gaining a mind of one's own." As Raya puts it: though intellectuals may love the expression "in the beginning was the word," the truth is that in the beginning was *labor*, the *deed*—and not just as source for someone else's word, but *as Subject*. Raya takes us from the 17th century through the 18th, and we meet everyone from the indentured servants of the American Revolution to Mary Wollstonecraft—but she dwells on the 19th and 20th centuries because it is there that we have, finally, the *mass movements* as creative power. The first great women's strike in America of millworkers in 1824 and the climax in the First Female Reform Association in 1844, the 1848 revolutions in Europe and the Seneca Falls Convention in America, are all put in the historic framework not only of Marx's discovery of a new continent of thought, but of Flora Tristan's call for a Workingman's International that predated Marx's call by two decades, to demonstrate that when the desire for freedom is this powerful, it is "in the air" everywhere at once, and the intellectual catches it in thought because so many workers have done it in deed for so many years before. And the story does not stop there. We see what happens when the revolutions of 1848 are defeated. The counterrevolution takes its toll, but something new that has been born cannot be totally crushed, it still stirs underground—and it bursts forth in everything from the Taiping Rebellion in China to the Civil War in the U.S., only *after* which can the National Labor Union arise. This great bursting forth of the labor movement is not "impersonal"—we see it in the struggles of Augusta Lewis who helped to organize the first printer's union when the Knights of Labor had 50,000 women members, and Clara Lemlich who called for the first general strike the East Coast ever saw, and Rose Schneiderman who organized 120,000 as a funeral for the 146 workers, mainly women, who died in the Triangle Fire, not only to mourn but to express solidarity with the unorganized workers of 1911.

Or take the lecture on the *BLACK DIMENSION*, which Raya presented as a good time to learn a new language—the language of thought, Black thought. She developed the concept of "time as the space for human development" by concentrating on specific historic turning points and what they meant. It was because of their integral connection with each of these historic points that six Black men were brought into this lecture: Nat Turner, 1831; Frederick Douglass, 1848 and 1867; W.E.B. Du Bois, Marcus Garvey, and Claude McKay, 1919; and Frantz Fanon, the 1960s. The theme throughout was the activity of Black women not only as bravery but as thought, and their story not only as suffering but as creativity, the creativity of new ideas and of new forms of struggle. Thus, it was after Nat Turner's hanging that the question to be answered was how to transcend the isolated slave revolts in order to end slavery, and the new form created was the Underground Railroad, of which the most famous conductor was Harriet Tubman. But when we hear of her in history, she is not presented as a thinker and a leader—of both men and women, both Blacks and whites. In the same way when we hear of Sojourner Truth we hear of her courage, but not of her tremendous thought, or the philosophy she carried in her very name. Nor are we made aware that though only a Black man, Frederick Douglass, would agree to chair the first meeting of the women to discuss their rights *as women*, by the time it came to 1867 even Douglass said that though he agreed "in principle" that the women should have the vote, it was not the time. It was then that Harriet Tubman and Sojourner Truth refused to accept his leadership, terming even the Black man "short-minded" and remaining with the white women in their struggles to the very end.

When we get to the '80s and '90s and the Blacks are supposedly free but have not got their 40 acres and a mule—they get instead the KKK and lynchings as the way of white civilization—a new stage begins. At the turn of the century Du Bois begins to fight against Booker T.

Washington's philosophy, and the Niagara movement is organized. We do not hear of Ida B. Wells, a cofounder of the organization and editor of their publication—but it was she who separated from Du Bois because she thought the organization too mild. Du Bois believed that every culture has its "talented tenth," and it is the Black intellectuals who will bring freedom to the masses. She didn't. And we will soon see how the talented tenth, in fact, worked *against* the masses. We will see that just as the 19th century was a century of genius, the 20th century divides into two, not on the question of "genius" but on the question of nationalism and internationalism. The two Black men who enter history here are Marcus Garvey and Claude McKay. Garvey was a relatively uneducated West Indian and McKay was a poet, a Marxist, an internationalist. Like Du Bois he was an educated intellectual, but unlike Du Bois he recognized what Garvey represented—the Black pride expressed in nationalism and the creativity that saw six million Blacks flock to Garvey in 1919 when the KKK had blood flowing in the streets and everyone was saying the Blacks couldn't be organized. Contrast that to Du Bois who was so ashamed of Garvey and the "uneducated" ones that he actually tried to help the government deport Garvey.

How clear it is that literacy has nothing to do with creativity is shown in everything from the 1929 Aba Riots in Nigeria, when the Nigerian women the British tried to tax defeated not only British imperialism and their own chiefs, but created a solidarity among all the tribes, to the strike in North Carolina in 1937 when the Black tobacco workers were told by everyone that they couldn't win—in the South, all women, and all Black—and thereupon organized themselves and won. At every stage we have a history of the bravery and the thought and the philosophy of the Black women—who have not hesitated, either, to break with their own Black men, whether it was Amy Jacques Garvey in 1919, who edited a woman's page in the *Negro World* and, criticising the Negro men as too halting, wrote "Mr. Black Man, watch your step!"—or whether it was the Black Panther women who challenged the Panther men when they were ready to give over the women's time on an agenda to Aptheker.

The women who fill the '60s are so great and so many it is impossible to begin to name them, but they stretch from Gloria Richardson, Daisy Bates, and Rosa Parks all the way to Joan Little. When we see, despite all this history, a book produced called *Chronicles of Black Protest* that does not include a single woman's voice—not even Harriet Tubman or Sojourner Truth, who rate only a picture—it becomes clear why Doris

Wright's question—"When the time comes to put down the gun, will you shove a broom in my hands?"—is not a matter of putting a precondition on her activity for revolution, but a matter of posing the question of What Comes After? as *the* question we have to answer *now*.

It is again the relationship of theory to practice that is the red thread running through the lectures on Women Theorists Today and on Literature and Revolution, but the excitement is heightened, perhaps, because so much of the material Raya developed was totally new to all. At the lecture on the *WOMEN THEORISTS TODAY* we were told from the start that we would be discovering what is meant by theory *rooted in philosophy* and "theory" which is not. For that we had to turn first to Marx and grapple with the fact that even he, though he had already discovered his great new continent of thought in 1844, as late as the 1860s when he was writing *Capital* still considered theory different from practice, an "argument with other theoreticians." It was only after seeing the actual struggles for the shortening of the working day, which Marx called greater than the Declaration of the Rights of Man, that *Capital* was reworked and that great new section on The Working Day added, while the arguments with other theoreticians were moved to the very end. The question we must ask is, what would your job be as a woman theorist, 100 years later, *if* you believed Marx's concept of theory is the right one? Simone de Beauvoir spends one single sentence in *The Second Sex* on the Paris Commune of 1871. There were 3000 members of the Women's Union for the Defense of Paris. And there were great women like Louise Michel, a poet, a teacher, a worker. Yet all Simone de Beauvoir can say is that for every Louise Michel (whose greatness she cannot deny) there were thousands of women who were backward! *The Second Sex* was published in 1949, when workers were posing the highly philosophic question of what kind of labor human beings should do, but none of this enters her thinking. None of the revolutions or revolutionaries mean anything to her. Not Dmitrieva, not Flora Tristan, not Rosa Luxemburg. She says the women who began the 1917 Russian Revolution didn't really know what they were doing. And whom does she praise? Some of the greatest women, to her, were Stakhanovites! Her "theory" leads her to wind up calling women's oppression man's burden—and because it is his fault, we supposedly must wait for man to free us. She has missed entirely the new stage of Women's Liberation that began in the '40s when women were driven into the factories and then out again at the end of the war. She follows Sartre and his Existentialism every step of the way. Hell is other people, and to her woman is Other, the Second Sex, the subordinate one. Betty Friedan couldn't shine her shoes, but she got her number in the interview recently published in the *Saturday Review of Literature.* Or take Kate Millett's *Sexual Politics.* Millett does see the relationship to history, but it is not the history of class struggles she recognizes. She divides history into two parts, on the basis of women—up to 1930, which she calls revolution, and from 1930 on, which she sees only as counterrevolution. But she thereby misses out on everything from the CIO to the Spanish Revolution in the '30s alone—and when you come to the new stage today you cannot find where it comes from. She thinks Simone de Beauvoir is great—which only shows that intellectuals "understand" intellectuals better than what comes from below.

If we move to Juliet Mitchell's *Woman's Estate,* we come face to face with Structuralism applied to the Women's Liberation Movement. Althusser says if you combine the economics of Marx with Freud, you'll get great things. Mitchell sees the "moment" that produces revolution as when a great leader tells you what to do. She winds up being a real imperialist chauvinist, concluding that only the advanced women of the West can start the revolution, and she says that *never* does class consciousness come from being at the point of production; the party alone brings you class consciousness. She quotes Lenin's *What Is To Be Done?,* disregarding the fact that Lenin changed his mind ten times after he wrote that.

What is there unifying all these women? The revolutionary petty-bourgeois intellectuals, themselves victims of the division between mental and manual labor, are always ready to hand over the role of workers' self-emancipation to The Party. They do not see the human dimension as the movement of masses in the act of uprooting the old and creating the new, but as "the existential project." But the most serious to contend with is *Sheila Rowbotham,* who is a near-Trotskyist. She takes up 300 years of history, but one look at the titles of her chapters reveals that they are completely absent of any philosophy. She is an historian, but because she doesn't see any movement in history, her conception of revolution goes back to "consciousness." In the February Russian Revolution, the women were brave but not conscious of what they were doing. She agrees that women do have to organize autonomously, but she brings them right back to the need for the party and the consciousness that the leaders will bring. In 280 pages of history, Rosa Luxemburg is not even mentioned, just because she didn't write directly on women; there is no recognition that her theory of spontaneity is one of the most important for us to take up in our age, and especially on women. She winds up, like Mitchell, concluding that the Black and Oriental women are not up to the demands our age is making. For her, "feminism and Marxism cohabit uneasily," and she gives us *preconditions* for revolution. Rather than Women's Liberation being an Idea whose time has come, Rowbotham presents it as an abstraction imposed on women. To her, Women's Liberation is a Particular form that concretizes the Universal of the new society. But, unless it is further concretized in the Individual, we will never get there—and Rowbotham cannot move to that because she denies the four forces of revolution that we recognize, the workers, the Blacks, the youth, and the women, and without these forces you have to wind up relying on the elite party to bring you socialism. Indeed, this is what all the women theorists wind up with. And what contrasts to them all is the new kind of creativity we have seen expressed by the Three Marias and especially by Maria Barreno.

The lecture on LITERATURE AND REVOLUTION was even more breathtaking in its scope . . . We were shown that great crises, such as the eve of Civil War or Revolution, permit the artists to perceive reality in a new way and that new characters that are created not only give a perception of that period, but an anticipation of the new. Raya started at the very beginning, 500 B.C. which was the height of Greek philosophy—and the beginning of its end. From there she discussed everything from the *Oresteia* in which your desire to see Orestes judged not guilty is so great you don't even recognize the male chauvinism in Athena's speech—to Virginia Woolf's *A Room of One's Own*, which Raya considers one of the finest pieces of literary criticism ever written—to all the personal relationships that are so different during great revolutionary periods. Thus not only did William Blake borrow from Mary Wollstonecraft and dedicate one of his finest poems to her, but we find that in the same group in London in 1792–93 there was Mary Wollstonecraft, William Blake, Tom Paine, and William Godwin, all under the impact of both the American and the French Revolutions. Raya discussed in detail *Wuthering Heights*, writen by Emily Brontë on the eve of the 1848 revolutions, which is recognized now as important, but only because it was by a woman writer; it has not yet been recognized as being on the same level of greatness, if not greater, than Thackery or Dickens of her own age. De Beauvoir says that Cathy's cry "I am Heathcliff" is the greatest sentence in the book, but says nothing about Heathcliff's much more revealing cry for Cathy never to leave him. All miss that the author creates entirely new characters and steps over tremendous barriers by creating ghosts when necessary. Marx said you can learn more from great novels than from classical political economy. For when you are a genius, the tale escapes you; there is a movement to the creation of the plot and the characters that makes you see more than you intended to see. (Raya read footnote 83 from *Marxism and Freedom* on form and content—which, incidentally, is a footnote to the section on fetishism of commodities!)

She took up the greatness of the American period on the eve of the Civil War, when *Moby Dick* was written, and elaborated on this period of Poe, Hawthorne, Melville, and Brook Farm, with special attention to Margaret Fuller, a journalist, a historian, and a great author who wrote directly on *Woman in the Nineteenth Century*. The sweep Raya covered was so great it cannot even be "listed," but it took up every century right up to our own day. And on the American scene she dwelt especially on the Black writers and the Harlem Renaissance that developed between the First and Second World Wars, with which the Black dimension brought us something entirely new in language. The Black women poets were seen as greater than the men, with Gwendolyn Brooks and Audre Lorde singled out especially and some of their poems read out. And finally, Raya related it all to how Hegel deals with literature when he takes up the Greeks and Shakespeare and sees that it is the stage of consciousness at a specific period that creates the form of expression, so that at one point there is the move from epic poetry to drama, and the chorus is seen as the whole people participating. When Hegel takes up tragedy we see that Lysistrata is not just a question of women vs. men, but women vs. war—the women are definitely at a higher stage than the men. We see that it is when new societies are being created that new forms of literature are created. The question at the present moment is whether we, also, are going to have a new form appear. This is why Raya felt that *The Three Marias* is not only something totally new in literature, but perhaps the greatest thing that has arisen. The Marias see all of literature as one big letter one person has written to another, and in writing to each other they reveal what women have been through the years. Raya read some of the most beautiful and powerful sections from this work—and it was unmistakable that these women wanted a totally different revolution that would not be distorted but be the beginning of something totally new in all relations.

Which brings us, finally, to the very first lecture—and to the final one; the two are as intimately connected, I feel, as are the first and last chapters of *Philosophy and Revolution*. The very first lecture on *RUSSIA, 1917; GERMANY, 1919; PORTUGAL, 1975*, had plunged us into revolution as act and as consciousness—but so tightly merged that each became something other than what it started out, as dialectics led the participants to great, new creativity. Raya took up 1917 as Revolution, 1919 as Counterrevolution, and 1975 as ongoing Revolution, which has yet to run its course.

Just the telling of the tale of the first five days of the February Revolution in Russia 1917 revealed how it was that the women textile workers in Petrograd who went on strike against the advice of all, including the Bolsheviks, not only transformed a quiet celebration of International Women's Day into a revolution, but thereby transformed history. (Yet this is the very act that some of the women theorists are now saying proved only their courage; they "didn't know what they were doing.")

Turning to Germany, 1919, we examined the revolution not alone as act, but as leader, force, reason, and martyrdom. It is impossible to summarize briefly all the material Raya developed on Rosa Luxemburg both as activist and theoretician—from her fight in 1899 against the revisionists, led by Bernstein; to her activity in the 1905 Russian Revolution and her development of the theory of the General Strike (which brought in the question of spontaneity and organization); to her return to Germany and the beginning of her fight with Kautsky in 1910, four long years before the outbreak of World War I and Lenin's break with Kautsky; to her 1913 theory of accumulation and discussion of imperialism, her wrong position on the National Question, but her unswerving hailing of the 1917 Russian Revolution; her long years in prison and the short two and a half months she lived after her release from prison in 1919, during which brief period she nonetheless managed to establish an independent Communist Party and called for Workers' Councils. As Raya put it, there is nothing more stupid than those who do not take her up just because she did not write directly on women, for we can learn more from her greatest mistakes than from all their "wisdom." What stood out in Raya's recounting of Rosa's life—and death—was the complete inseparability of her activity and her theory. (Yet this was the woman that some of today's women theorists either ignore or, like Simone de Beauvoir, say merely "followed" Liebknecht. A self-portrait reproduced in Nettl's work which Raya displayed made it especially disgusting to think of de Beauvoir's designation of her as "ugly.")

The Third Act was the Portuguese Revolution of our own period—in which we would see the revolution as masses in motion and face the question of "What happens after?" Having seen the revolution as Actuality in 1917 and as Reason in 1919, we now would see how, long before it appears, the revolution is present in the restlessness and the questioning from below. Raya reviewed what it meant for three women in fascist Portugal, the "Three Marias," to get together and talk and produce a great work, which was called "erotic" and for which they were thrown in jail. It was here that we had to turn to the question of what is a "philosophy of liberation"—and return to Marx's discovery of a whole new continent of thought in 1844 and his Humanist Essays in which he had posed as the most fundamental relation of all the relation of man to woman. We were shown that from 1843 when Marx broke with bourgeois society, to 1883 and his death, whether it was the National Question, or the relationship of man to woman, whether it was the dialectic of development in thought or in action, what was fundamental was the dual rhythm, the second negativity, the breaking down of the old AND the creation of the new, which is the longer and the far more difficult task. It was this that we had to consider when witnessing Portugal, where the first Women's Liberation demonstration after the 1974 overthrow of fascism was attacked, not by fascists but by Communists. The establishment of new human relations could not be left for the day after the revolution, and Women's Liberation cannot be viewed as a "deviation" from the revolution, but the *proof* that new human relations are being established.

It was this to which we returned again, directly, in the final lecture on *PHILOSOPHY AND REVOLUTION*, as we reviewed the double rhythm of the movement from practice to theory and from theory to practice, each of which is irreducible, and the unity of which is what, alone, creates something new.

We were shown 1789 as more important for us than 1776 because 1789 was against the enemy inside and created a new way of knowing. We were shown the French Revolution as not only giving birth to Hegel's great philosophy, but to everything from Mary Wollstonecraft's writing in Britain to Beethoven's music in Austria. We were introduced to Hegel's categories in the *Phenomenology of Mind* and to the new alienations that Spirit is constantly experiencing. We saw tragedy as facing the fact that one age is passing and another coming, and great literature as arriving when you have great crises in the objective world. We saw time as both the continuity of history and as the place for human development. We were faced with why none of the women theorists have seen what has come from the movement from practice, and how it is *philosophy* that creates the humus for everything else. We reviewed the three most important Hegelian categories of Universal, Particular, and Individual, and saw Universal as what we are striving for, but as abstract; Particular as the first concretization; and Individual as the highest point of the concrete when you are actually *living* the new relations. We saw 1968 as supposedly the highpoint of the New Left Revolution of the '60s, but were confronted with recognizing that 1970 was the highpoint of the counterrevolution—not because of Kent State only, but far worse because of Jackson, Mississippi and the break that came *within* the movement between white and Black. And we were able to see that this is what has also happened in the Women's Liberation Movement, which has suffered from its own "fixed Particular." After Raya went into Sartre's male chauvinism with some amazing quotations from his works, we could understand that the fixed Particular for Simone de Beauvoir was Existentialism, just as for the other women theorists it has turned out to be "party-to-lead" because they all consider women as backward. Their maternalism is worse than paternalism—and their direction is all away from the actual movement from below.

After the impact of these six tremendous lectures, the final paragraph of *Philosophy and Revolution* surely had a deeper meaning for all: "Ours is the age that can meet the challenge of the times when we work out so new a relationship of theory to practice that the proof of the unity is in the Subject's own self-development. Philosophy and revolution will first then liberate the innate talents of men and women who will become whole. Whether or not we recognize that this is the task history has 'assigned' to our epoch, it is a task that remains to be done"...

Yours,
Olga

II

Women's Liberation in Search of a Theory: The Summary of a Decade

August 26, 1980 will mark a full decade of Women's Liberation as a new *mass* freedom movement. It was Aug. 26, 1970 that 50,000 women marched down Fifth Avenue in New York to celebrate the 50th anniversary of suffrage in the U.S. and stunned the world by transforming the first "Women's Strike for Equality" into the largest women's march in U.S. history. In the ten years since then, the movement has reached every continent and touched every facet of life, forcing even the UN to declare, in 1975, an International Women's Year—and then rename it International Women's *Decade*.

We have seen massive marches for the right to abortion not only in West Germany but in Catholic Italy; speak-outs on rape everywhere from the U.S. to India; feminist publications appearing everywhere from Africa and Peru to the underground in Russia.

In the U.S., from the very beginning of the decade, minority women organized their own groups: Chicana feminists and North American Indian women in 1970; Puerto Rican women in 1972; the National Black Feminists in 1973. A new dimension in class struggles burst forth all over the land: from textile workers to telephone operators and from office workers to welfare mothers, the unorganized began organizing themselves, and the organized began forming women's caucuses within their unions. The questions they demanded be answered were not only equal wages but sexual harassment by company or union officials or fellow workers alike. There was nothing—from attitude to the family to sexual preference; from art to health care; from affirmative action to language—that the Women's Liberation Movement did not raise.

But what most distinguished the WLM of the '70s from the New Left of the '60s—out of which it was born, and which it was challenging to end the separation of "thinkers" and "doers"—was that none had to be convinced that activity alone will not do it, that theory is needed. The search can be seen in the veritable explosion of both activist papers and academic studies, in theoretical journals like *Quest* and *Signs*, and in the more than 15,000 courses in Women's Studies established by 1978. Nowhere was the thirst for ideas more evident than in the outpourings to all the varied conferences that continuously astounded the "organizers"—whether that be CLUW in 1974 or the Socialists-Feminists in 1975, the IWY Conference in Houston in 1977 or the Second Sex Conference in New York last year.

Yet, at the end of so magnificent a decade, the WLM faces a counterrevolution—from within and from without—so strong that in the U.S. not only does the 1973 Supreme Court victory on abortion stand in danger, but we cannot even guarantee ratification of the ERA in a northern industrial state like Illinois—while in Portugal and Iran, where women's demonstrations challenged the incompleteness of those revolutions, the whole revolution now stands in mortal danger.

Never was there a more urgent need to finally find a theory that can match all the new beginnings in practice. Never was it more clear that the question which demands to be answered at this point is not even so much *what* theory as what *is* theory. It demands a second look at today's Women's Liberation theorists with those eyes.

THE SECOND SEX, THIRTY YEARS LATER

The three-day conference last September at NYU, called to discuss the significance of Simone de Beauvoir's *The Second Sex*[1] 30 years later, was organized around 22 papers, 30 workshops, and five general sessions. The 1000 women who participated were all seriously trying to work out a feminist theory. Yet none questioned why a conference on the threshold of the 1980s should be "inspired" by Simone de Beauvoir's Existentialist philosophy which, in 1949, was but a *transition point* from the old to the new, as she opened wide a heretofore undared discussion of sexuality. It was that topic that inspired today's WLM, not de Beauvoir's conception of woman as "Other." And it is that topic, sexuality, that is still in need of a relation to revolution. We will surely never find it in the Sartrean Existentialism that de Beauvoir followed so faithfully.

In the 814 pages of *The Second Sex*, never once do we see woman as active, thinking *subject*. Woman is always the *object* that terrible things are done to—and primarily because she supposedly allows it to be that way. Indeed, she tells us that the slaves were always conscious of their oppression, the proletariat has always been in revolt, but woman? "No desire for revolution dwells within her." (p. 52)

Because "creativity" means to her only works of art or of literature, not new human relations, she can insist that "as long as woman has to struggle to become a human being, she cannot become a creator" (p. 672), when the truth is the exact opposite. There is such a total absence of appreciation for any mass movement that it extends even to the leaders of those movements. Thus, Rosa Luxemburg, the great leader of the 1919 German Revolution, merely battled "beside Liebknecht" and supposedly demonstrates "that it is not the inferiority of women that has caused their historical insignificance; it is rather their historical insignificance that has doomed them to inferiority" (p. 122). None of the revolutions count for anything.

All the great women of history whose names are sprinkled on page after page are, we are told, "isolated individuals" as we are asked: "for one Flora Tristan or Louise Michel, how many timid housewives begged their husbands not to take chances?" (p. 567). But it is not only the true history of the great Paris Commune of 1871[2] that de Beauvoir ignores—the 3000 women of the Committee for the Defense of Paris, working women for the most part, who not only took their places on the barricades but who organized their office to remain open around the clock during even the most critical days of battles. More important, it is the true history of her own age she does not see.

The first edition of *The Second Sex* came out in 1949 just when, in industrial America, the miners in their great Automation strikes were challenging nothing less than what sort of work human beings should do; a whole new Third World was being born; and on the level of the WLM itself, the women who had been drawn into the factories in World War II were challenging the attempts to shove them back to the kitchens again. Everywhere the movement from practice was raising the most highly philosophic questions—but none of this penetrated de Beauvoir's thinking, despite the fact that of all the women theorists the WLM has embraced, she is the only one who is a philosopher.

Nothing better proves that it is not *any* philosophy that is needed, but one that will enable you to catch in theory what masses in motion have been doing and thinking in practice, create new categories, and thus help move the revolution forward. Nothing better demonstrates that it is not the historic epoch you are born into, but your relationship to that movement from practice, as well as to the movement from theory, that determines what voices you hear, what facts you find, and even what words mean.

How else can you explain that de Beauvoir could conclude her voluminous epic with the magnificent statement of discovery Marx had made in his *Economic-Philosophic Manuscripts* of 1844: "The direct, natural, necessary relationship of man to man is the relationship of man to woman . . ." and so twist its meaning that she "restates" it to be an affirmation of *her* philosophy that "it is for man to establish the reign of liberty"!

From beginning to end for the Existentialist de Beauvoir, woman remains Other, the *Second* Sex.[3] How, then, could none of this come out for examination, let alone critique, even "Thirty Years Later," at a conference of women theorists?

And what of the historians at that conference? Have they done any better than the philosopher?

GERDA LERNER, ACADEMIC HISTORIAN

Gerda Lerner has written no less than four books specifically on the history of American women and is considered a "pioneer" in the field. How could she be allowed to get away with the vulgar anti-intellectualism she displayed there, continuing to fight Freud and

Marx alike, not on the ground of their ideas, much less their historic period and relation to objectivity, but merely on the grounds that they are men?

It is her latest book, *The Majority Finds its Past: Placing Women in History*,[4] a collection of 12 essays written over the past decade, that most clearly reveals her false thesis of "history," in the very manner in which she changed the title of her 1977 documentary *from* "Women in the Making of a Nation" *to* "The Female Experience." In a "flash of insight," she tells us, she rearranged all her material according to "female life stages (Childhood, Youth, Marriage and the Single State, etc.) and to stages of the growth of feminist consciousness." (p. xxx)

"What is needed," she insists, "in order to correct the distorted picture presented by traditional history is women-centered analysis. *What would the past be like if man were regarded as woman's 'Other'?* Even to pose such a question . . . shifts one's angle of vision." (My emphasis, p. xxxi). What we wind up with is a vision not only shifted, but so twisted that the dialectic of history—the history of mass struggles of women and men for freedom—becomes a history of the "tensions" between two separate cultures, "male and female." The result is that, far from "Placing Women in History," Gerda Lerner wrenches women out of it.

While she correctly exposes that "the rich history of the abolition movement has been told as though women played a marginal, auxiliary, and at times mainly disruptive role in it," nowhere do we get a whiff of the dialectical, historical, and *continuing* relationship between the freedom struggles of Blacks and of women. Nowhere is the Black Dimension seen as the catalyst for liberation—not only as the slave revolts were the ground out of which white Abolitionism was nurtured; not only as Abolitionism itself thus became a whole new dimension of American character *practicing* interracial equality; but specifically as regards women's liberation. Nowhere are the Sojourner Truths and Harriet Tubmans seen as the speakers, the "generals," the leaders, who inspired the white women to *be* more than "auxiliary." The Women's Rights Movement arose *out of* the Abolitionist Movement. There is no such thing as Black history that is not also white history. There is no such thing as woman's history that is not the actual history of humanity's struggle toward freedom.

Both *Black Women in White America* and *The Female Experience: An American Documentary*, as documentary histories, are collections of magnificent scope. But because this academic historian sees them only as that—voices, and not the Reason in all the great struggles that *are* history—she can actually call the work she did on *Black Women* nothing more than a "detour" on her way to her original "theory" of women's history (p. xxix).

No wonder she can write that "The speech by the former slave, Sojourner Truth, belongs here not so much because of its content, but because of its tone." And this is the speech where Sojourner is criticising no one less than Frederick Douglass after the Civil War, for being "short-minded" because he asked women to wait for their enfranchisement, while Sojourner was insisting that women, too, must have their rights!

Lerner's disdain for Marx is not just because he is a man. It is because for Marx theory flowed out of the actual thoughts and actions of women and men shaping history, whereas for Lerner she, not the women who speak in her books, is going to be the original.

The sad truth is that it is not only the white WLM theorists who have not caught the creativity of the mass movement. We have yet to produce the Black woman theorist who has been able to develop what Toni Cade attempted to show in *The Black Woman*, her 1970 anthology of voices that were demanding to be heard; to catch in theory what the Rosa Parks, Fannie Lou Hamers, Daisy Bates, Gloria Richardsons, and countless others were acting out in life in our own age.

What enabled Marx to "transform historic narrative into historic Reason"—his total philosophy of revolution—is what still eludes nearly all the new women theorists. And not only those who reject Marxism as a theory for Women's Liberation, but even those who are seeking to join socialism and feminism.

SHEILA ROWBOTHAM, SOCIALIST HISTORIAN

Sheila Rowbotham's *Women, Resistance and Revolution*[5] remains the most serious work of all the women theorists, not only because she is a Marxist and the one best representative of the generation that gave birth to today's WLM *out of* the New Left, but because she has traced, through 300 years of history, not merely the oppression but woman's *resistance* to that oppression. Indeed, so organic does Rowbotham see the resistance that she states categorically: "there is no 'beginning' of feminism in the sense that there is no beginning to defiance in women."

Her 247 pages of text are filled with names and dates and events that leave no doubt about that thesis. And she is especially attuned to recognize the importance of the working-class dimension. There are hundreds and hundreds of important historic "facts." But all the events are told as if each happened apart from the other. *There is no movement.*

Thus, though we learn about Flora Tristan's proposal for a Workers' International in 1843 on one page; and the activity of Jeanne Deroin, a self-taught working woman who was active in the women's clubs that sprang up in 1848 on another; and of American Abolitionism on still another—there is no sense of what the 1840s represented as a momentous historic *age* that produced not only the Seneca Falls Convention, the 1848 Revolutions in Europe, and the anti-slavery movement in America—*but Karl Marx's break from bourgeois* society in 1844 and his world-shaking discovery of what Raya Dunayevskaya has called a whole "new continent of thought."

It is Rowbotham's failure to see Marx as that founder of a total philosophy of revolution for our age that is her fatal error. It is not that she has not studied Marx's work. She writes of everything from the early *Economic-Philosophic Manuscripts* to the *Communist Manifesto, German Ideology,* and the powerful pages in *Capital* where Marx describes the working conditions "of sewing girls, silk workers, bleachers, straw-plaiters, and other women." She acknowledges his support for a women's section of the International, his praise for the women of the Commune, his encouragement for the intellectual development and activism of his own daughters.

Yet she insists on viewing Marx as a "bourgeois man in the 19th century"! Because she equates Marx's profound view of the Man/Woman relationship in his 1844 Humanist Essays as no more than the development of a "theme generally discussed in utopian socialist writing on women's liberation"—rather than seeing it as a breakthrough to the conception of just how total must be the uprooting of this exploitative society if we are ever to achieve a new human society—she limits Marx to being nothing more than a theoretician of "class struggle" rather than philosopher of a whole "new continent of thought." That is precisely why, though she passionately wants to "connect" what she feels are the two dimensions of her own being—feminism and Marxism[6]—she winds up concluding, in the final four pages of her whole book: "This is a book in which feminism and Marxism come home to roost. They cohabit in the same space somewhat uneasily ... the connection between the oppression of women and the central discovery of Marxism, the class exploitation of the worker in capitalism, is still forced. It is still coming out of the heads of women like me as an idea."

But it is *not* an outside mediator that brings Marxism and feminism together. *It is life.* To insist that "women have come to revolutionary consciousness by means of ideas, actions and organizations which have been made predominantly by men" (p. 11) is to wrench women out of the real history of humanity's struggle toward freedom every bit as much as does Simone de Beauvoir or Gerda Lerner. To see only that women have been "Hidden from History" and not that they have been *hidden from philosophy* means that you have not grasped what it means that throughout history women have been not only force but Reason, revolutionaries in action *and in thought*. What is urgent for today's revolutionaries to grasp is that only when a whole new category has been made of that cognition, i.e., Woman as Reason and as Revolutionary Force—as only one woman philosopher, Raya Dunayevskaya, has done[7]—have women finally become part, vital part, of the philosophy of freedom.

Without that philosophy, "resistance" never moves to "creativity"—the creation of the *new*. Without it, the challenge to the Left to practice new relations *now*, not "after the revolution," out of which today's WLM was born, retrogresses to as empty a thesis as the pamphlet, *Beyond the Fragments*, which Rowbotham produced in 1979, seven years after her serious work on *Women, Resistance and Revolution*. It is not that the question of "form of organization" that she raises there is unimportant. It is that the question is what form of organization will elicit the new voices and ground its theory in *that* Reason rather than attempt to "harness" the new passions of Women's Liberation—and youth, and Blacks, and labor—to *its* "leadership."

Only that kind of theory and organization can help move the WLM forward. What the decade of the WLM as a mass movement proves, more than anything else, is that *without* such a philosophy along with activity for liberation, we will not stand still, but go backward. With it, we can help create a new, truly human world.

NOTES

1. Simone de Beauvoir, *The Second Sex* (Alfred A. Knopf, 1953), originally published in France by Librairie Gallimard, 1949. Paginations in this article from Bantam Book edition, 1968.

2. In *The Women Incendiaries* (Braziller, 1966; Gallimard, 1963), Edith Thomas has documented the magnificent history of the women of the Commune in such moving detail that one feels exactly what Marx described in *The Civil War in France* as: "Working, thinking, fighting, bleeding Paris . . . radiant in the enthusiasm of its historic initiative!"

3. And how do we explain that women theorists like Margery Collins and Christine Pierce can write so devastating a critique of the male chauvinism of Jean-Paul Sartre as their "Holes and Slime: Sexism in Sartre's Psychoanalysis" (included in *Women and Philosophy*, Putnam, 1976) without a single word of criticism of de Beauvoir, who shared exactly the same philosophy of Existentialism?

4. Gerda Lerner, *The Majority Finds its Past* (Oxford University Press, 1979).

5. Sheila Rowbotham, *Women, Resistance and Revolution* (Random House, 1972).

6. In her paper, "The Feminist Challenge to Socialist Thought and Practice," Joan Landes has contributed a serious discussion of what she pinpoints as "the most marked difference between the present and the past ... the rise of an autonomous socialist feminist tendency within the women's liberation movement." Yet, she too labors unsuccessfully at making a "synthesis" of socialist and feminist thought, primarily because, like most of the WLM, she considers Marx and Engels as one. What is needed is not synthesis but *divide*—between Marx's own philosophy and all others. (For a full development of this, see Raya Dunayevskaya's "Marx's and Engels' Studies Contrasted" in *News & Letters*, Jan./Feb., 1979.)

7. For her development of this philosophy, see Chapter 9, "New Passions and New Forces," in *Philosophy and Revolution* (New York: Dell, 1973); "The WLM as Reason and as Revolutionary Force" in *Notes on Women's Liberation* (Detroit: News & Letters, 1970); "Women as Thinkers and as Revolutionaries" in *Working Women For Freedom* (Detroit: News & Letters, 1976); and three draft chapters from her new work-in-progress on *Rosa Luxemburg, Women's Liberation and Marx's Philosophy of Revolution* (printed in *News & Letters* Jan./Feb. 1979; Jan./Feb. 1980; March 1980).

CHAPTER 13

New Passions and New Forces: The Black Dimension, The Anti-Vietnam War Youth, Rank-and-File Labor, Women's Liberation*

... So empirical-minded is the American youth, Black included, that even revolutionaries who have separated themselves from Communism of the Russian and the Chinese varieties have fully and uncritically embraced Castro. So exhilarating was the Cuban experience that they never questioned the direction, much less the philosophy, of its development since achieving power. One famous exception seemed to have been the young Black Communist philosopher, Angela Davis, who from prison posed the question "What happens after?": "the most difficult period of all is the building of the revolutionary society after the seizure of power."[1] This did not, however, predominate over her Cuban experience: "my first prolonged contact with a socialist country through my own eyes and limbs, I might add, since I cut cane for a while." Contrast this view of a leader with the view of a Black woman from the ranks of the Women's Liberation movement:

> I'm not thoroughly convinced that Black Liberation, the way it's being spelled out, will really and truly mean *my* liberation. I'm not so sure that when it comes time "to put down my gun," that I won't have a broom shoved in my hands, as so many of my Cuban sisters have.[2]

For that matter, once Angela was freed, she refused to sign the appeal of a Czechoslovak fighter for freedom, Jiří Pelikán, who had written to her: "We too have many Angela Davises and Soledad brothers."

---

*Excerpts from Chapter 9 of *Philosophy and Revolution—From Hegel to Sartre, and from Marx to Mao* (New York: Dell, 1973); 2nd edition (Humanities Press; Harvester Press, 1982), contains new Introduction by author. International editions: Spanish (Mexico, D.F.: Siglo Veintiuno, 1977); Italian (Milan: Feltrinelli, 1977); German (Vienna: Europa Verlag, 1981).

As against the voices from below, the whole of Régis Debray's *Revolution in the Revolution?*[3] burns with zeal, "to free the present from the past" (pp. 19–91). This is further bound by a "principal lesson" (pp. 95–116) and held on to tightly as the spokesman for Castro expounds "some consequences for the future" (pp. 119–26). In place of "traditions" or theoretic abstractions we must face the facts, "the concrete," *the* experience (Cuban), topped by "the military foco." Anything, anything whatever that stands in the way of this veritable miracle, "the military foco," is to be thrown into the dustbin of history. In the guise of nontheory the French philosopher thus presents us with a "theory" that departs in toto from Marx's most fundamental concept, that of a social revolution. He proclaims a "new dialectic of tasks" (p. 119): unquestioning obedience to the "Equivalent Substitution" (military command). Outside of the penchant for monolithism—"There is no longer a place for verbal ideological relation to the revolution, nor for a certain type of polemic" (p. 123)—which characterizes this manual on how "to make" revolution, its 126 pages are an endless pæan of praise for the guerrilla: "the staggering novelty introduced by the Cuban Revolution is this: the *guerrilla* force is the party in embryo" (p. 106).

So supreme is the military as means and end, as strategy and tactic, as leadership and manhood itself, that it does indeed swallow up not only theory and party but the masses themselves:

> One finds that a working class of restricted size or under the influence of a reformist trade union aristocracy, and an isolated and humiliated peasantry, are willing to accept this group, of bourgeois origin, as their political leadership (p. 112).

At this point enters the Leader Maximum, for the end result of the Army's replacing the Party, replacing the Proletariat, replacing the Peasantry, is that all are replaced by the know-it-all, see-it-all, be-it-all "Equivalent Substitution."

Now, suppose that, for the moment, we are willing to forget that the first modern theorist and greatest practitioner of guerrilla warfare was *not* Fidel Castro, but Mao Tse-tung; suppose, further, that we close our eyes to the truth that "the present" (1967) was *not* a Cuban Revolution but the ongoing Vietnam War of liberation engaged in direct combat with the mightiest world imperialist, the U.S.A.;[4] and finally, suppose we agree that a guerrilla force is "the party in embryo"—where exactly do all these suppositions lead? If the achievements are the proof that "*insurrectional activity is today the number one political activity*" (p. 116), does the old Stalinist monolithism of forbidding factions in order "to free us" from "the vice of excessive deliberation" thereby become "the present," "the theoretical and historical novelty of this [Cuban] situation" (p. 123)? And do Marx's and Lenin's deliberations on revolution, as actuality and as theory, become consigned to "the past" and allow Debray to point "a warning finger . . . to indicate a shortcut"? Guerrilla warfare is a short-cut to nowhere. It is a protracted war that leads more often to defeat than to "victory," and where it does lead to state power, hardly keeps the revolution from souring.

When Ché spoke with his own voice rather than Debray's, he did not flinch from direct confrontation with Lenin's theory by consigning it to the past:

> This is a unique Revolution which some people maintain contradicts one of the most orthodox premises of the revolutionary movement, expressed by Lenin: "Without a revolutionary theory there is no revolutionary movement." It would be suitable to say that revolutionary theory as the expression of a social truth, surpasses any declaration of it; that is to say, even if the theory is not known, the revolution can succeed if historical reality is interpreted correctly and if the forces involved in it are utilized correctly.[5]

Were we even to forget the martyrdom of Ché Guevara in the very period when Debray's nimble-penned panacea became the New Left's manual on how "to make revolutions," our post-World War II world is not short of guerrilla wars, from the Philippines to Burma, from Malaya to Japan, that have failed. The post-World War I world, on the other hand, exuded true magic, the "magic" of the Russian Revolution, which set the world aflame. Even today, with a half-century's lapse and the first workers' state having been transformed into its opposite, a state-capitalist society, the perspectives unfolded by 1917 remain the greatest form of world revolution. This is the Marxist heritage, the past from which Castro's chosen theoretician wishes "to free the present." Marx's concept of revolution—great masses in motion, in spontaneous, forward movement—is not something that can be "made" from above.

When that Black Women's Liberationist expressed a fear that when it comes to putting down the gun, she may once again have a broom shoved into her hands, she was expressing one of the most anti-elitist new forces and new passions that had come on the historic stage and were raising altogether new questions. It is true that, on the whole, these were questions addressed to the private capitalistic world, specifically the U.S. But the women were saying: "We will no longer be objects—mindless sex objects, or robots that keep house, or cheap manual labor you can call in when there are no men available and discard when there are." These women were also demanding their heads back, and it is this which surprised none more than the New Left, since though born out of the New Left, it was the New Left men whom Women's Liberation opposed. The same women who had participated in every phase of the freedom movements refused to continue being the typists, the mimeographers, the "ladies' auxiliaries" to the Left. They demanded an end to the separation of mental and manual labor, not only as a "goal," not only against capitalist society, but as an immediate need of the Left itself, especially regarding women. Nor were they afraid to attack the male chauvinism in the Black movement as well. Black and white women joined together to do battle with the arrogance of a Stokely Carmichael, who had said that "the only position for women in the movement is prone."

So uncompromising as well as adamant was their attack on elitism and authoritarianism that the very structure of the new Women's Liberation groups, the small groups that sprang up everywhere, were an effort to find a form that would allow for the self-development of the individual woman. They disregarded the established women's groups because they too were structured and too concerned with the middle-class professional women. They wished to release all women—most of all Black, working-class, Chicana, Indian.[6] Whether it was a question of the right to abortion, or equal pay, or having control over their own lives, the single word was NOW. Freedom meant now, today, not tomorrow, much less the day after. "Now" meant not waiting for the day of revolution, much less excluding from the political struggle the question of the relationship of man to woman. Women no longer considered that question a merely private matter, for that was only the standard way of making women feel isolated and helpless. The very fact that freedom was in the air meant that she no longer was alone, that there were thousands forming a movement, a force. Individuality and collectivity became inseparable from the mass demonstrations in August 1970. And for the first time also, history was not past but *in the making*. And now that they were making it, there was no feeling that they were lost in a collectivity, but rather that each was individualized through this historic process.

Thus, in spite of adverse publicity about "ugly girls burning bras" and whatever other nonsense the male chauvinists played up in order to make the movement look silly, more and more women kept joining it. Different kinds of women who had never joined anything before became activists—and thinkers. In addition to those who called themselves members of the movement, thousands more expressed the same ideas, from the welfare mothers' organizations to the new drives to unionize women's industries and fight the discrimination sanctioned by existing unions. And the many voices expressing the ideas of Women's Liberation were the result not of women reading Kate Millett's *Sexual Politics* or the hundreds of less serious works on the subject, but of the hunger for new roles in society and new relationships for them here and now.

Instead of grasping the link of continuity of today's strivings with that which Marx saw emerging, or of listening to new voices, today's "Marxists" themselves are the best examples of Marx's concept of ideology as false consciousness. They look upon themselves as the leaders, or at least the politicos, who can offer "a rational reassessment of feminist ideology" and look down upon today's new women rebels as apolitical, as if that meant they had nothing to say worth listening to and that there were no objective validity to the movement. It is true that with the mass demonstrations by women, especially in New York in 1970, all parties want *to use* them. That precisely is the trouble.

The uniqueness of today's Women's Liberation movement is that it dares to challenge what is, including the male chauvinism not only under capitalism but within the revolutionary movement itself. To fear to expose this male chauvinism leads to helplessness. To face reality, and to face it not through sheer voluntarism, but with full awareness of all the forces lined up against us, is the one way to assure the coalescence with other revolutionary forces, especially labor, which is so strategically placed in production and has its own Black dimension. But the fact that it will not be possible fully to overcome male chauvinism as long as class society exists does not invalidate the movement any more than any struggle for freedom is invalidated. On the contrary, the very fact that there is a widespread Women's Liberation movement proves that it is an idea whose time has come and that it is an integral part of the very organism of liberation ...

It is true, of course—and indeed there would be something fundamentally amiss if it were otherwise—that Marx and Lenin solved the problems of their age, not ours. But powerful foundations have been laid for this age which we would disregard at our peril, even as it would be fatal not to build on the theoretic-practical Humanist ground rediscovered since the mid-1950s, and which Marx in his day called "positive Humanism, beginning from itself." The restatement, by the mature proletarian revolutionary author of *Capital*, of the young Marx's exuberance of 1844—"the development of human power which is its own end"—demonstrates beyond the shadow of a doubt how Europe's 1848 revolutions, America's Civil War, 1861–65, and the Paris Commune, 1871, verified Marx's "new Humanism." Any *other* foundation, any *other* ground, such as "nationalized property," with or without military "focos," can only lead to still another tyranny.

There is no way to end the reappearance of still another exploitative, alienated, and alienating society except through a social revolution, beginning with the relations between people *at the point of production*, and continuing as that elemental outburst involving what Lenin called the population "to a man, woman, child" which ends once and for all the dichotomy between mental and manual labor so that "individuality," as Hegel put it, is "freed from all that interferes with its universalism, i.e., freedom."

To labor under the illusion that one could pick up theory "en route" and thereby avoid going through "the labor of the negative" in the theoretic preparation for revolution as in the actual class struggles is every bit as false a consciousness as that which befalls the ruling class.

As against the concept that endless activism, though it be mindless, is sufficient "to make the revolution," what is needed is a restatement for our age of Marx's concept of the "realization" of philosophy, that is, the inseparability of philosophy and revolution.

The mature Marx, like the young Marx, rejected Feuerbachian materialism and held instead that the Hegelian dialectic of "second negativity" was *the* "creative principle," the turning point which puts an end to the division between mental and manual labor. The mature as well as the young Marx grounded "the development of human power which is its own end" in the "absolute movement of becoming." Only with such a Promethean vision could one be certain that a *new* Paris Commune would not only be "a historic initiative—working, thinking, bleeding Paris ... radiant in the enthusiasm of its historic initiative"—but continue its self-development so that a totally new social order on a world scale was established.

The *new* that characterizes our era, the "energizing principle" that has determined the direction of the two decades of the movement *from practice*, simultaneously rejects *false* consciousness and aborted revolutions.

The reality is stifling. The transformation of reality has a dialectic all its own. It demands a unity of the struggles for freedom with a philosophy of liberation. Only then does the elemental revolt release new sensibilities, new passions, and new forces—a whole new human dimension.

Ours is the age that can meet the challenge of the times when we work out so new a relationship of theory to practice that the proof of the unity is in the Subject's own self-development. Philosophy and revolution will first then liberate the innate talents of men and women who will become whole. Whether or not we recognize that this is the task history has "assigned" to our epoch, it is a task that remains to be done.

NOTES

1. "Angela Davis Speaks from Prison," *Guardian*, December 26, 1970. See also Angela Y. Davis, *If They Come in the Morning* (New York: Joseph Okpaku, 1971).
2. Doris Wright in *News & Letters*, August-September, 1971.
3. Translated from the author's French and Spanish by Bobbye Ortiz (copyright c1967 by Monthly Review Press; New York: Grove Press, 1967). The page numbers following in the text are to this book.
4. Which did not stop the glib French theoretician from pontificating that since the Vietnamese guerrillas had not from the start brought "autonomous zones into being," their creation was therefore no match for the uniqueness of Castro's concept of "self-defense": "In Vietnam above all, and also in China, armed self-defense of the peasants, organized in militias, has played an important role . . . but . . . in no way did it bring autonomous zones into being. These territories of self-defense were viable only because total war was being carried out on other fronts . . ."
5. Ché Guevara, *Notes for the Study of the Cuban Revolution*.
6. See *Notes on Women's Liberation: We Speak in Many Voices* (Detroit: News & Letters, 1970). See also Toni Cade, *The Black Woman* (New York: New American Library, 1970). The flood of books on Women's Liberation is nearly endless; only a few are listed in the bibliography.

PART III
Sexism, Politics and Revolution—Japan, Portugal, Poland, China, Latin America, the U.S.—Is There an Organizational Answer?

CHAPTER 14

The New Left in Japan: Achievements and Goals*

A lecture tour through Japan is an exhilarating experience for one coming from the United States where Marxism is not exactly the most popular doctrine. In contrast to the political atmosphere in the States, where even the youth with a cause feels it necessary to vie with non-committed groups in denying an "ideological" foundation for his struggle for freedom, the New Left in Japan is all proudly Marxist, "anti-Stalinist and anti-imperialist, East and West." These sharp outer differences notwithstanding, there is a deep affinity of purpose between the New Left in Japan and in the United States. Both the date of birth—1960—and the parallelism of actions—great mass demonstrations in Japan against the American-Japanese Security Pact and, in the U.S., the sit-downs signalling the start of the Negro Revolution—symbolize the beginnings of a whole new epoch of development in both countries.

The 700 that came out, Dec. 4, to hear my first talk at the Telephone and Telegraph Workers' Union hall in Tokyo were representative of the whole spectrum of the New Left. This was seen both from the introductory speeches which showed that, although the meeting was under the auspices of *Zenshin*,[1] independent Marxists were also there, and it was made clear from the questions and discussion which followed the talk on "The Negro Revolution, the New Left, and Marxism in America." Furthermore, the questions disclosed an intense desire to develop relations with the second America—the America of the Negro Revolution, of the Free Speech Movement, of rank-and-file labor struggles, of the anti-Vietnam War teach-ins as well as the analyses of these developments by Marxist groups. And the preponderant presence of youth was made manifest by what I would call the sheer

---

*Excerpts from the report on a 1965–66 trip to Japan, printed in *The Activist*, Oberlin College student journal, Spring 1966.

adventure of philosophic explorations, ranging from the historic gulf that separates the "Oriental concept of Void and Nothingness" from the "European (Hegelian) concept of negativity" through Sartre's Existentialism,[2] to the concrete urgency with which the Hungarian Revolution invested the Humanism of Marxism.

The focal point of the discussion, however, remained the need for revolutionary regroupment, the need for solidarity between freedom fighters the world over—between workers and students and those who were fighting for and had won national independence from Western imperialism that would not fall prey to Stalinism of either the Russian or Chinese variety.

I do not mean to give the impression that the whole of the New Left is anti-Stalinist. The oppressive air of Maoism which dominates the Communist Party of Japan (JCP) hangs heavily also over a good part of the intellectual left. As was evident from another meeting, this time at the Waseda University, which was attended by nearly 1,000 students on Dec. 19, more than a little residue of Stalinism is imbedded also in some anti-Stalinist groupings ...

The Waseda University Students Paper invited me to write for it. In the article, entitled "The Humanism of Marx is the Basic Foundation for Today's Anti-Stalinism," ... I wrote:

> ... it is not some "bourgeois scholars" who brought Marx's Humanism onto the historic stage, but masses in motion, masses in motion against established Communism, masses in motion against American imperialism, masses in motion against British, French, Belgian imperialism, masses in motion against all existing societies. Stalinism, be it in Russian or Chinese garb, should not be allowed to sully Marx's concept of revolution and vision of the "all-round" man ...
>
> There must be no more Hiroshimas and Nagasakis. And something a great deal less honorary than "a degenerated workers' state" should be reserved for retrogressionists, for any who expound the barbarous view that a "new civilization" can first be built on the ruins of what would be left of the world after a thermonuclear war ...

I. Hiroshima Internationalism

The deep internationalism of the Japanese youth can be seen in the peace rally held in Hiroshima on Dec. 8. If you recross the international date line, you'll find it is Dec. 7 in the States.

Now, anyone feels very small and very humble when he arrives in Hiroshima. A visit to the Peace Museum is a most harrowing and

The New Left in Japan

sobering experience, guaranteed to fill your night with ghoulish nightmares, and by morning kindling such wrath in you against America for that fiendish act of dropping the A-bomb that you are quite ready to forget that you too are American, and that there is a second America, one that is determined that there be no more Hiroshimas, no more Nagasakis.

It seemed inconceivable that the very city that American imperialism atom-bombed would hold a rally in commemoration of all who died the night when Japanese imperialism attacked Pearl Harbor. Yet that is exactly what took place in Hiroshima on Dec. 8, 1965 . . .

Besides the peace rally, there was a public meeting under the auspices of the Marxist Student League, the Marxist Young Workers' League, and *Zenshin* that was attended by about 300. There were also smaller meetings with the students and the student press of Hiroshima University who were interested in all the details of the Berkeley Revolt.

The most impressive part of those meetings with *Zenshin* which concerned themselves specifically with those questions on which we did not agree—the theory of state-capitalism and my emphasis on the working out of the philosophy of Marxism for our age as taking precedence over the question of "the vanguard party"—was the presence of workers from all basic industries, auto, electric power, shipyards, etc., etc. They were concerned with establishing relations for action, as the Nagasaki Shipyard workers with those in the Clyde in Scotland where Harry McShane had distributed leaflets calling for common action between Scottish and Japanese shipyard workers. And there was also deep concern with ideas.

In contrast to what is the situation now among trade unions in the U.S., the political groups in Japan have shop papers that are openly Marxist. Just as a group among the shipyard workers—the Social Science Research Club—were the ones to translate and publish a Marxist-Humanist analysis of *The Soviet Economy and the Law of Value—A Revision or Reaffirmation of Marxism?*, so auto, coal, and steel were most interested in publishing *Workers Battle Automation* by Charles Denby, editor of *News & Letters*. In what other countries did groups of trade unionists publish such theoretical as well as class struggle analyses? And where else would a Marxist group that does not fully agree with another Marxist grouping in a different country publish the other's views precisely on the points in disagreement—state-capitalism, and the philosophical essays on *Marx's Humanism Today* and the *Afro-Asian Revolutions?*

That this dynamism of ideas characterizes not only workers who are "politicalized" was most clearly evident in Toyota.

II. TOYOTA LABOR SPEAKS

Toyota, "the East Detroit" of Japan, is a perfect example, and by now a very rare one, of the telescoped, brutalized industrialization of Japan when it was still a feudal country. In Toyota the fantastic remnants of feudalism and paternalism underlie one of the most automated industries, auto. Not only is it a company town such as I have seen in mining towns of West Virginia and Kentucky, or like some of the textile towns in Japan; it has some features that are more like a prison than a town.

Thus the workers not only live in houses owned by the auto company, but these houses are within a compound to which no entrance may be gained, not even by the relatives of the employees, except with permission of the company. Those employees who have a college education live in separate compounds from those with only a high school education; married couples live in different areas from the single men, and the single men can have no female visitors.

Not only that. What calls itself a union, run by the right wing of the Socialist Party, tolerates these conditions and even manages "to show them off" to the "progressive labor leader" (Reuther) of its sister-city in the United States, Detroit.

It seems that Reuther took the grand tour of the factory, in the company of what the workers consider a company-union but Reuther considers an example of "Western democracy." He left a picture of himself in the union hall which testifies to his visit. What the workers resented was Reuther's acquiescence to their conditions of labor, and to the town as a whole, which management dominates.

Yet, out of this constricted milieu, one worker, not connected with auto, arose to challenge the economic domination and political monolithism that the auto firm imposed on the town. Masashi Toguchi who had once been a Communist Party member, but broke with it, decided to run for City Council.

Toguchi ran as an independent. The attack Toguchi launched against auto management and its stranglehold over the workers, as well as against the do-nothingness of the union, was concretized in two slogans: "Down with the Fences!" and "Let's Make Love!" He won handily.

I was invited down there on a Sunday, the workers' only day off. The topic at the afternoon meeting concerned American labor, concentrating on the one hand on the birth of the CIO, and on the other hand, on the wildcats against Automation, which were as much against union as against management.

The New Left in Japan

I had brought greetings for the Toyota auto workers from a group of rank-and-file auto workers in Detroit, and this was promptly translated into Japanese and read to the 150 who came out to hear the afternoon talk.

The thing, however, that brought the house down was the Detroit workers' expose of Reuther and the revelation that they hated him as much as did the Japanese workers.

The evening meeting was on straight theory—the void in the Marxist movement since the death of Lenin. But make no mistake about it, Toguchi is completely opposed to Stalinism in general and the JCP in particular. What concerns him is a genuine proletarian revolution.

What the workers discussed that evening was how to realize the humanism of Marxism in practice, how to move in their daily struggles when they have stacked against them the company, the government, the union, the Communist Party (CP)

III. ZENGAKUREN, MARXISM, AND THE ACADEMIC MILIEU

... The highest point reached by Zengakuren (All Japan Federation of Student Governments) was in that pivotal year 1960 when it led mass demonstrations against both U.S. imperialism and its own Kishi government. And because by then the Zengakuren was not merely a student movement, but a political one that truly represented the majority of the people, they succeeded in stopping Eisenhower's projected trip to Japan, and in forcing Kishi to resign.

These, however, were not its greatest achievements. The greatest achievement was this: Outside of the bourgeoisie, every strata of the population, labor and women included, came alive.*

---

*My discussion about the activity of the women was by no means limited to discussions in Japan. I kept raising the international aspect on my return because of the unevenness in the development of Women's Liberation everywhere. In a talk to WRAP (Women's Radical Action Project) at the University of Chicago in April of 1969, during the demonstrations around Marlene Dixon's tenure, the question came up again. Here is what I said then:

> I was invited to Japan in 1965 to make a tour around *Marxism and Freedom* when it was translated into Japanese, and I had many meetings with the left of the left of the left, the left of the Zengakuren. The women had been every bit as active as the men in the struggles there. Indeed, the Zengakuren demonstrations against Eisenhower led to one death and that was a woman, Michiko Kanba, a student from Tokyo University. Yet, I was there for two weeks before I heard a woman take the floor. I finally asked them where they were keeping the women? The men said that though they had known I was a woman before I arrived, to actually see me standing up there lecturing for hours every day was a "shocking sight." At one meeting I finally got some women to open up (and that's only because they were

(continued bottom, next page)

In those struggles against the American-Japanese Security Treaty, as both symbol of continued American domination and the resurgence of its own bourgeoisie, the self-development of the so-called common man reached so high a point that it created a true basis for independent Marxism . . . [but] the very success of its ventures meant the end of one type of cohesiveness. The political tendencies within it, the very ones that helped lead it away from the CP, now found their theories tested in practice, and prepared to shift their concentration from the student movement to the class struggle, and "the building of a revolutionary Marxist party" . . .

Merleau-Ponty once expressed the true purpose of philosophy most succinctly and profoundly when he stated that it must be "spontaneity which teaches." 100 years before Merleau-Ponty, Marx, in arguing against those who wanted "to negate" philosophy by, as he put it, "turning one's back on philosophy . . . and murmuring a few trite and ill-humored phrases," insisted that the only way "to abolish" philosophy is "to realize it," that is to say, make the theory of liberation and freedom itself real. To grasp the meaning of spontaneous action and have philosophy merge with praxis is the only way to realize it. Each by itself is one-sided; only in unity can reality be transformed and thus philosophy realized. It is toward this end that the New Left strives. Therein lies the affinity of ideas between the New Left in Japan and in the United States.

NOTES

1. *Zenshin* (Forward) is the organ of the NC-JRCL. To avoid confusion which would arise from the fact that the Japanese Revolutionary Communist League contains the Trotskyist grouping as well as those like *Zenshin* and *Liberation* who have split not only from the Communist Party but from Trotskyism, we will refer to each group by the name of its organ.
2. I should add that I began to see why my work, *Marxism and Freedom*, when translated into Japanese, became *Alienation and Revolution*.

---

teachers, but not college teachers). They said that there isn't any woman in a leadership role in the party, and they were just not as free as women in America. Well, it is true that women in America speak up more. But Marx insisted that no matter how free we think we are, we shouldn't fool ourselves that the ideas of the ruling class aren't the ideas of society—and no matter how hard we work, there will be certain taints that we carry with us . . .

CHAPTER 15

Will the Revolution in Portugal Advance? Under the Whip of the Counter-Revolution*

The revolution in Portugal was born in the African Revolutions.[1] The counterrevolution in Portugal is "coinciding" with the U.S.A.-CIA-South African conspiracy to try to recolonize Angola. As against the revolutionary appeal coming from Black Africa as well as Portugal, South African apartheid has increased its falsehoods along with its power, trying to make itself "part" of "The West."

Thus, Admiral Bierman, South African Chief of the General Staff, wrote in 1972: "It is imperative that a superpower would be involved in the strategy of the Southern hemisphere ... We must persuade the West that communist penetration into the Southern hemisphere is a direct threat to Western Europe and the rest of the free world." It is this which is now appealing to the Ford-Kissinger-CIA dirty tricksters and deep organic imperialists ...

THE NOV. 25 COUP: BEFORE AND AFTER

The counterrevolution that put down the alleged "extreme Left attempt at coup d'etat" in Portugal is unfolding on all fronts, from the imposition of "discipline" on factory workers to the purging of MFA (Armed Forces Movement) and re-establishing of a military hierarchy loyal to "it"—the capitalist government ...

The Rightist move backward—the Nov. 25 coup—instead of being seen and fought as the whip of the counterrevolution that it is, is being whitewashed by the press as if that was the way to avoid a bloody Chile-type coup. But the only reason they do not dare yet roll history

---

*Excerpts from a "Political-Philosophic Letter" written January, 1976. The Letter was translated into Portuguese, for circulation among Portuguese revolutionaries, in the spring of 1977.

backward that far is because the mass movement is still intact, has not been taken over by any existing parties . . .

The truth is that even under Spinola's "leadership," the Portuguese Revolution did not begin as no more than an ordinary coup d'etat . . . A deeper look at new beginnings will, of necessity, lead us to the spontaneous mass movement: land seizures by revolutionary sections of the poor peasantry as well as the great proletarian strikes, of which there were no less than 100 the very first month after the overthrow of the fascist regime—the youth as well as Women's Liberation Movement, which has been paid least attention, though it is a pivotal force.[2]

When the Socialist Party-Communist Party had, in 1969, organized the Democratic Women's Movement, it was strictly limited to economic issues . . . not that "Equal Pay for Equal Work" was ever enforced even in 1974–75. Still, that movement, from above, kept eyes turned away from "feminist" issues, such as right to abortion, or other man/woman relations, though some Portuguese men were backward enough to oppose their wives using contraceptives because it could supposedly make them impotent! Even when women were complaining they were as afraid of their men at home "as of bosses in the factory," it did not move those "advanced politicos" to change the nature of their organization. The Women's Liberation Movement (MLM) thereupon arose on new ground, ground that didn't separate philosophic foundation from feminism or class struggles.

New Forces of Revolution, Focus: Women, Youth, Peasants

Amilcar Cabral, back in the 1960s when the Portuguese economy seemed to experience its greatest "development" with the multinationals moving in on Portugal, said that Portugal, as the weakest link in world imperialism, "could not afford neo-colonialism." The only ones who seemed to listen to the African revolutionary were the Portuguese students, whose strikes came to a climax in 1968 and were against conscription as well as for academic freedom.

The more foreign capital began to move into Portugal as a safe haven for profits and low-paid labor, the more contradictions undermined the regime.

Take the question of the 1973 Middle East War with the accompanying Arab quadrupling of oil prices. On the face of it, it seemed to have no relationship to anything happening in Portugal. But, in fact, fascist Portugal, with its monopoly CUF and in collaboration with two Swedish and two Dutch shipyards, had built the great showy Lisnave dry docks because they expected a most profitable tanker business.

Will the Revolution in Portugal Advance?

The complex at Sines was based on refining and petrochemicals and the expansion of motor vehicle assembly plants. But where a 25 percent increase in tanker business was expected, a 10 percent drop in oil purchases was the consequence of the quadrupled oil prices. The Western economic crisis, which was global, deeply affected Portugal, facing defeat in Africa and massive unemployment and strikes at home.

The human factor of this equation was not only the suffering. Some new forces of revolution were born. First, no less than one and one-half million (out of a population of 8.5 million) had seen service in Africa where they had been politicized by the national liberation movement. Secondly, the miserable conditions in Portugal sent Portuguese workers also to West Europe. By 1974 no less than 900,000 Portuguese had emigrated to West Europe, with 700,000 in France and 150,000 in West Germany. This move to the big cities abroad for employment was glossed over as if it meant economic development at home. Actually, the great number that left agriculture—there was a drop from 50 percent to 30 percent in agricultural production—meant not industrial development at home, but agricultural collapse.[3]

All these factors brought the women into production—industrial, agricultural—and into unemployment. They were the first to be hit by unemployment which, by 1975, numbered no less than 500,000. The women who established the Women's Liberation Movement (MLM) did not think that all their problems were "solved" by the existing parties and unions. Which doesn't mean they didn't actively participate in all of them. It does mean, as was proved all over again at the May 1, 1975 demonstration where they were attacked by the Communist Party and other so-called Left men who did not stop from also attacking their children, that not only was an autonomous movement of women necessary, but the Old Left had to answer *today*: what happens *after* the revolution on the most fundamental Man/Woman relationship?

An MLM leaflet, calling for equal pay for women at the Via Longa brewery and Pao sugar factory, was forced to state: "It is not only the bosses that are exploiting us; it's our own comrades that are refusing equal pay."

Or take the question of agriculture and the most reactionary Catholic hierarchy. Ironically, the entry of foreign capital—U.S., West German, Swedish, Dutch, French—built up not only big industry, like the Lisnave shipyards or the new airport at Farno, but also (in this case West German capital) an irrigation scheme in the Alentejo, which is exactly where the majority of workers were women, where the greatest activities, including the seizure of land, were most militantly fought for by women. Along with the militancy was the demand for a philosophy to fight against the ideological power of the Catholic and fascist tradition which had forced women into submission to God, man, family. They have a long tradition of strikes, arrests, imprisonments. Whether it is in the Alentejo district, where out of 10,000 unemployed, 8,000 were women; or in the cities where, besides industrial struggles, women are very important in health care service; or in ideological struggles, where surely one of the most revolutionary groupings, PRP/BR is headed by a woman—Isabel do Carmo—there is no way to escape the *new*, the pivotal role of women, the youth both on campus and in the army, or the poor peasants. On Feb. 9, 1975, 30,000 farm workers in Alentejo demanded confiscation of the properties of the owners attempting coups.

Instead of keeping away from "feminist" questions, the Old Left better learn to recognize new forces of revolution and new ways of emergence of those forces. Before the April 1974 overthrow of the fascist regime, undercurrents of revolt arose among women, from literature to actual class struggles.

Thus *New Portuguese Letters* (published in the United States as *The Three Marias* and by no means "just literature"—though great literature it is) posed questions of human relations far more profoundly than the Old Left had. The freedom of the "three Marias" from jail was by no means due only to the overthrow of the Caetano regime, but to the protests by the *international* Women's Liberation Movement.[4] The symbol the women's movement, in agriculture especially, had chosen was Catarina Eufemia, assassinated by the National Guard during a strike for the eight-hour day.

Women became especially important in 1973 when a labor shortage sent them into textiles and electronics, and directly into the fight against the multinationals: Timex, ITT, Plessy, and the garment industry (where Swedish capital owned 15 of the 25 major companies). It is in textiles and electronics and shipyards where the grass roots workers' movement first erupted and where none questioned the militance of women workers. But they were asking not only for a fundamental change in labor conditions, but for different relations at home.

Or take agriculture. Women's wages averaged only 50 escudos a day, 50 percent lower than men's. Just as in Lisbon, women workers took over a laundry plant to make it a free service so that "working class women will be liberated from housework," so they were among the most active in the peasant seizures of land and cultivating it on a cooperative basis. The peasants came in their tractors to take part in the Aug. 20 political demonstration to unite with the working class tenants and squatters who were occupying houses. At Caixa the peasants occupied the land of the Duke of Lafoes and turned that into a cooperative . . .

DUAL POWER? APARTIDARISM (NON-PARTYISM)?

. . . Of all the parties that arose the one that was most indigenous and revolutionary was the PRP/BR (Revolutionary Party of the Proletariat/Revolutionary Brigades).[5] So characteristic of the revolutionary situation is non-partyism (*apartidarismo*) that this group, a splitoff from the CP, tried to assign priority not to the party, but to the spontaneous mass organizations. They called for and were instrumental in organizing Revolutionary Councils of Workers, Soldiers and Sailors. The critical question became: were they really developing spontaneously and on a national scale? Was it the type of mass outpouring, and an arming of the working class, that one could say these instances of self-activity created actual dual power?

It simply wasn't true that there was such a self-mobilization of the masses that actually challenged the new but still very much capitalistic government. Nor was it true that even the most "revolutionary" sections of the MFA equalled the armed people, quintessential for a social revolution. And least of all was it true that the Constituent Assembly was anything approaching such high rhetoric. The vote was just a vote, a mere consultative one at that, that didn't challenge continued army rule. To say, as one[6] of the Trotskyist groups maintained, that the Constituent Assembly was a "step toward a workers' and peasants' government," is utter nonsense, reformist euphoria . . .

DIALECTICS OF THEORY

Our acts of solidarity with the Portuguese Revolution must not be separate from a serious theoretical summation of where the Portuguese Revolution was stopped and how to try to advance under the whip of the counterrevolution. As a first step in that direction and in the hope that the discussion will dialectically develop, in Portugal most of all, let us begin with one of the points raised in the Draft Program of the Revolutionary Party/Revolutionary Brigades: "It is also the organization capable of making a synthesis between theory and revolutionary practice."[7]

That cannot just be stated. It must be *worked out*, beginning with the voices and actions that came from below and their question asked of "what happens after?," even as they raised the struggle for workers control of production, Revolutionary Councils, and the ways of self-defense to fight the myriad forms the counterrevolution is imposing—as Portuguese and as part of world capitalism—as it conspires to get back total power . . .

Instead of quoting endlessly what Lenin said on the Party in 1903—a position he many times revised[8]—why not see how Lenin reorganized his thought when he was first confronted with the betrayal of the German Social Democracy and raised the perspective, "Transform the Imperialist War into Civil War," not just as a slogan, but the new *philosophic*, dialectical question of transformation into opposite.[9] By 1917, "All power to the Soviets" was rooted in the philosophic reorganization and its political expression in *State and Revolution: that there can be no new society unless production and the state is run by the population "to a man, woman and child."*

To reduce that to a question of the Party, the Party "to lead," as everyone from the Communists and Maoists to the Trotskyists (of all varieties) is doing, is to doom the resurgence of the revolution.

Stop to think as well as to do . . .

NOTES

1. See especially the African struggles before 1974. *The Struggle for Mozambique* (Baltimore: Penguin Books, 1969) by Eduardo Mondlane, then FRELIMO president, is the most comprehensive by an African leader and contains the first theoretical section also on Women's Liberation, plus quotations from women leaders. See also *Return to the Source: Selected Speeches of Amilcar Cabral* (PAIGC) (New York: Monthly Review Press, 1973). Cabral also wrote the foreword to Basil Davidson's *The Liberation of Guinea* (Baltimore: Penguin Books, 1969), which has the most beautiful pictures, including that of Carmen Pereira, a leading political commissar. As it happens, the current *New York Times Magazine* section (Jan. 4, 1976) carries an article, "Suddenly, Angola," which contains a poem by the third of the leaders of Portuguese Africa, Dr. Neto of the MPLA, whose most recent interview is reported in the Jan. 3, 1976 issue of the *Manchester Guardian*.
2. *Portugal: A Blaze of Freedom*, Big Flame Publications (632 Bristol Rd., Birmingham 29, England), is both the most objective and comprehensive revolutionary study. It is the only one of the analyses that has a substantial section on the role of women, and its glossary doesn't suffer from the sectarianism of either International Socialists that doesn't mention Trotskyist groups, or the Trotskyist groups, which go on endlessly just on themselves.
3. See "The Thorns of the Portuguese Revolution" by Kenneth Maxwell in *Foreign Affairs*, Jan. 1976.
4. When Maria Barreno, one of the authors of *New Portuguese Letters (The Three Marias)* was in the United States, she not only insisted that the international women's movement had much to do with freeing her and her co-authors from jail, but insisted: "I believe in feminism because for me it is the hope to change society." Her speech is reproduced in *News & Letters*, April 1975.
5. Both PRP/BR's Manifesto and many other documents of the Portuguese Revolution

have been reproduced by the People's Translation Service (1735 Allston Way, Berkeley, Cal. 94703) in *Portugal: Key Documents of the Revolutionary Process*.

6. There are two Trotskyist groups in Portugal, one headed by the majority of the Fourth International Secretariat (Mandel), and one by the Socialist Workers Party (Joe Hansen). See *Intercontinental Press*, Sept. 8, 1975 for "In Defense of the Portuguese Revolution," by Pierre Frank, Livio Maitan, and Ernest Mandel (24 pp.) and the endless one about all the differences between the Fourth International and the SWP (70 pp.) in the Oct. 13, 1975 issue of *Intercontinental Press*, "For A Correct Political Course in Portugal," by Gerry Foley, Joseph Hansen, and George Novack.

7. The Sept. 10 Revolutionary United Front Manifesto is included as a separate page in the People's Translation Service, *Portugal*.

8. For the modification of the party concept, 1903–1923, see Ch. XI on "Forms of Organization: The Relationship of the Spontaneous Self-Organization of the Proletariat to the 'Vanguard Party' " as well as Ch. XII on "What Happens After" in my *Marxism and Freedom*, pp. 177–209.

9. Along with *Lenin's Philosophic Notebooks* (included in Vol. 38 of his *Collected Works*), see his Critique of Bukharin's *Economics of the Transition Period*, reproduced as Appendix to that work (New York: Bergman, 1971).

CHAPTER 16

*The Revolutionary Activity of Polish Women**

The celebration of International Women's Day this year may not, on the surface, appear to be directly related to the momentous events in Poland, on which the eyes of the entire world are focused. Yet it is precisely the revolutionary activity of the Polish women that both illuminates the depth and power of Solidarnosc as a movement striving to achieve a whole new society of "Bread and Freedom"—and, at the same time, reveals contradictions that need to be faced, by calling into question whether these women have been recognized as the great revolutionary force they are.

Indeed, none have focused on the women. Yet they have been crucial to the struggle from the very beginning and remain so in the unyielding resistance to the counter-revolution that began the moment martial law was declared. The general strike in the Lenin Steelworks Plant in Cracow at the end of December was led by Andrzej Chudaszek and a woman leader, Halina Bortnowska—and that it was carried through to the end was attributed mainly to her. At the Wujek mine in Silesia, where one of the bloodiest confrontations occurred, the miners had been given an ultimatum to vacate the mine in one hour. Women immediately blocked the way, some lying down in front of the advancing army tanks. When they were swept away by a water cannon, other women picked up tear-gas grenades and threw them back at the police. In Gdansk, 3,000 women armed with flowers and Solidarity bulletins faced the tanks ready to crush the Lenin Shipyard gates. In Katowice, women blocked the way outside the occupied steel mill. And in the underground, Alina Pienkowska and Joanna Duda-Gwiazda remain among the leading activists, calling for continued resistance and describing events in the detention camps—such as the hunger strike of Anna Walentynowicz.[1]

---

*A report sent to Raya Dunayevskaya by Urszula Wislanka, a young Polish feminist in exile, March 1982.

135

If we follow the dialectic of the events, we will see that, from the beginning of the movement, it is not only as sparkplug or as leader, but as masses in motion that the women have been integral to this revolution—both as workers and intellectuals, and both as Force and as Reason.

The birth of Solidarity in 1980 was sparked by a strike at the Gdansk shipyards over the firing of Anna Walentynowicz, a crane operator who, each year, had placed a wreath at the gates where the workers were killed in the 1970 revolt. Throughout the course of the Gdansk strike which created Solidarity, women took part in all the activities.

Alina Pienkowska "thought of everything. She got the rubber stamp, issued passes, collected food from people, opened a place to accept gifts, made sure the Strike Committee had access to the broadcasting center. In a word, she took care of the administration of the strike."[2]

Joanna Duda-Gwiazda immediately started organizing support for strikers from people around the city: financial help, food, blankets, distribution of information.[3] In a textile town, the first act of solidarity was organizing help for the many single mothers, taking care of the children while the women were striking, recognizing financial difficulties of single mothers and organizing material help, establishing cooperatives of women taking turns standing in store lines . . .

Women were also central in working out one of Solidarity's most urgent questions: the form of its own organization. The concept is now known as "horizontal solidarity" and includes all employees from a particular geographic area. The first known instance of horizontal solidarity happened in Swidnik where the women health workers in the local clinic took their demands to the helicopter factory workers saying: Since we're too small to strike—and those who would suffer the most are the patients—include our demands with yours. The workers did, and in the process discovered that there are a lot of issues people raise which affect more than just a particular plant. Thus horizontal solidarity was a way of ensuring that the whole of society was included in the organizational expression of the movement that was not separated from its political, i.e., democratic character . . .

It was in the wake of the 1976 Polish revolt in Radom and Ursus that a new link between workers and intellectuals was forged when a new organization arose called KOR—Committee to Defend Workers. After all of the imprisoned workers were freed, KOR continued its activity, publishing its own uncensored bulletins and helping to publish *Robotnik*, a paper where workers spoke for themselves. Again, it was three women—Helena Luczywo, Ludwika Wujec and Irena Woycicka—

who took responsibility for systematically writing, editing, and producing *Robotnik*.[4] When *Tygodnik Solidarnosc* (Solidarity Weekly) interviewed them, here is what Irena Woycicka had to say about working out that relationship: "To help the Radom and Ursus workers financially and legally was relatively easy. But to understand each other, to get information—that was much more difficult."

By working out, on the basis of workers' own stories, such documents as the Charter of Workers' Rights, the intellectuals who edited *Robotnik* helped lay the ground for the future development of Solidarity.

The uncensored press proliferated; the ideas of "social self-defense" spread over Poland. When the government in the summer of 1978 introduced a new retirement tax for farmers, the peasant women took social self-defense in their own hands. First they chased off the tax collectors. Listen to this report:

> On 25 June in Gorny and Ostrowek there appeared a tax collector who took property from the boycotting farmers . . . When he came to Kowalski's farm he saw women from the whole village at the doorstep. They didn't look at him all too favorably and there was some talk about some sickles which each household has. What happened is not exactly known, but what is known, is that though the tax collector got there, he never entered . . .[5]

Then, to make sure the government heard how angry they were, they organized a milk strike—they refused to deliver milk to the state collection points. The strike was entirely successful, and only after that did the women go to their local priest asking him for help in organizing social self-defense. The peasant movement, crowned with the recognition of Rural Solidarity, had its beginning in the activity of those women.

Modeling their activity on KOR's "flying university," where the intellectuals would go and deliver lectures, wherever and whenever it was possible, on subjects frowned on by the government (such as history), the Farmers' Self-Defense Committee decided to set up the People's University in January, 1979. It was accomplished with the cooperation of intellectuals from Warsaw, particularly Marzena Gorszczyk-Kecik, who was a major power behind the initiative and subsequently was charged with organizing the meetings of the university. Rural Solidarity, built on these foundations, has never lost its relation to the workers, so that after the declaration of martial law, they brought food to the workers in occupied factories. That aid to the resistance was given despite the church's repeated calls for "calm."

But then, some opposition to the church has always existed in the workers' and particularly women's activity. In October, 1981, the women textile workers in Zyrardow refused to follow the church's advice to postpone their demands and end their strike. They struck because there was no food—a strike the government declared "political" and therefore illegal. The women refused to recognize any distinction between political and economic despite threats from the government and the church's appeal that they go back to work. They even defied their own leadership, which, fearful of the consequences, had advised them to stop their strike.

With the tremendous activity of women there also had arisen the beginnings of a Women's Movement. Sigma was the first of Poland's feminist groups, organized in November, 1980. They intended to publish their own newspaper, telling the history of women and their ideas. Their demands included equal pay, development of social programs for women, and increase in men's responsibility for their children. As for abortion, Krystyna Kowalewska, one of the founders of Sigma, puts it clearly: "Many of our demands conflict with the position of the church. For example, abortion. The church has clearly spoken against it. We can't accept that."[6]

Abortion has been used as a political weapon between the church and the state with complete disregard for women's freedom. The church opposes abortion, while the state does not allow any other forms of birth control, forcing women to go through an endless series of abortions. The Russian feminists' description of abortion clinics as "mince-meat machines" is also true in Poland. The feminists made the question revolutionary by making it a question of human choice, opposed to both church and state manipulations...

The women of Poland, as everywhere, know reality in a way that men don't. Listen to a woman from Lodz, interviewed July 30, 1981:

> Take my husband: he's always worked on the first shift. He never waits in line. He knows there is nothing (in the shops), I told him. But he really isn't informed. He can only say the refrigerator is empty. Men don't like to wait in line... It's like with the salaries. Lodz receives the least because they give us light industry. Which light industry? We work in clouds of dust, in humidity, under an infernal noise!... They think that because we're women, they can pay us less!... Lodz and the light industry of Silesia have the lowest salaries in the country.[7]

Or listen to Alina Pienkowska:

> In August, 1980 the women in Gdansk were very active in building Solidarity and in the strike . . . They fought for the rights of all human beings. Naturally an improvement of the position of women depends on the improvement of the general economic situation. But we have not been able to win our concrete demands that are important to us women . . . Taken all in all, I have come to the conclusion that we must struggle more for the women's cause.

NOTES

1. The *Washington Post*, Jan. 17, 1982, has an eyewitness report of the events at the Wujek mine. For a description of the most recent events in Poland, which also brings out the new forms of resistance, see "Counter-revolution drives the revolution underground; the resistance continues" by Raya Dunayevskaya, *News & Letters*, Jan.-Feb., 1982.
2. Quoted from "Glos Anny" (Anna's Voice) in *Gwiazda Polarna* (Northern Star), Nov. 10, 1981. This weekly paper is published in Stevens Point, Wisc. For more of Walentynowicz's own description of the beginning of that strike, see the "Woman as Reason" column by Terry Moon, *News & Letters*, Jan.-Feb., 1982.
3. See the eyewitness account reported by Ewa Milewicz, a member of KOR and NOWA, in *Biuletyn Informacyjny*, Aug.-Sept. 1980. This paper was published by KOR outside the censored press.
4. For reprints from *Robotnik* and other articles, see *Today's Polish Fight for Freedom*, a bilingual pamphlet which I edited. It was published by News & Letters in the spring of 1980 before events exploded in Poland.
5. *Glos* (Voice), Aug.-Sept. 1978. *Glos* was one of the uncensored papers published in the aftermath of the 1976 revolt.
6. *Connexions*, May 1, 1981.
7. *L'Alternative*, Nov.-Dec. 1981.

CHAPTER 17

Alienation and Revolution: A Hong Kong Interview*

"There is no word in the Chinese language that is the exact equivalent for the word, alienation. The ideograms spell out: separation and distance." The young refugee from mainland China hesitated as she searched for words to describe what was happening there, and why she had fled to Hong Kong.

Let's call this refugee Jade, and let me admit at once that, in a few instances, Jade is a composite of several people I interviewed. This method of reporting the discussion with refugees serves as protection for them. Moreover, many of the stories do fit into one another since they are typical of those who, though they are now refugees, had not streamed out of China when the Communists first came to power.

WENT BACK TO CHINA

On the contrary, in the early 1950s they went back to what they considered to be their homeland. "We wanted to do something for our country. We wanted to live as free men and women. No one who has to live all his life in a colony can feel free. Even when he has the proper credentials to stay in Europe or in the United States, he remains always an outsider, a 'foreign student'."

"As a Chinese," continued Jade, "I couldn't stand living in this colony where citizenship was denied me.

"Peita (Peking University) was my dream. We all felt ourselves the children of the May 4 (1919) Movement. Its new name was communism, but I do not think that most of us were communists. Humanist tendencies are very strong among the Chinese. I think the intellectuals went with Mao against the nationalists because of his democratic ideas;

---

*This interview with a refugee from mainland China appeared in *News & Letters*, June-July 1966. It was included in *Sexism, Politics and Revolution in Mao's China* (Detroit: Women's Liberation, News & Letters Committees, 1977).

141

we all thought of communism as the truest democracy. In any case, I disliked, intensely, the merchant class. Almost everyone in Hong Kong sells something, and I certainly didn't want to be any sort of tradesman."

Jade's enthusiasm for the Maoist regime had not begun to wane until mid-1958. I asked her what impact the Hungarian Revolution had made on China. She replied: "I don't think the Hungarian Revolution was in the consciousness of the masses. There were dissatisfactions with conditions in China. Many, especially the older ones—at least at first it was the older ones—felt that after seven years of strict military rule it was time to relax the control. I had also heard that in Yu-men there was a strike of some oil workers. I had heard it from Lin Hsi-ling, the most famous student critic at Peking University. She was all the rage among us during the 'Let one hundred flowers bloom, let one hundred schools of thought contend' debates in the spring of 1957. She was a very powerful orator and kept us spellbound for three and even four hours at a time. She could speak for that long a stretch of time. We would laugh when she derided the superior air of Communist Party members and the system of ranks in the Party.

"It was she who told us that a book critical of the Stalin era had been published, but it was sold only to cadres above the 11th rank. It's true she also mentioned the Hungarian Revolution, but if I remember right, this came only after the Party began accusing its critics of wanting 'to imitate Hungary'. But Lin Hsi-ling herself had drawn a distinction between the Russian Communist Party, which put down the Hungarian Revolt, and the Chinese Communist Party, which initiated the hundred flowers discussion. As I remember it, what she complained of mostly was that the 'contending and blooming' was confined to the upper strata, insisting that only when the masses are free to air their views can the problems that beset us be solved. But all this was said in order to assure our road to genuine socialism.

"Insofar as I was concerned I still thought that was exactly where we were going. Nor did I think it wrong to make some university lecturers clean spitoons. To me it was a sign of breaking down mandarinate society that had always plagued Chinese civilization. Thus I participated actively in the anti-Rightist campaign in mid-1957—I was then in Shanghai. In 1958, when the Great Leap Forward was launched, I volunteered for work on one of the big dams. It was only there that my disillusion began."

"ALL LABOR WAS FORCED LABOR"

She stopped talking and seemed suddenly to be far, far away. I looked at this intense young woman who was less than five feet tall and weighed about 85 pounds. I asked her how could she do the arduous and menial work of building a dam. She replied, "It isn't the menial work that upset me. It was the utter human waste, the bureaucratism, the inefficiency. We were transported by truck, and when we reached the place, we found that nothing was ready for us. Neither a place to live nor even the tools with which to work. It was the most primitive labor imaginable, as if we were to build the whole dam by hand. We lacked even such simple devices as a block and tackle to lift heavy rocks. These had to be pushed into place by sheer brute force.

"Also, although work didn't start until ten in the morning, we had to get up as early as five o'clock because we had no less than 20 miles to walk daily from where we slept to where we worked. All we had when we stopped for lunch was some bread. We did eat better when we finished work at sundown, but we had to reassemble for meetings. We didn't know which was the hardest to bear—the labor, the food, or the meetings. We had to describe what we did that day, and we had to speak about our attitude to what we did.

"Although I had volunteered for the job, I now began to feel as if all our labor was forced labor. I kept my tongue, but you couldn't always keep quiet since, if you kept silent, your team leader would see you afterwards and ask what was the matter. I began to feel like I was nothing more than an ant, and that not only because of the unthinking mass labor, but because you so often said, yes, when you meant, no, that you lost all confidence in yourself. Every day it got harder to think any thoughts of your own. There was many a day when I wanted to bury myself in that dam.

"Finally, my health began to break down. I got what they call a nervous stomach. It got so that I couldn't eat the food at all. After a few months I couldn't bear it any longer and asked to be returned to Peking. Surprisingly, my team leader agreed to that on the condition I wouldn't immediately return to the university and that I shouldn't reveal that I quit. She said I really needed some rest before returning to school.

"For the first time since I had been so actively engaged in the anti-Rightist campaign I began to realize what they—I had now begun to put a distance between myself and the regime—feared most was the reaction of the youth. Of all the surprises during the Hundred Flowers campaign what must have shocked them most was the attitude of the youth, for the very generation that was a product of the new People's Republic had become its severest critics.

"In my opinion," Jade concluded, stressing the word, my, as if the counterposition of an individual's view to that of the state and the

Party was the highest possible daring, "in *my* opinion," she repeated, "the designations of the Right and Left were used only afterwards. At the beginning of the Hundred Flowers debates it was so obvious that the most brilliant students, those who had been the most dedicated Communists and who had been the most prized by the regime, and who themselves kept stressing that they were Communists and wanted no return to the old, had nevertheless become the most severe critics. As I told you, I volunteered for the building of the dam and I truly thought that it was a way not only of building up my country, but of 'uniting' mental and manual work. But now every one of my bones ached, and my brain, too, was tired, tired, tired."

STUDIED "MAO'S THOUGHT," BUT NOT MARXISM

Jade stopped talking. I felt that the telling of the story of the dam was an actual reliving of that shattering experience, and I didn't wish to break the silence. After a few moments she resumed talking, this time about how she used the period of rest to begin studying Marxism. Paradoxical as it may sound, it seems that Marxism was not taught to one and all; it was reserved for "the cadre"—the Communist Party and Communist youth members. "Well, you know, not everybody did consider himself a Communist. Actually only a very small percentage of the Chinese people are Communist Party members. We all, of course, had to know the latest pronouncements of the Communist Party and be acquainted with 'Mao's Thought' on current subjects, but as for serious study of Marxism, that's a different matter."

"I was peeved. I had not been taught Marxism in Hong Kong or in the United States, and I was determined to study it by myself now. Businessmen, for example, could attend the Democratic People's After Hours Political Education School and in four months come out as experts in Marxism, but it was not easy for me to get into a class that studied the original works of Marx.

"I found out what the ten basic books were, and I asked for these from the library: four volumes of Mao's *Selected Works*; two pamphlets by Lenin—*Imperialism* and *State and Revolution*; two books by Stalin—*Foundations of Leninism* and *History of the Communist Party of the USSR*; and two volumes of the *Selected Works* by Marx and Engels. There are not many Chinese translations available of the original works of Marx. It is, however, possible to buy some books in the bookstores on the famous Wang Fu Ching Avenue in Peking if you can read a foreign language, and if you have the money. It is fun to go into those bookstores.

"I was told I should concentrate on Mao's Thought; that theoretically, the two most important essays are 'On Practice' and 'On Contradiction', as well as one of the latest, 'On the Correct Handling of Contradictions Among the People'. These, plus Stalin's *History of the Communist Party of the USSR*, were the sum total of what constituted to them 'Marxism-Leninism'. The trouble was, the more I read, the more I began to doubt some of Mao's statements, because my own experience which kept intruding into my study didn't jibe with his practice or theory. But I didn't dare to say so out loud, not even to myself."

SINO-SOVIET CONFLICT ERUPTS

"I had first heard about disagreements late in 1958, when P'an Tzu-nien, an editor of *Hsinhua* (the official news agency), listed ten points on which Soviet Russia disagreed with the People's Republic. He had begun reeling them off as the Great Leap Forward, the Three Red Banners, the 'non-dialectical' approach to technicians who, the Russians said, should be judged not on how 'Red' they are, but how expert they are, and so forth and so on.

"However, the real shockers did not occur until 1960—and those we heard first not officially, but through the grape-vine—and those concerned an exchange of gunfire between Chinese and Russian border guards and the departure of the Russian technicians with their blueprints. All work had to stop. The campaign then began full force against the Russians. We had no specific love for them; there had actually been very little contact between Russians and Chinese, but the regime itself had always played up the Russians as the greatest friends we had, and Stalin's *History of the Communist Party* had been studied as much as any work by Mao. And now all we heard about them was that they were 'revisionists'. Somehow, instead of hatred against the Russians, a feeling of utter isolation descended upon all of us.

"Then something else took place that set me thinking. African students began coming to our university. We were very interested in them, their countries, their revolutions, but we were not permitted to fraternize with them. They were ghettoized both as to living quarters and any socializing. Meanwhile, living conditions in China had become so difficult that we wanted to ask these new arrivals for things we were short of, like soap. And we were stopped from doing that. So once again, we felt very frustrated. I felt more strongly than ever that things were reeling backwards. At the same time my health hadn't improved much; it seems I was now stuck with a bleeding ulcer. I wanted to flee. I began to plan my escape. It took me two years to achieve it, and yet . . ."

Jade stopped and looked at the mountain at the top of which one could see the radar of mainland China. She resumed talking as if she was talking only to herself: "And yet, I wasn't back in Hong Kong very long—I only came last year, you know—when I began to feel all the old alienations that drove me from this island to the mainland. I'm referring not only to the British colonial administration, but the so-called independent British scholars—and they are not as poor a breed as the Americans who seem to have so exhausted themselves in learning the Chinese language that they do not bother to learn anything about the Chinese people.

"It's funny, their attitude to their 'specialty', China, seems to be like that to a skill, like oil drilling. People exist for them as so many millions—a figure, a figure they wish they could cut, that's all. They don't exist as people with feelings, thoughts, aspirations. Not a single one of them is a Marxist, for example. OK, I can understand that. What I cannot understand is their cynicism. It seems to be one big joke for them, but Marxism isn't one big joke to the Chinese people. No wonder Mao feels so sure that no outsiders will ever get to first base in China, much less win the leadership over the Chinese."

MAOISM IS RETROGRESSIONISM, NOT REVOLUTIONARY

Heretofore I had intervened only in order to ask questions, but I felt it necessary at this point to make my own position clear. I told her that what she knew about me was that I was an American; what she didn't know was that I was a Marxist-Humanist. And as a Marxist-Humanist I wished to state most categorically that Mao was no sort of Marxist. Quite the contrary. Were it not for the fact that he had state power over a vast land of 700 million human beings, no one would pay any attention to his sophomoric essays—"On Practice," "On Contradiction"—much less consider them original contributions to the Marxism of our age. As for "How to Handle Contradictions Among the People," that is not only a revision of Marxism, it is the pronouncement of an exploitative tyrant who is so drunk with power that he thinks that the objective contradictions of capitalist production can be abolished by fiat. Mao decrees so, and so it is.

The shocker, to me, I concluded, was *not* the power conflict between those two state-capitalist societies, Russia and China, that euphemistically call themselves Communist. The shocker was ingrained in Mao's contention that "for decades"—and "even a century"!—the class struggle would continue "in all socialist countries ... as an objective law independent of man's will." Far from being a new theory of revolution, that is the most sinister of all theories of retrogression.

At this Jade fairly jumped out of her seat, exclaiming: "Retrogression, that's it. That really is it. Mao is a retrogressionist! That's the word that escaped me when I said everything seemed to be reeling backwards. That word never came into my consciousness because I was afraid to face its consequences, though I had felt for some time that Mao was the real revisionist. Retrogression, that really sums up 'Mao's Thought.' " Jade took my book, *Marxism and Freedom*, out of my hands and began glancing at the chapter "The Challenge of Mao Tse-tung," saying "I must translate this and get it into the mainland." She kept stressing, over and over again, that Mao was the retrogressionist, not the Chinese masses: "Marx's Humanism will raise their spirits once more, and then history can move forward. The youth stand ready to make a new revolution."

No wonder, I thought to myself as the interview drew to a close, that some Chinese refugees consider the American scholar no more than a new form of the CIA. It is, after all, impossible to bridge the gulf between a tired exponent of "the end of ideology" age and the energetic revolutionary who had suffered through more than a decade of "Mao's Thought" and hard labor and still dreams of new revolutions. No doubt Jade exaggerated the proximity between philosophy and revolution. But the Maos fear their youth, and not those who bemoan their fate at the hands of "the gods that failed." For the dreams and energies of youth are the stuff revolutions are made of, totalitarianisms undermined, Maos overthrown. .

CHAPTER 18

Sexism, Politics and Revolution in Post-Mao China *

I

Chiang Ch'ing, Hua Kuo-feng in Post-Mao China

The present vilification of Chiang Ch'ing as the leader of the "gang of four"—which pictures the alleged radicals as the worst of "capitalist roaders," who had brought China to the verge of catastrophe until saved by Hua Kuo-feng—tells a great deal more about the contradictions tearing at post-Mao China than the victors in this power struggle intended to disclose. Ironically, into this game of power politics in China comes a small-time "Western" entry—Roxane Witke's biography *Comrade Chiang Ch'ing*,[1] which the author prefers to call "a history of the revolution largely from Comrade Chiang Ch'ing's point of view." Because this simplistic work is further befogged by a bourgeois concept of feminism as against the genuine revolutionary feminist viewpoint and actual struggle of a Ting Ling, it becomes necessary to disentangle the three to get at the root of what characterizes not just *post*-Mao China, but Mao's China itself...

Here is how Hua wound up the whole of the speech and thus the two remaining tasks—"to learn from Tachai" to strive "to push the national economy forward," and finally "to study conscientiously and well the works by Marx, Engels, Lenin, and Stalin, and Chairman Mao's works": "Immediately after smashing the 'gang of four', the Central Committee adopted a decision on the publication of the Selected Works of Mao." Hua then singled out from the new Volume V—actually writings from 1949 to 1957—"Chairman Mao's brilliant work" "On the Ten Major Relationships"[2] which is "to guide all" in the fight against Russian revisionism and "the smashing of the gang of four."

---

*Excerpts from two articles in *News & Letters*. The first appeared in two parts, July and August-September 1977; the second in two parts, January-February and March 1981.

Now, what was so crucial about 1962? I don't mean its significance insofar as the annals of Chinese Communist history are concerned, which record 1962 as the Socialist Education Campaign. I mean its significance for Chiang who felt very much discriminated against and underestimated in her own right rather than just as the wife of Mao. It is true that when she begins her story—"Let me dissect myself before you"—Chiang starts with her childhood and details all her suffering. The "true story" is also that she was a revolutionary long before she came to Yenan and married Mao. Indeed, once she became the dominant force in the arts during the Cultural Revolution, she wreaked vengeance on those Communist leaders who hadn't given her her due in the 1930s.

But what predominated in all her actions and ambitions was to be a leader *in Mao's eyes*, and in 1962, for the very first time, *Mao* permitted her to draft a policy statement on the arts known as the May 16th Circular (p. 304). This, then, becomes the year her self-development reaches the high point from which what Mao was later to call her "wild ambitions" took off. So much so that, much as she knows and believes Russia is the enemy, the Sino-Soviet conflict which predominated in those very years—1960–1964—plays a subordinate part to her never-ending preparations for what would, four years later, become her zenith: "The Great Proletarian Cultural Revolution."

Unfortunately, that view holds true not only for Chiang, but for her professor-biographer who had five years to research something she certainly knew about before she ever started. But we get not one whiff from Witke of the serious theoretical debates of the Sino-Soviet conflict when Mao first began to challenge Russia, not just for Sinification of Marxism, but for *world* leadership. Yet it is this, *this precisely*, which preceded the Cultural Revolution and was its leitmotif, and without which it is impossible to understand the changing global relations that, at one and the same time, made it possible for Chiang to exercise influence as Mao's health was failing, *and*, while Mao was still alive, led to the beginning of the end of Chiang's reign.

Instead, we get a sort of Chinese version of Roxane Witke on male chauvinism. Male chauvinism surely is rife in China, and Chiang suffered from it at various times, even as all suffered from Chiang's philistinism. Shouldn't the author have been more perceptive as to the reasons why Chiang herself did not attribute what she considered her overly-long march to power to male chauvinism? What point is there to interpreting Chiang's competitiveness with Mao as "teaching the Chairman not only to love her as a woman, but also to respect her as a political figure not to be monopolized by any one man" (p. 449)? And what, exactly, does the phrase "not to be monopolized by any one man" mean at a time when the author does make clear that the measure *Chiang* thought she was creating was nothing short of "eventually changing the nation's life"?

A more objective and sharper picture of some of Chiang's history emerges from two photographs (among the series following p. 220) than from the lengthy, distorted story of a distorted life. Both are from the decisive years of the War of Liberation, 1947–1949, after Chiang Kai-shek bombed Yenan to smithereens, and Mao began the final march to power. One shows Chiang as a young soldier following Mao in that march. (She was also a "political instructor" to the People's Liberation Army.) The other is a picture of Chiang as clearly more than secretary to Mao—although Mao himself was later to denigrate that role of secretary.[3] It was a most productive period in Mao's life as he both fought and theorized on a guerrilla war and the perspective he saw for the new society he meant to build and called "New Democracy."

When one considers that it was after those two decisive years, followed also by what is called "incognito" work in land reform and marriage reform, that, as her health failed completely and she was shuttled between hospitals in Peking and Moscow, Chiang was stripped in 1951 of all her posts, one must conclude that there is a greater tale against Mao as male chauvinist than ever there was against Chou Yang in the 1930s upon whom Chiang later wreaked her vengeance.

Again, it was not a bourgeois feminist but a great revolutionary writer and feminist—Ting Ling—who dared challenge Mao directly both in Yenan and in the 1950s, and who summed up the fate of the leaders' wives in a single phrase, "Noras who came home."[4]

Chiang Ch'ing rode the crest of the so-called Cultural Revolution, as autocrat over the arts, directly into the very core of Party-Army-State power—membership in the Politburo. By the time of Lin Piao's downfall and Mao's complete reversal of Sino-American relations when he rolled out the red carpet for Nixon in 1972, Chiang took advantage of the presence in China of the host of U.S. journalists, scholars, and what not, to seek out one Sinologist, Roxane Witke. Professor Witke had been commissioned to report on "Chinese female masses," and Chiang asked her to record her solo flight to the echelons of power. The fact that Ms. Witke held that Chiang had "inspired" the "Cultural Revolution"[5] and held leadership in her own right in a "very patriarchal society" surely did earn Chiang a sympathetic ear.

Unfortunately, the wheels of bourgeois research and publishing grind very slowly. By the time—five years later!—the "week-long interview" was expanded to a 550-page book on what Professor Witke fancies is "a history of the revolution largely from Comrade Chiang Ch'ing's point of view" (p. 14), Chiang Ch'ing had been arrested and vilified as a "traitor," not to mention a "maggot." When the "Cultural Revolution" first unfolded in mid-1966 and catapulted Chiang front center stage, she seemed to have no historic past... The height of power she achieved during the Cultural Revolution was the beginning of the end for Chiang.

The first flurry of mild anti-Chiang posters appeared in 1973–74, when Mao was still alive and when rumors first surfaced about the biography she was recording via a bourgeois writer. Whether or not Mao inspired those first attacks, Hua now claims that Mao saw through her "wild ambitions" and warned her against her "faction of four" in 1974.

A new period had begun at the 10th Congress of the Chinese Communist Party, when the undercurrent of revolt in the military following the downfall of Lin Piao compelled the rehabilitation of many of the former Communist Party leaders who had been removed from their posts during the Cultural Revolution. Where Mao did this reluctantly, Chou hailed it as a sort of "savior" for the development of the national economy. Indeed, he raised Mao's main "enemy," Teng Hsiao-ping, to Deputy Prime Minister. Mao could not have been all that hostile to Chiang in 1973–74. And 1975 proved it.

What was at stake was something greater than Chiang. It was a possible global realignment. First, Mao absented himself from the Fourth National People's Congress, which drew up a whole new Constitution as well as both a Five and a Twenty Year Plan for the development of the national economy. Mao did not attend that Congress. Instead, he was meeting with every reactionary world leader, from Franz Josef Strauss of West Germany to the disgraced ex-President Nixon, not to mention taking any side, any side whatever, including that of apartheid South Africa's role in Angola, so long as Russia was recognized as "Enemy No. 1."

The year 1975 had revealed great unrest in China. There were many strikes and bank robberies. At the same time Russia was winning victories in not only Africa, especially in Angola, but also in Europe. China felt "surrounded." The climax came in the first spontaneous, genuine mass demonstration at the grave of Chou En-lai in April 1976. Instead of facing the reality that it was a spontaneous outburst against the regime—the ruling "radicals" controlling the mass media—Mao

Tse-tung moved, this time with the great aid of Chiang, to remove Teng. Hua was to replace him. That was Mao's last hurrah. It was not exactly an anointment of Hua as Chairman, but that top cop knew how to take the "interim" position, and so organize the Party bureaucrats, the military, and state bureaucracy behind him as to need no more than a month after Mao's death to displace in toto all those who had control of mass media and may have opted for total power.

His pre-emptive coup succeeded so well that there is no doubt whatever that, whether or not Mao meant to cut Chiang's "wild ambitions" as far back as 1974, Hua surely had it all planned long before Mao died. Why then is he still so preoccupied, in 1977, to totally smash "the gang of four"? *Well, it isn't the "four."* It is the Chinese masses who are asked to produce more and ever more as China rushes to "overtake" the U.S. by the end of the century. It is Hua's "interpretation" of Mao's "Ten Great Relationships." . . .

It all spells out state-capitalism entrenched and looking for a global role. It isn't that Chiang Ch'ing had fundamentally any different perspective, but she surely had greater belief in "superstructure." It is this fetish that sealed her fate.

The military-industrial-political complex had no difficulty whatever in getting the "mass media" to toe its line once it won total state power. It promptly branded Chiang a "maggot."

One famous Sinologist, Simon Leys, attributes part of the emptiness of *Comrade Chiang Ch'ing* to the author's being "somewhat blinded by her feminist bias."[6] In truth, however, it isn't Ms. Witke's "feminist bias"; it is her petty bourgeois *kitsch* that kept her from penetrating what was actually happening among the masses, women included. Thus, as part of her 1972 assignment, she interviewed women other than Chiang Ch'ing, but, again, it was the pseudo-leaders, rather than the masses, as was the case with her report, "Wu Kuei-hsien: Labour Heroine to Vice-Premier."[7] Here she becomes so great an apologist for Mao's China that she designates the case of that Chinese Stakhanovite thusly: "In today's China she represents women in total control."

And how did that display itself? Well, she quotes Wu Kuei-hsien as saying that she prefers to remain with her First National Textile Mill of Hsienyang rather than go to the center of power because of the work she puts in. Thus, "I have one child born last year. That kept me away from work only one month; I did not need the usual 56-day leave."[8] As for her self-development intellectually, we get it straight from Professor Witke that Wu was grappling "in plain language with the contradiction between thought and action, idea and practice . . ." and therefore she wanted to work out "her dialectical examples from cotton spinning and weaving..."

That, dear reader, is not the product either of Ms. Witke's "feminist bias," or Chiang Ch'ing's "wild ambitions." Rather, it is the product most directly of Mao's retrogressionism.

NOTES

1. Roxane Witke, *Comrade Chiang Ch'ing* (Boston: Little, Brown and Co., 1977). Pagination below is to this volume.
2. *China Quarterly*, March 1977, carries both "On the Ten Major Relationships," as edited by Hua and thus now the official version of the Mao Tse-tung speech of April 25, 1956, and a comparison of it and other versions by Stuart R. Schram.
3. In a March 1964 speech, Mao said: " 'On the Current Situation and Our Tasks' was spoken by me in 1947. Someone transcribed it and it was revised by me. At that time I had contracted a disease whereby I could not write... But if you never take the initiative and rely on a secretary, it is just like having a secretary assume your responsibility for leadership work." (*Miscellany of Mao Tse-tung Thought, II*, p. 338. These volumes are the English translation of the Wan-sui documents, those that appeared in China under the title *Mao Tse-tung Ssu-hsiang Wan-sui*.) This is the speech Chiang was so proud of having taken down "word for word."
4. Ibsen's *A Doll's House* enjoyed popularity in Japan, and the heroine Nora who slammed the door on housewifery was used by Ting Ling in her piece on International Women's Day, "Thoughts on March Eighth," (first published in *Jiefang Ribao—Liberation News*—Yenan, China, March 9, 1942), where she saw wives of leaders as cruelly taken advantage of as they became "Noras who returned home." The article was used in the campaign against Ting Ling, who was purged from the Chinese Communist Party in 1957 for criticizing the views of the party on marriage and love at the time of the Hundred Flowers campaign. The best pamphlet on *Ting Ling, Purged Feminist* was issued in Japan (Feminetern Press, Box 5426, Tokyo). When American feminists who themselves suffer from Maoism issue anything by her, as the feminist journal *Signs* did, Autumn 1976, the "explanatory" note is disgusting as they try to conclude that, though right, Ting Ling was nevertheless evidently wrong, or untimely, or whatever.
5. For a more comprehensive view of the "Cultural Revolution" see both the chapter on Mao Tse-tung Thought in my *Philosophy and Revolution* (New York: Dell, 1973) and my essay "Post-Mao China: What Now?" in *New Essays* (Detroit: News & Letters, 1977). For a view of China's foreign policy, some ten chapters devoted to that are well worth reading in *The Chinese Party in Power, 1949–1976* by Jacques Guillermaz.
6. See "China's Fallen Empress" by Simon Leys, *New Republic*, June 25, 1977.
7. "Report from China," *China Quarterly*, December 1975, pp. 730–740.
8. As against Ms. Witke's apologia, see my Hong Kong interview with Jade, printed in *News & Letters*, June-July 1966, and Jade's report of the achievements and retrogressions since the Chinese Revolution, "Women's Liberation in China," included in *Notes on Women's Liberation* (Detroit: News & Letters, 1970).

II

China's "Gang of Four" Trial Charade

... Let's now take a look at the simple incommensurability of the dates in the trial of Lin and the trial of Jiang suddenly turned into a single amalgam. First came the 1971 Mao-Lin dispute, which ended in the death, or murder, of Lin Biao (Lin Piao). Jiang Qing (Chiang Ch'ing) was in the forefront of the campaign of calumny against Lin that followed. What followed in immediate post-Mao China was that Jiang was arrested by the top cop, Hua Guofeng (Hua Kuo-feng) who helped give the present 1981 ruling clique the appearance of "legitimacy," since he supposedly had Mao's blessing to become Chairman. Where is he now? It was nearly four years between the arrest and the trial of the so-called Gang of Four. And the one who did the arresting is now nowhere around.

Does anyone doubt that it is really Mao Zedong (Mao Tse-tung) who is on trial? Ah, there's the rub. Those in power now, like those who stand accused now—including Mao himself—are the ones who, at one and the same time, both initiated and destroyed the Cultural Revolution.

What remains absent from all reports is any view of the objective world situation, be that in 1966 or in 1971; in 1975 when Mao was still alive or in the immediate post-Mao China, 1976, when Jiang was arrested. If, however, we hold fast to the objective world situation, it will not be too difficult to unravel all the plots and counterplots which developed during the so-called Cultural Revolution.

They came to a climax, not in any sort of "uninterrupted revolution," but in Mao's counterrevolutionary rolling out of the red carpet for Nixon after Nixon finished the mad bombing of Cambodia. Nixon's bombing of Cambodia had been followed by his tilting to Pakistan— which was bloodily attempting to stifle the newborn nation of Bangladesh—in order to get Mao's approval for Kissinger's trip to meet Zhou Enlai (Chou En-lai) and plan for that super spectacle: Nixon's trip to China.

By the end of the current trial, considerable sympathy was extended to Jiang Qing because she alone, of both the so-called Gang of Four and the military adherents of Lin Biao,[1] displayed some strength of character not only in opposing the accusations against her, but in calling the judges "counterrevolutionaries," whom she challenged to behead her: "Revolution is no crime. To rebel is justified," she shouted. Glaring at the presiding judge, Zeng Hanzhou, she continued: "During the war it was I, the only woman comrade, who followed and accompanied Chairman Mao to the front. At that time, where were all of you hiding?"

To say, as the prosecutor put it, that she was invoking the name of the Great Helmsman only to save her skin—an accusation *Business Week* (Nov. 24, 1980) repeated—is both to miss the point that it was

Mao who did the commanding and Jiang who obeyed unquestioningly, and to try to deprive Jiang of the dignity that a belief in your principles gives you—no matter how wrong those principles may be. It is this which in her two-hour defense also enabled her to be sarcastic of the entire charade that was going on, which featured her, as she put it, as if she were "some kind of devil with three heads . . . Tell the Monkey King to come and teach me how to grow several more heads, is that it?"[2]

Unfortunately neither the courage, nor the sarcasm, nor the fact that she certainly didn't plot any assassination of Mao, can in any way clear her of the responsibility for the horrors of that so-called Cultural Revolution. The 20,000-word indictment charged that no less than 727,420 Chinese were mercilessly persecuted, and that 34,272 died. But the only grisly proof of Jiang's "direct crimes" was the constant display of a picture of the bruised corpse of the former Coal Minister, Zhang Linzhi, whom, it was charged, she had ordered to be beaten to death.

What preceded all of this and intensified the differences between Lin and Mao was the question of relations with U.S. imperialism. It wasn't that Lin disagreed about relations with Russia; he was in the forefront of calling Russia Enemy Number One. But his position was that not only does Russia's "hegemony" have to be challenged, but so does U.S. imperialism's. To the extent that both the U.S. and Russia were held out as the enemies of the masses, Lin was as adamant as Mao against Russia. There was no difference between Lin and Mao either in the initiation of the Cultural Revolution or in suppressing it when it began to have a momentum of its own.

Again Jiang marched to their tune, adding a few vicious persecutions of her own in the arts. Whether she did or did not, by then, sprout some "wild ambitions" of her own[3] is not what brought on the crisis in China . . .

After Mao had put down the self-created turmoil called the Cultural Revolution—and after he not only "rehabilitated" Deng Xiaoping (Teng Hsiao-ping), but what is a great deal worse, started to play with U.S. imperialism—there was no sort of revolutionary legacy he could possibly leave the Chinese masses. Thus it was that in 1975, while staying away from the National People's Congress run by Zhou and Deng with its "four modernizations," Mao met with Franz Josef Strauss!

It is wrong, however, to think that, because the scholars were deluded by Mao, the journalists have done any better in presenting the opposite side of the coin. Instead of overestimating Mao, they underestimated the entire Chinese revolutionary experience, though that was national.

In the *New York Times* of Jan. 2, 1981, Flora Lewis came up with the most superficial of all scenarios: "Winston Churchill got it backwards when he described the Soviet Union as a 'riddle wrapped in a mystery inside of an enigma'. It's the other way around; inside is the infighting to be expected, and the mystery wrapper is to conceal the fact that there really isn't much higher meaning . . . I think we'll manage understanding better if we remove the veils from our own dazed eyes . . ." The only trouble is that it isn't the eyes that are dazed, but the thought. The crisis in China would hardly be as intense as it is now if it had no "higher meaning" than the "infighting to be expected."

When the first spontaneous mass demonstration in Mao's China sprang up on April 5, 1976—in honor of Zhou Enlai who had died and was still being slandered by Mao, Jiang, et al.—Mao embarked on his last hurrah. Whether inspired by Jiang or otherwise, he ordered the demonstration put down and Deng, who was blamed for instigating it, removed. Within a few months, Mao himself died, and Jiang was left to hold the bag. In no time at all, she was arrested.

Whether or not Jiang escapes death now in order, as Deng put it, not to make a martyr of her, and whatever punishment is meted out to Lin's adherents, the point at issue is not those few who are now in the dock. What is at issue is, where is China going now, nationally and internationally? Are there still illusions that when one has some H-bombs, the backwardness of the economy, including the military, doesn't matter half as much as who becomes the ally, be it back with Russia or with the U.S.?

The truth is that it's not what is being decided at the trial that is decisive. The truth is that the only way to change direction, be it Maoist or Dengist, is to listen to the voices of revolt. China has a history of peasant revolt that is second to none, and it has a history of proletarian and youth revolts that have not stopped, either with Mao's last hurrah or Deng's removal of the Democracy Wall.[4] It is they who have not yet said their last word.

NOTES

1. Actually, the first in the series of arrests following the army's suppression of the Cultural Revolution was that of the genuine Leftist, Chen Boda (Chen Po-ta) who was the head of the whole Cultural Revolution Group. Chen Boda had been Mao's political secretary ever since the mid-1930s in Yenan. Indeed, there is no doubt whatever that many of Mao's speeches were written by Chen—whereupon he was the very first one Mao arrested and started vilifying.
2. The *Manchester Guardian* of Jan. 4, 1981 explains that "the reference is to a mythical figure who could grow as many heads as he chose, who would need to help her if the court had its way."
3. The expression is supposed to be Mao's in a letter to Hua Guofeng, whom he allegedly

designated as his successor. This period of vilification is briefly reported in *Comrade Chiang Ch'ing* by Roxane Witke (Boston: Little, Brown and Co., 1977).

4. See *The Revolution is Dead, Long live the Revolution: Readings on the Great Proletarian Cultural Revolution from an Ultra-Left Perspective*, compiled and edited by a group of independent socialists in Hong Kong, "The 70's," May 1976. Section Three consists of the views of the Chinese "ultra-leftists" in their own words. This same group, renamed "The 80's Front," also has translated into English a bulletin of documents from the outpouring of opposition during "Peking Spring" (1979); see *Peking Spring* (The 80's Front, c/o 1984 Bookshop, 180 Lockhart Rd., 1st Floor, Wanchai, Hong Kong).

CHAPTER 19

*International Women's Year: Where To Now?**

Nearly 20,000 women converged on Houston, Texas for the International Women's Year (IWY) Conference Nov. 18–21. Since delegates to the government sponsored and funded affair numbered only 2,000, it is clear that the activist observers, who had to pay their own way, felt that just being there could help transform the meeting into an event that would change the face of the United States on the question of women's liberation. They were right. They created a momentum far beyond the "National Plan of Action" devised by the appointed commissioners.

Despite the fact that the well-organized and efficiently run conference had worked to have all 26 Resolutions of the Plan voted as presented, the disabled, then the minority, and then the older women wrote entirely new ones for themselves that gave far more concreteness to women's rights than the abstract cornerstone of the entire convention: the ERA.

It was the Substitute Resolution on Minority Women that was the highlight of the conference in everything from style to substance to comprehensiveness. Five women presented it. The Black woman who rushed to the mike to offer the substitute yielded to the Asian woman, who spoke and then yielded to the Hispanic woman, who spoke and yielded to the Native American, who spoke and yielded to Coretta King, who completed it. The Native American spoke of their children who are taken away; the Hispanic of the deportation struggles and the question of bilingual studies; the Asian woman of sweatshop working conditions; and Coretta King of their demand for firm government support for affirmative action. No wonder she ended, not on how much

---

*From *News & Letters*, December 1977.

was achieved these past 10 years, but by declaring that "We still have a long way to go."

Because these new substitute resolutions that were passed so overwhelmingly were so concrete, it was clear that it was not what was done there at the conference that was the most important, but what remains to be done afterward. That task was recognized as the one to be done by themselves, not left to those "above." It was the recognition of Self as social being, Women's Liberationists in action.

The euphoria created by the massive attendance, the fact that the delegates were so well-organized that the feared *direct* confrontation with the ilk of the KKK did not happen, and the need for and achievement of unity on the question of the ERA, did create altogether too much enthusiasm for the "leaders," so that a person like Rosalynn Carter, who came as "personal emissary" of the President, was never challenged on his backward move refusing federal funds for the poor needing abortions.

The anti-Women's Liberationists held their own counter-meeting of some 10,000 men and women, from around Texas and Utah mainly—especially male-dominated in its counterrevolutionary philosophy of unfreedom, as represented by the KKK, Birchers, Conservative Union, as well as the most right-wing members of the Catholic and Mormon Churches. But the presence of the counterrevolution was felt within the IWY hall, too. What male chauvinist thought that a whistle was needed to try to keep the right-wing women delegates in line to vote against every and all resolutions?

Unfortunately, the majority delegates—mainly white, middle-class, career women, aiming for political jobs and running for electoral office—were so anxious that all behave as "ladies" that they would not entertain a motion to expel the Mississippi delegation, though it included KKKers. Actions like that not only held back the confrontation of ideas, but permitted the delusion that the counterrevolution was not a threat. None bothered to mention that police cars with KKK insignia patrolled the streets surrounding the conference and struck terror among lesbians, nor that the other "rally" referred to the IWY as "International Witches' Year"!

On the other hand, it was the threat of the counterrevolution that did mobilize the conference and brought a leader like Betty Friedan, who had feared touching the lesbian question, to change her mind and urge adoption of the motion not only for "reproductive freedom" (the right to abortion on demand), but also the right of "sexual preference" (lesbianism). Both motions passed overwhelmingly.

International Women's Year: Where to Now? 161

When one of the reactionary women said that the conference was dominated by "lesbian abortionists," one feminist writer, Lucy Komisar, smiled, "Well, they can't be both, can they?" The significance of this incident isn't the "sense of humor" the *New York Times* reporter emphasized, but the seriousness of the activists; the range of ages—literally from 16 to 80; the connection with history's path, not because the Smithsonian Institute let them use the gavel Susan B. Anthony had used in 1896, but because her niece-namesake, 61, was there—and because the young women who had never heard of either one were the ones who were carrying the struggle far beyond what it was at the end of the 19th century.

That is what brings us to the question of the left and the ideological battles that, unfortunately, *didn't* take place.

At the 1975 IWY international conference in Mexico City, many of the delegates were wives of state rulers, parroting the political line of their respective husband-rulers, whether that be Mrs. Sadat or Mrs. Rabin. Unlike them, these middle-class white women were moved by the controversial questions and by the minority and other women to neither stick only to their own 26 Resolutions, nor be so totally elitist as not to hear some of those voices from below. They knew these voices had no intention of remaining silent once the conference was adjourned, and legislation tries to take over and stall and stall and stall.

The sad part, then, was that the left itself would try either to limit itself to single issues like ERA or right to abortion or action against deportation; or to think of themselves as "grass roots" rather than recognizing the actual grass roots whose concreteness was the ground for a battle of ideas.

Women's Liberation-News & Letters Committee did raise the question of Woman as Reason. The manner in which Iranian women showed their interest in *Marxism and Freedom*, and Black women their interest in a pamphlet like *Sexism, Politics and Revolution in Mao's China* saying, "Sexism is everywhere," showed the universality and interconnectedness of rights with revolution.

The counterrevolution with their slanders against the very subject of the conference did change the question from any single issue to the totality of revolution. That unfolds an entirely new banner: Woman as Reason and as Revolutionary. Nothing short of it will help uproot this exploitative, sexist, racist society.

CHAPTER 20

The Latin American Unfinished Revolutions

The phenomenon of a Third World *within* the U.S.—which had been raised at the International Women's Year Conference in 1975—became especially intense during the 1970s. What follows are: 1) excerpts from a Political-Philosophic Letter written May 15, 1978, which shows how the whole question of Latin America was related also to the question of Eritrea. These excerpts include the Appendix to that Letter—an exchange of correspondence in the 1960s with Silvio Frondizi in Argentina; 2) excerpts from an article written in 1979 by Marta Lamas, a Women's Liberationist associated with the Mexican journal, *fem*; and 3) a 1981-2 exchange with the Peruvian feminists around ALIMUPER.

I

Excerpts from a "Political-Philosophic Letter" on The Latin American Unfinished Revolutions

May 15, 1978

Of the more than two dozen talks I gave on this spring's lecture tour—ranging from "Gramsci's Philosophy of *Praxis* vs. Eurocommunism" to "Frantz Fanon, Soweto and American Black Thought"; and from "Rosa Luxemburg and Today's Women's Liberation Movement" to "Today's Global Crisis, Marx's *Capital* and the Epigones Who Try to Truncate It"—the talk that produced the most probing discussion was the one given at California State University on "The Latin American Unfinished Revolutions: Where to Next?" This was due to the fact that the discussion on it transformed the question, "Where to Next?", from one of "programs and tactics," as was the case heretofore, to one of methodology and a philosophy of revolution.

THE CUBAN REVOLUTION BEFORE AND AFTER RUSSIA'S ENTRY

In the 1960s the discussions around the New Divide—the Cuban Revolution—were nearly totally uncritical both because of the great enthusiasm over its success against both Batista and that Goliath 90 miles from its shore, U.S. imperialism, *and* because of the hope that it would initiate a new age of revolutions on no less than a tri-continental Third World range. But the *new* question posed in the 1970s was: How could it be that Cuba—which made its revolution by its own force and its own *Reason* which Fidel had declared to be "Humanist"[1]—was now so blatantly tail endist to Russia, *globally*, as to declare Ethiopia a "land going toward socialism" and oppose the Eritrean liberation struggle Fidel had so long championed?

This is not to say that those now asking that question had opposed the Cuban Revolution when it first took place. Quite the contrary. They had opposed any who dared question a single aspect of it, whether that was the transformation of guerrilla warfare into *the* universal for uprooting any and all class societies, or Cuba's relationship to Russian Communism. But now one African called the Cubans "mercenaries," and I strongly objected to the designation, explaining that, no doubt if I were Eritrean, I could easily sound as Maoist as those who declare Russia to be "Enemy No. 1," but that choosing the "lesser evil" has always brought to the fore the greater evil, be it U.S. imperialism or Russian.

The young man replied that, first, he was not Eritrean, but Ethiopian; and that a genuine social revolution is exactly what the liberation struggles *within* Ethiopia aimed at, as against Col. Mengistu. But, continued the young man, the truth is always concrete, and, concretely, the Cubans are not revolutionaries but *counter*revolutionaries in Ethiopia.[2]

THIRD WORLD-ISM AND "DEPENDENCY THEORIES"

Where, in the 1960s and early '70s, discussions in the Left centered around "Dependency Theories,"[3] today discussion is around the unfinished nature of all Third World revolutions. That is to say, previously U.S. imperialism alone was held to be the enemy, its tentacles so massive that, it was concluded, there was no substantive native capitalist class, and therefore the class struggle road to revolution was inapplicable in the underdeveloped countries. Today, Third World-ism is declared to be sheer "euphoria."[4]

This particular aspect of the discussions was induced by Gérard Chaliand's *Revolution in the Third World*. It is by no means a work by some reactionary outsider, but a Left "participant-observer" as he rightly designates himself. It is true he is not a Marxist, and is so anti-Leninist as to often hyphenate Lenin's name with Stalin's. Moreover, he disregards totally the global extension of the theory of revolution to the Orient by "non-party masses," developed by Lenin in the Theses on the National Question at the 1920 Communist International Congress, and other writings that flow from it.[5] When Chaliand does speak of the relevance of Lenin's view to the underdeveloped countries of our era, he seems to skip a near half-century of fundamental changes in the world, especially Mao's transformation of Lenin's concept of proletarian and peasant revolution into guerrilla wars, that Mao designated as "people's wars" in which he accepted "patriotic" capitalist nationalists. To cap it all, Chaliand entitles the crucial section "The Leninist Bureaucracy and Foreign Policy: China Since the Cultural Revolution"!

Nevertheless, for today's Left, Chaliand speaks as an "insider," a Leftist who had been a prominent exponent of Third World-ism and who lived with revolutionaries in the field—in Latin America, in the Palestinian Resistance Movement, and in the jungles of Africa. It is this that makes Chaliand's book a serious contribution to the present discussion of what to do now that the revolutions in the Third World have remained unfinished.

He answers unequivocally with what he calls "Guerrilla Inflation: The Foco Theory as a Theory of Failure." He shows that, first, the only peasant and urban guerrillas that had any success were those that were social as well as national struggles, that is to say, class battles.[6] Secondly, he now acknowledges that "the most important weakness is the conceptual" (p. 179). In a word, where in the 1960s and early '70s activism was about the only guideline—whether that concerned Cuba, Africa, and the Middle East, or whether that related to the industrialized countries, especially France, May 1968—Chaliand concludes that, both to understand *what* happened and to see the direction we are heading, objectively and subjectively, we can no longer evade the "conceptual."

Unfortunately, far from drawing the "conceptual" to a logical conclusion as a total philosophy of liberation, Chaliand himself reduces it to "social and political terrain," which is hardly more than Trotskyist paraphernalia . . .

MARX'S THEORY OF REVOLUTION, AND SILVIO FRONDIZI

. . . The specific terrain of Latin America brought to my mind the development of the Argentinian revolutionary, Silvio Frondizi. In

February 1952, on the eve of the first revolts from under Russian totalitarianism—the June 1953 uprising in East Germany—Frondizi began a new type of digging into the origins of Marx's new continent of thought he called a "new Humanism." Frondizi wrote:

> The recent publication of the *Economic-Philosophic Manuscripts of 1844* and of *The German Ideology* serves to illuminate many important aspects of dialectical materialism, making urgent and indispensable a new study of theory that would take into account the humanism in them and in *The Holy Family*, *The Jewish Question*, the introduction to the *Critique of Hegel's Philosophy of Right*, as well as the later economic works that, far from contradicting the philosophical principles affirmed in the early works ... illuminate and enrich them.

Silvio Frondizi was a serious Marxist, an activist. In a land where the Left confusedly hoped after World War II that Peron might be an effective force against U.S. imperialism, Frondizi had instead, by the 1950s, organized a group to seriously study dialectics and print Marxist studies in Argentina.

In the early 1960s, Frondizi moved toward accepting the theory of state-capitalism. (I append part of my correspondence with him when he was translating *Marxism and Freedom*[7].) ...

What the 1970s brought forth that was new is by no means limited to the question raised by the Ethiopian student at California State University on Cuba's role in Ethiopia. Quite the contrary. What is new are the new groups that are appearing from the Left, who want to see with eyes of today the past two decades that would not separate the Latin American struggles from those in East Europe, or the Black revolution in the U.S. from the present struggles in South Africa, or new class struggles in West Europe from the so-called "ultra-Lefts" in China, much less allow Women's Liberation to be relegated to "the day *after*" the revolution. The new is that the struggles must be considered *as a totality*, and as a totality from which would emerge new beginnings.

It is on this question, precisely, that Frondizi still has a great deal to contribute. The Argentinian fascists who murdered Silvio Frondizi on Sept. 27, 1974 could not kill those new beginnings.[8] New dialogues have been opened which must be continued, whether it be on the question of a total philosophy of liberation that would not allow philosophy and revolution to be separated, much less be taken out of global context, or whether it be on the strategy of foco-ism, or genuine proletarian revolution. I trust that this is but the beginning of a dialogue with the new Latin American revolutionaries.

NOTES

1. See Fidel's speech, summer 1959, reproduced in *The New Left Review*, Jan.-Feb. 1961.
2. *Gramma* first revealed Cuba's participation in Ethiopia this March. See also the London *Economist* report reproduced in the *Toronto Globe and Mail*, May 6, 1978.
3. See *Latin American Perspectives*, No. 11, Fall 1976, especially the following two articles: "Dependency Theory and Dimensions of Imperialism" by Timothy F. Harding, and "Capitalist Development, Empire and Latin American Underdevelopment: An Interpretive Essay On Historical Change" by Frederick S. Weaver.
4. See *Revolution in the Third World: Myths and Prospects* by Gérard Chaliand (New York: Viking Press, 1977).
5. See my analysis of those Theses in relationship to the African Revolutions of our day in *Nationalism, Communism, Marxist-Humanism and the Afro-Asian Revolutions*.
6. See my analysis of Debray, Ché and Castro's foco theory in Part III of *Philosophy and Revolution*, "Economic Reality and the Dialectics of Liberation," especially pp. 276-278.
7. Now available in Spanish: *Marxismo y Libertad* (México: Juan Pablos, 1976) and *Filosofía y revolución* (México: Siglo XXI, 1977).
8. See *News & Letters*, Nov. 1974, both for further quotations from Frondizi and an "In Memoriam" article which states:

> Having lost its fascist head, Peron, Argentina now wobbles between open civil war and total fascist barbarism. At present, Mme. Peron's goon squads are doing in extra-legal fashion what they dare not yet do legally and openly: exterminate their opposition. There is no question that the violence now wracking the southern end of South America, including Brazil, Uruguay, Argentina, and Chile, is part of an attempt to prevent the Latin American revolution from completing its links. A pro-fascist combination of military forces, oligarchs, U.S. imperialists, and CIA ferret out left-wingers and independents, then torture and assassinate them

APPENDIX: Excerpts from an Exchange of Correspondence with Silvio Frondizi

Buenos Aires
March 28, 1963

Dear Miss Dunayevskaya:

... I want to tell you that I'm very interested in the Spanish translation of your book because I hope it will turn out a success. I am willing to undertake this and I think the publication may include all the appendices you would decide. Although we have the original of the "Political and Economic Manifesto," and its English, Italian and Spanish translations, I think it is always interesting to consider a new version. We also have the French and Italian editions of the "Lenin's Philosophic Notebooks," but haven't the Spanish translation of these. Your pamphlet "Nationalism, Communism, Marxist-Humanism and the Afro-Asian Revolution" may be included in our publication too.

I'll have all our materials sent to you as soon as possible, except those which are out of print. You will advise that some of them are not in fashion, but you may take the opportunity to know what have we done as yet.

We shall take it our business to do whatever you suggest about this matter and to begin a regular exchange of materials.

I'll be hoping to hear from you soon and I should like to meet you here for in-person discussion between us.

Most truly yours,
Silvio Frondizi

Detroit
April 2, 1963

Dear Dr. Frondizi:

...I think it would be an excellent idea to include the pamphlet on the Afro-Asian Revolutions because all of this does apply to Latin America as well as to Africa. I am including herewith one of the letters of Africa that I had written when I was there, plus the pamphlet. Under separate cover we will also send you all of our other publications.

Will you write a special introduction for the Latin American edition? I certainly hope so and I too will wish to write a special preface. I will not comment on the trip because I don't see it as an immediate possibility, unfortunately, because of the cost. No doubt, however, by the time the book has been translated, I hope to be there. Will you please inform me what type of publisher you have in mind? How long do you estimate the translation and the printing will take?

Fraternally yours,
Raya Dunayevskaya

Detroit
May 29, 1963

Dear Com. Frondizi:

Thank you very much for inscribing your *La Realidad Argentina* to me and forwarding to us your other books as well as those of your collaborators, Marcos Kaplan and Eugenio Werden. It is most exciting to find that in the same two decades—1943–1963—in which our ideas were formulated, so were yours. While, in its main current, the Marxist-Humanism, internationalism and revolutionary aspirations are on the same level—or, as you phrase it in "Doce Años de política argentina," "que aspira a superar las limitaciones y la antitesis de stalinismo

The Latin American Unfinished Revolutions

y del trotzkismo"—the different origins and environment of the American and Argentinian Marxist-Humanists should also show themselves. What is quintessential is that, finally, after a theoretic void begun with the death of Lenin and never ended, a dialogue between us should begin on the serious level of bringing out a Spanish edition of *Marxism and Freedom*, with, I hope, an Introduction for the Latin American readers by yourself. Naturally, at the same time, I will see that your works get read by our people and, while the situation in this country hardly allows for translation and publication of your works, I shall certainly try to see what I can do.

If you will permit me to call to your attention the method of my book, I believe we will also be able to see wherein the emphasis you have put in your works differs. Your group impresses me as being serious and all intellectual; ours is serious but it is nearly 50 percent proletarian. Hence, while we have theoretical works like *Marxism and Freedom* and the pamphlet on the Afro-Asian Revolutions, and presently the National Editorial Board's statement on *American Civilization on Trial*, we have not only the unique combination of worker and intellectual in the monthly paper, *News & Letters*, but also such pamphlets written by workers and Negro youth as *Workers Battle Automation*, *Freedom Riders Speak for Themselves*, etc. It is this concentration on letting the workers speak for themselves that has also influenced the writing of the major theoretical work, as you can easily see by the break in style in Section Two on the American Scene of Part B, "The Problem of Our Age: State Capitalism vs. Freedom."

This same concentration on the working class' self-activity explains why the reestablishment of the Humanism of Marxism in the United States dates itself, on the one hand, to the miners' strike against Automation in 1949–50, and to the East German revolt against Russian totalitarian "norms of labor" in 1953, on the other.

Your concrete theoretical analysis—whether your own "La Realidad Argentina," "Doce Años de política argentina" and "La Revolucion Cubana," or Marcos Kaplan's "Economía y Política del Petroleo Argentino" (1939–1956)—therefore were of greater value to us than the philosophic statements, whether of Rousseau, Locke, or dialectical materialism. This is *not* because philosophy is not of the essence to us as an organization and to the epoch as an age that must still achieve its revolution. Rather it is because your latter works trace a philosophic development, in and of itself, whereas our philosophic theses relate directly to the present stage of political and proletarian development.

Let us take, as one example, Humanism. Of course it can be traced from Rousseau, and surely we come closer yet to Marx through Feuerbach. And I agree with you that Rudolfo Mondolfo is surely underestimated in Europe and not known at all in the United States. I remember being impressed with his "Marx and Marxism," especially his attack on the current pretenders to Marxism as against "genuine Marxism which is animated by a deep historical consciousness and the highest demands for freedom." Nevertheless the stress on Feuerbach did not help the Marxism of the late 19th century not to betray *nor*, which is more important, Lenin be able to find his way back to the Hegelian dialectic as self-development, self-activity, self-movement and the humanism that followed *without breaking with the whole philosophic foundation of the Second International, even in its revolutionary internationalist days, of counterposing materialism to idealism instead of seeing them as synthesis.*

In any case—to return to the method of *Marxism and Freedom*—the 1844 Manuscripts are dealt with, *not* in relationship to either Rousseau or Feuerbach or, for that matter, the dialectic of the Greeks upon which Marx also surely depended, but as they arose in the beginnings of the factory age. That is to say, the Industrial Revolution, on the one hand, stimulated the American Revolution and English classical political economy with its theory of value; and, on the other hand, impelled the great French Revolution, the Hegelian dialectic, and the utopian socialists and vulgar communists. Out of all these forces plus the actual class struggles of the 1830s came Marx's Humanist essays, the anticipation of the 1848 revolution.

The next "break" in Marx comes as a result of the American Civil War, the struggle for the eight-hour day and birth of the First International, and the Paris Commune. These forces help him theoretically break with his former method of presenting his *Critique of Political Economy* as a dispute among theoreticians, to *Capital*, as a history, not of theories, but of production relations. The Humanism and Dialectic of *Capital* reestablishes, therefore, the Humanism of 1844 on a very much higher level, right within his most "economic" work.

To me, Lenin's need to break with his own philosophic past has the most cogent effect on us today, and is seen, not so much in his break with the Second International which betrayed, but with his own Bolshevik colleagues, especially the main theoretician of the party, Nikolai Bukharin, whom he considered suffering from "economism" and not "fully a master of the dialectic." In this Lenin predicted all state planners of today. Naturally he couldn't know them as we who have suffered from Stalinism know them, but the anticipation of state-capitalism and degeneration of Russian Revolution in his last speech had never been mastered by Leon Trotsky. Though he had remained the one symbol of opposition to the Stalinist bureaucracy, it turned out to be no more than a footnote to history, and now the Trotskyists are nothing but left-wing whitewashers of both Russian and Chinese Communism.

Finally, the Humanism gets to the American, East German, and Hungarian Revolution scenes, and it is on such a need for a new humanism that I end the book. I do not go into the French "resuscitators" of Humanism in the mid-1940s who used it only to whitewash Stalinism—and later the American state department through "Congress of Cultural Freedom." I do have in a recent Two Worlds column the new spate of books on the Early Essays of Marx, but on the whole I will not argue with those who speak one way when they talk abstractly (as Lefebvre, Merleau-Ponty, let alone that Stalinist apologist Sartre) and act quite differently on the political and organizational front. I would rather stick with the proletarians and follow *their* real movement for the reconstruction of society.

Do please let me hear from you as to the actual possibilities of bringing out the Spanish edition this year. As you noted from the various people who introduced the American and Italian editions of my work, they were *not* co-thinkers. This is why I look forward so much to your introducing the Spanish edition so that both you can say what you feel in it applies to the Latin American scene—and we get both Praxis and News & Letters Committees as the organizations to whom theory means something of great importance.

Fraternally,
Raya Dunayevskaya

Buenos Aires
June 14

Dear Miss Raya:

Yours of May 29 reached me yesterday . . . I want to tell you that it's really exciting to find we had both met in the same point around the same time.

According to my opinion there are many possibilities of bringing out the Spanish edition of your work this year, on account of the dynamic conditions of the Argentine affairs; I shall take it my business to introduce the publication and will be very pleased to do it.

I cannot explain my opinions about the subject matter in your letter to you now, but I shall do it when I recover my health. On Sunday 9 I was set at liberty after some days being arrested on account of a short course of lectures on neoliberalism, neocatholicism and neomarxism in the Cordoba University. My detention turned out a great success. On Monday of this week, I have retaken the professor's chair in the Buenos Aires University.

Most truly yours,
Silvio

II

Translated excerpts from an article by Marta Lamas which appeared in the Mexico City daily paper, *El Universal*, February 6, 1979

Yesterday Raya Dunayevskaya, well-known Marxist theorist and distinguished member of the U.S. organization, News and Letters Committees, arrived in Mexico. As the leading theorist of this group, which has been in existence more than 20 years, she has developed a position that has come to be called "Marxist-Humanist." Her interpretation and practice of Marxism is markedly different from the interpretation of others like the Trotskyists and Maoists...

Two of her books have been translated into Spanish and published in Mexico: *Marxismo y Libertad* by Juan Pablos and *Filosofía y Revolución* by Siglo XXI. In keeping with her position that theory can develop fully only when it is based on what the masses are thinking and doing, Dunayevskaya ties her theoretic work to the activities of the different committees and submits her writings to the discussion of workers, minority groups such as the Blacks and Indians, youth and women...

Feminism plays as important a role in the committees as it does in the theoretic work of Dunayevskaya. Considering it one of the "new passions and forces" Marx predicted would rise and become a spark of revolution, Dunayevskaya has devoted many analyses and essays to the theme of the women's movement and its relation to the other freedom movements. In her discussion of revolutionary feminism she emphasizes their attack on the male-chauvinism and sexism that still exists within revolutionary organizations. For her the attack by women against the elitism and authoritarianism of the male Left means they are demanding freedom now, not tomorrow. According to Dunayevskaya, "now" means that "they will not wait for the day of the revolution, much less exclude the problem of the relationship of man to woman from the political battle." What signified one of the first steps to fight male-chauvinism in the "new left" was not accepting the silence imposed on discussions of personal life but beginning to talk about it. The man/woman question changed from being a private matter to being a political matter which could be discussed and analyzed. For Dunayevskaya the uniqueness of today's Women's Liberation Movement consists "in that they dare to challenge male chauvinism within the revolutionary movement itself."

The visit of Raya Dunayevskaya to Mexico is an important event for Marxist feminists. The chance to discuss and confront ideas with a woman who has dedicated her entire life to the fight for human liberation doesn't come along every day.

III

Excerpts from a Letter of October 12, 1981 from Raya Dunayevskaya to ALIMUPER (Alliance for the Liberation of Peruvian Women), Lima, Peru

... What a great American writer, Herman Melville, once called "the shock of recognition" is always an exciting experience, and never more so for me than when I first heard of your letter, asking permission to publish in Spanish some of my essays on Women's Liberation. You can gauge the importance we attach to that by the fact that my colleague is coming to carry on the dialogue with your organization in person.

You no doubt also know that I have finished my study of *Rosa Luxemburg, Women's Liberation, and Marx's Philosophy of Revolution.* Allow me to elaborate subjectively as well as objectively what the work means to me as a way of seeing whether it strikes a "shock of recognition" also in you. It never fails that, no matter how fully you know a subject, when a new force and Reason of revolution arises (as Women's Liberation has arisen in our age), you feel you have known nothing until that new moment of illumination.

It is then that the individual and the universal have merged in what Hegel calls the "birth-time of history", and that is why everything— the familiar as well as the unfamiliar—is so totally new. This is the way I felt about Rosa Luxemburg, about Women's Liberation, and about Marx's philosophy of revolution, though I have lived with those subjects my whole adult life. All are so intimately interrelated that it is impossible to assign a primacy only to one. And it became clear to me that not one of all the books on Luxemburg had grasped her as a total person and as a revolutionary. Even more is that true of the Women's Liberation Movement, which has such a vast untapped field to work out that the activities seem to overwhelm the philosophic ground needed.

That is why I feel it becomes imperative to grapple with the whole new continent of thought and revolution that Marx discovered, and why, in each age, he becomes more alive than in the age before. Because I tried to unite all three elements in my latest book, I feel it is not only relevant but urgent for our age. This is why I wanted to write to you about all this even before Anne arrives there; my book will be published next year, and I am very anxious to have it published as soon as possible in Spanish also.*

Yours,
Raya

Translated Excerpts from Introduction by ALIMUPER to "Woman as Reason and Force of Revolution" in Spanish, Lima, March 1982

Raya Dunayevskaya has dedicated the last four decades of her life to the Marxist movement, and in this period has achieved the development of a whole body of revolutionary ideas, the most important being Marxist-Humanist philosophy, properly called, as it applies to the working class, the Black dimension, and women's liberation in the United States of North America...

In October of 1981, on the occasion of a visit to Lima by Anne Molly Jackson, feminist, follower of Raya Dunayevskaya and militant of Women's Liberation-News and Letters Committees, ALIMUPER published Dunayevskaya's essays in Marxist philosophy entitled "Woman as Reason and Force of Revolution," thus initiating a series of "Feminist Notebooks."...

This second edition also contains the text of one of Anne Molly Jackson's talks on Rosa Luxemburg, which we have entitled "Rosa Luxemburg and Feminism." In this way we are responding to the interest that a wide public showed, an interest that demonstrates that readings on women and her problematic are well received by a great number of readers. This decidedly inspires us to continue striving to offer periodically readings equally as beneficial as this one.

---

*A Spanish edition of *Rosa Luxemburg, Women's Liberation, and Marx's Philosophy of Revolution* is due off the press in 1985 by Fondo de Cultura Economica in Mexico.

PART IV
The Trail to the 1980s: The Missing Link—Philosophy—in the Relationship of Revolution to Organization

SECTION I:
Reality and Philosophy

CHAPTER 21

Excerpts from a Radio Interview: On the Family, Love Relationships, and the New Society*

Question: Rosa Luxemburg wrote of the need for "dispelling the suffocating atmosphere of the present philistine family life." This is still a problem today and could be summarized, in my opinion, as heterosexism manifested in the nuclear family. We're still oppressed by reactionary socio-political values that retard social evolution to a more equalitarian and intelligent way of relating to people and the world in which we live.

When I think in terms of a socialist state, I think in terms of a society where adults, whether they be women or men, would be free to do what they do best, and their children would be cared for by people who are professionally trained to raise children, so that the children would have genuinely equal opportunities, regardless of their color or anything else. That to me would mean the dissolution of the nuclear family.

Dunayevskaya: ... On the question of the family, Marx expressed himself very openly. At the beginning of his revolutionary writings, in the 1840s, in the *Communist Manifesto*, he called for the abolition of the family. That was that. He said that anyone who thinks it isn't connected with class society, with monogamy, with property, is crazy. But the point was that he didn't want to create another universal as the "answer." It would be just as stupid to give the answer on the family as to think that the nuclear family and Christianity is *the* way. We should be very, very open.

In the 1960s, many people tried new lifestyles and "free love." When I was young, "free love" meant that you lived without a marriage license, without going to the priest or the state. You lived with your

---

*From a WBAI, New York, radio interview by Katherine Davenport aired on International Women's Day, March 8, 1984.

love, and if you didn't love him anymore you left him or he left you. In the '60s, "free love" meant living a different lifestyle, but I don't think all those new life-styles in the '60s were more revolutionary than we women who just limited it to not having to go to a priest for a license. There is no way of saying that this is "the" revolutionary way.

Or take the question of gay liberation. Some people try and say that because Marx didn't raise the question of gay that that means he was opposed. But it was another age that he lived in, and there was no gay liberation *movement*. Gays were in the closet. Marx certainly would have been for a great writer like Oscar Wilde doing whatever he pleased and not having all that trouble because he was gay. But you can't make your right to your own kind of love-making as if that is the answer for everyone.

People want to have a conclusion on the question of love—what is love, whether it's physical, whether it's emotional, whether it's total, and all that sort of thing. But I don't think it's correct for us to try and solve it for others. I think what we have to do is to create the conditions for everyone to be able to experiment with choices, in love, in the family—and I don't think we'll really have those choices until we get rid of capitalism.

Capitalism tries to use everything for its power. That's why Marx criticized science under capitalism and said it was not neutral—"To have one basis for life and another for science is *a priori* a lie." He said that phrase in the same essay, 1844, *Private Property and Communism*, in which he discussed how pivotal is the Man/Woman relationship, and not only the class struggle. And I used that sentence to show what capitalism had done with the splitting of the atom. Why did it take them 40 years to split the atom, after Einstein's theory of relativity? Because until the capitalists saw an immediate use for their power, they weren't going to develop it, and so the smashing of the atom became not the greatest productive force but the most horrible destructive force. That is going to be true all the time, if you separate science from life and don't do it for human beings to be able to have all their talents develop.

So in terms of new family forms, it's not a question of having a "scientific" answer. We can look at what has happened in revolutions. The question of the family is something the Russians did do a lot of experimenting with, after the Russian Revolution and before Stalin destroyed *Zhenotdel*, the Women's Department. Their conception was that it was very important to get the woman out of the kitchen, and that she should have all the experiences that the man had. After the child was two years old, there would be nurseries, so that the individual woman was not responsible.

But two kinds of questions came up, that the women themselves raised. One, the women began questioning the fact that their children were so much exposed to the ideology of the state, that they were always under the control of the state. The second question was that many women said, Yes, I would like the child not to be home while I am working, but I want to have my child at home at nights, or on weekends, or whatever; I want that kind of love relationship. In any case, there were still many things to straighten out—not excluding the fact that there were incidents where the husband literally killed his wife because she dared to live the new way!!—but then Stalin destroyed *Zhenotdel* and didn't permit the experiment to go on at all.

In the Chinese experiment, it happened also that the young Chinese women felt, My God, my child isn't going to know me at all, and I'm not going to know it. Yet I'm the one that bore him, because I wanted him, or wanted her.

So I don't think there is a way we can know the answers beforehand. We are so backward on the whole question that we will have to go through a lot of stages of actual experimentation, with people having the right to choose. There is just no way of giving the answers from above. That is why I emphasize that the expression "revolution in permanence" as *Marx* used it (*Marx*, and not Trotsky's "permanent revolution") was not just a political expression, the overthrow of the old regime. That is only the first stage. Now that you've gotten rid of what is, what are you going to do to create the new?

Marx's *Critique of the Gotha Program* is the finest critique in the sense of seeing that the revolution in permanence has to continue after the overthrow. Yes, there's the idea that there's a transition period, and the state will wither away—but in our age we know that we've seen an awful lot not of withering away but the state getting totally totalitarian. So the point is the recognition of what Marx meant by revolution in permanence, that it has to continue afterwards, that it encompasses the criticism that's necessary, the self-criticism that's necessary, and the fact that you have to be very conscious that until we end the division between mental and manual labor—and every single society has been characterized by that, and it was even in primitive communism—we will not really have a new man, a new woman, a new child, a new society.

So therefore you should know that the minute you win, your problems aren't ended. That's exactly what our age is facing: that the depth of the uprooting is not really seen, when it's considered just a question of overthrowing the oppressor, not the creation of the new society. You must never forget that the revolution in permanence refers to you too, not just to the enemy, and that it has to be continuous after the day of the revolution and the conquest of power, as much as the day before.

CHAPTER 22

The Grundrisse *and Women's Liberation**

I received a peculiar letter from the Sociology and Anthropology Clubs saying they couldn't make up their minds whether they wanted me to speak on the *Grundrisse*, which they were very interested in, or on Women's Liberation, which they were also interested in. My first reaction was that that was really crazy. How can you combine the two? Then I decided that it was a challenge that had to be met. So let's all meet it together.

It is true that the *Grundrisse* had nothing to do with the "Woman Question"; it certainly didn't deal with it in the form in which Marx's 1844 Humanist Essays did. That was where Marx first explained why he called his philosophy of liberation Humanism, stressing his opposition to vulgar communism—the idea that all you had to do to have a new society was to abolish private property. He insisted that until we did away with the division between mental and manual labor that characterizes all class societies, we could not be whole persons and have a new society, no matter what it was called. He pointed out that the most fundamental relationship is that of man to woman, and vulgar communism would not mean any change in that...

You have none of that in the 1857 *Grundrisse*, and yet the methodology is there. At this specific point when Marx was finally an "economist," finally "scientific," and supposedly freed from Hegelian idealism, he was at his deepest in the Hegelian dialectic. I want to begin today with what I used from the *Grundrisse* as the frontispiece to *Philosophy and Revolution*, on the "absolute movement of becoming"—and then carry it through both on the level of dialectics and on the level of women's liberation:

---

*Excerpted from a talk given to a group of sociologists and Women's Liberationists at New School for Social Research in New York in March 1974; transcribed and printed in the September and October 1974 issues of the *Detroit Women's Press*.

>...When the narrow bourgeois form has been peeled away, what is wealth, if not the universality of needs, capacities, enjoyments, productive powers, etc., of individuals, produced in universal exchange? What, if not the full development of human control over the forces of nature—those of his own nature as well as those of so-called 'nature'? What, if not the absolute elaboration of his creative dispositions, without any preconditions other than antecedent historical evolution which makes the totality of this evolution—i.e., the evolution of all human powers as such, unmeasured by any *previously established yardstick*—an end in itself? What is this, if not a situation where man does not reproduce himself in any determined form, but produces his totality? Where he does not seek to remain something formed by the past, but is in the absolute movement of becoming?

There is absolutely no expression in Hegel that is so deeply dialectical and so deeply the new humanism of the unity of the ideal and real as "the absolute movement of becoming." Let's take that at the point when it led Marx to what was new as compared to what it was in the *Communist Manifesto*, or in the 1844 Essays. Yet we will have to see why the dialectic of thought, as great as it was, could only come up to a certain point at which Marx, in turn, had to break with his own past and begin an entirely new dialectic of liberation—that is, the actual activity coming from below, the actual activity of class struggles.

Hegel said that if he had to put his entire philosophy into a single sentence, it would be that in contrast to all other philosophers, he held truth to be not just substance (whether that substance was God or Absolute or whatever you wanted to call it) but Subject. Marx concretized that Subject as the proletariat, the masses. The point was that you were not just the product of history; you were also the creator and the shaper of history. In the *Communist Manifesto* Marx supposedly had dropped all his Hegelianism and thrown the gauntlet to the bourgeoisie by claiming: "A specter is haunting Europe, the specter of Communism." The *Manifesto* had hardly got off the press when there was a revolution.

Now look at how we cannot help but be a product of the age we are living in. When it came to the Orient, at the time when he was writing the *Manifesto* Marx said that the Orient was "vegetating in the teeth of barbarism." But in the *Grundrisse* the Orient is presented not only as the longest continually existing civilization, but as in advance of us Westerners. Why were they in advance? Because after the 1848 revolutions in Europe were defeated there was retrogression everywhere. But in the 1850s in China there was the Taiping Revolt. Marx began saying that maybe the revolution could come through the Orient. In other words, here was an activity, an actual revolt; and while the American and British imperialists rushed gun boats to bring "law and order" to China, Marx kept saying that the Chinese *ideas* were bringing *dis*order to the West and hurrah for that!

In the sections on Pre-Capitalist Formations in the *Grundrisse* Marx brought in the new idea that not only were the Chinese revolutionary, but they were great as artisans. And whereas India, for example, had also fought British imperialism but imperialism had won, China had absolutely endless peasant revolts, and imperialism couldn't conquer them. So we see Subject as Orient.

Now let us look at Subject in the history of women's liberation, at what was new and great from its start in America—the Black Dimension. While the white women Abolitionists were busy making sandwiches to raise money, the Black women were speakers and "generals," were great Reason and not only force or muscle . . . Take Sojourner Truth's choice of her very name. Take how she handled the ministers who were taunting her, when she asked, "Don't you believe in Jesus?" And, when they said they did, how she told them, "Well, Jesus is the son of God and Mary. *Man* had nothing to do with it!" You may or may not believe in the immaculate conception, but the idea that a Black woman in the 1840s and 1850s could tell the white clergy they had nothing to do with religion—that is one of the most revolutionary things you could think of . . .

It was because of this Subject, this Black dimension, that the philosophic concept in the fight against slavery wasn't just that you would get rid of slavery, but that you would have entirely new human relations. The whole concept of absolute movement of becoming was there . . .

What is different and unique in the Women's Liberation Movement of our age is that it came from the Left. The women were saying: "We're all supposed to be socialist and free. How is it then that we women' keep cranking the mimeo machines and you men keep writing the leaflets?" And because you couldn't say these women weren't really political, weren't theoreticians and hadn't figured out the law of value, you had to begin posing that, if there was going to be a new relationship of theory to practice, the men had to start proving it right now. The women were demanding: "Don't tell me to wait until after the revolution; too many revolutions have soured. I want new relations right here, right now, right in my organization if I have one, right in my philosophy if I have a philosophy." So that what had begun in the 1960s—and was related this time to the Black dimension on a different level—was a question of what is the relationship of theory to practice when it is grounded in philosophy and when it isn't grounded in philosophy.

Let's now return to the *Grundrisse* on another level. The first was "absolute movement of becoming." Now let's see absolute in relationship to the new economics that Marx was discovering—the law of value and the law of surplus value, the relationship between constant and variable capital, the fact that it was always a question of dead labor, your own materialized labor, oppressing and sucking dry living labor. Why did Marx have to return to Hegel? Well, Marx complained to Engels that he didn't quite like the way the *Grundrisse* was going. The *Grundrisse* has 890 pages, and on the very last page Marx says that he really should have begun with the commodity, whereas he had only two pages on it at the end. Marx said the *Grundrisse* was shapeless—he called it "sauerkraut and carrots."

In other words, you had *appearance*—commodities or money, the market; and you had *essence*—the exploitation right at the point of production. And everything was mixed up together; the appearance and the essence weren't separated. What was even more important—because Marx had been talking of the fact that equality in the market means nothing since that appearance is exactly what hides the actual exploitation and unpaid hours of surplus labor—was that Marx suddenly saw that the form and the dialectic of both appearance and essence and what would be the Absolute meant a relationship of theory and practice . . .

When it comes to our age, as we have said, what is unique is what has arisen from the fact that the new women's movement came from the Left. We have to ask: Was the Left really considering woman as Reason and not just as muscle? The relationship of all the other forces for revolution—labor, Black dimension, youth—how are they going to coalesce? What will be the philosophy that will bring them together?

Let me tell you about Simone de Beauvoir in the 1950s. De Beauvoir had written the *Second Sex* and we, Marxist-Humanists and others, were trying to fight that question out because a new element had arisen with World War II when the women were driven into the factories and were now proletarians, fighting not just for equal wages but as part of the workers' revolt. Yet Simone de Beauvoir's conclusion, after she exposed how horrible men are, is that since it's the man's fault that we haven't got as far as we should be, the men must free us. When I described this to the Black factory women I was working with they told me: "It's just like 'white man's burden'." It was fantastic because the women were saying, no sir! If we let man do the emancipating, we will never get emancipated. It's our job to do it. You couldn't build a mass movement, in the factory or out, whether it's the proletariat, or women, or any nationality, asking someone else to free you, instead of seeing the job as self-emancipation.

In the 1960s, the *New Left Review* tried to impose Althusserism on the women. In his *Reading Capital*, Althusser says you have to read "into" Marx; you have to do the same thing Freud did in listening to his cases' problems. Where does it all wind up—this listening but reading into? This overdetermination—that one single thing can suddenly be the important thing, instead of what Marx was really talking about, the actual class forces that are fighting to overthrow the old and create totally new foundations? It all ends up by Althusser saying to skip Chapter One of *Capital*.

To the contrary, Marx had said the last two pages of the *Grundrisse*, on the commodity, is exactly what had to be brought forward. In many respects *Grundrisse* is greater than *Capital* because when you first speak out, it's with everything that is in your head. *Capital* doesn't take up other forms of production like pre-capitalist forms, or art—but *Capital* remains the greater because of what Marx brought forward there: the commodity and the fetishism of commodities. We have to dig into that to bring us both to our world and to what the *New Left Review* is trying to do with Women's Liberation . . .

Some women—the latest is Juliet Mitchell in *Woman's Estate*—are trying to say that what Althusser had done with his interpretation of contradiction and overdetermination makes it possible to think that labor isn't pivotal. But what they don't openly say is that what they want you to do is follow that particular chauvinist, Althusser. What is important now, in relation to Women's Liberation—and particularly so in America, because both the Black dimension in the women, and the Black dimension in labor, and the Black dimension as a national question, are right here, not only in 1861 but in the 1960s and right now—is to begin to see that women must have the philosophy of liberation in general, in particular, in essence, and in mind. It is critical not ever to separate theory from practice or philosophy from revolution, because unless you have that unity you will just end up once more feeling good because you have told off the men, but not having established anything new for woman as Reason.

CHAPTER 23

*Marx's "New Humanism" and the Dialectics of Women's Liberation in Primitive and Modern Societies**

I

Bureaucracy, as the focal point of this year's international conference, gains a special significance because it takes place in the year of the Marx Centenary when, for the first time, we have a transcription of Marx's last writings—*The Ethnological Notebooks of Karl Marx* (transcribed and edited, with an Introduction, by Lawrence Krader and published by Van Gorcum in 1972). This allows us to look at Marx's Marxism *as a totality* and see for ourselves the wide gulf that separates Marx's concept of that fundamental Man/Woman relationship (whether that be when Marx first broke from bourgeois society or as seen in his last writings) from Engels' view of what he called "the world historic defeat of the female sex" as he articulated it in his *Origin of the Family, Private Property and the State* as if that were Marx's view, not alone on the "Woman Question" but on "primitive communism."

To this day, the dominance of that erroneous, fantastic view of Marx and Engels as one[1] (consistently perpetuated by the so-called socialist states) has by no means been limited to Engelsianisms on women's liberation. The aim of the Russian theoreticians, it would appear, has been to put blinders on non-Marxist as well as Marxist academics regarding the last decade of Marx's life, when he experienced new moments in his theoretic perception as he studied new empiric data of pre-capitalist societies, in works by Morgan, Kovalevsky, Phear, Maine, Lubbock. In Marx's excerpts and comments on these works, as

---

*Paper delivered to an International Conference on "Ideology, Bureaucracy and Human Survival", September, 1983, during the Marx Centenary, at the New School for Social Research, New York. A slightly edited version was published in *Praxis International*, an international-Yugoslav dissident philosophic journal, in January 1984.

well as in his correspondence during this period, it was clear that Marx was working out new paths to revolution, not, as some current sociological studies[2] would have us believe, by scuttling his own life's work of analyzing capitalism's development in West Europe, much less abrogating his discovery of a whole new continent of thought and revolution which he called a "new Humanism." Rather, Marx was rounding out 40 years of his thought on human development and its struggles for freedom, which he called "history and its process," "revolution in permanence."[3]

What was new in Marx's Promethean vision in his last decade was the diversity of the ever-changing ways men and women had shaped their history in pre-capitalist societies, the pluri-dimensionality of human development on a global scale. Marx experienced a shock of recognition in his last decade as he studied the new empiric anthropological studies and saw positive features—be it of the role of the Iroquois women or the agricultural commune and resistance to capitalist conquest—which bore a certain affinity to what he had articulated when he first broke with capitalist society and called for "a human revolution."

The result was that in that decade, 1873–1883, he, at one and the same time, introduced new additions to his greatest theoretical work, *Capital*, and projected nothing short of the possibility of a revolution occurring first in a backward country like Russia ahead of one in a country of the technologically advanced West. Clearly, there was no greater "empiricist" than the revolutionary dialectician, Karl Marx! Marx did not live long enough to work out in full those paths to revolution he was projecting, but we can see, in the correspondence he carried on at that time, the direction in which he was moving. Thus, we read his sharp critique of the Russian Populist, Mikhailovsky, who attempted to attribute to Marx the making of a universal out of his "The Historical Tendency of Capitalist Accumulation." Marx insisted that it was a particular historic study of capitalist development in West Europe, and that, if Russia continued on that path, "she will lose the finest chance ever offered by history to a people and undergo all the fatal vicissitudes of the capitalist regime."[4]

That letter was unmailed, but one of the four drafts he had written on the same subject to Vera Zasulitch, who had written to him in the name of the Plekhanov group which was moving to Marxism, was mailed. And the most important of all his written statements on this subject is the Preface to the Russian edition of the *Communist Manifesto*.

What the post-Marx Marxists have made of all this can be challenged by our age, not because we are "smarter" but because we now have Marx's Marxism as a totality, and because of the maturity of our age when a whole new Third World has emerged and Women's Liberation has moved from an idea whose time has come to a movement. The challenge to post-Marx Marxists to do the hard labor needed to work out Marx's new moments in that last decade is occasioned, not as a minor "demand" for an explanation as to why the unforgivable 50-year delay in publishing what had been found by Ryazanov in 1923, nor is the challenge limited to what the post-Marx Marxists did not do about the *Ethnological Notebooks*. The point is that even when the unpublished works of Marx, such as the *1844 Economic-Philosophic Manuscripts*, did come to light soon after they were retrieved from the vaults of the Second International by Ryazanov, under the impulse of the Russian Revolution—and even when they did create lengthy international debates—certain limitations of the historic period in which those commentaries on the work appeared point up the greater maturity of our age.

Take Herbert Marcuse's analysis of those Essays.[5] It was certainly one of the first, and a most profound analysis "in general," but he managed to skip over a crucial page on the Man/Woman relationship. On the other hand, Simone de Beauvoir, who does not approach Marcuse's Marxist erudition and is not a Marxist but an Existentialist, singled out precisely that Man/Woman relationship from Marx in her *The Second Sex*: "The direct, natural, necessary relation of human creatures is the *relation of man to woman*," she quotes on the very last page, and stresses its importance by writing: "The case could not be better stated."

Unfortunately, what follows that sentence and completes her final paragraph runs counter to Marx's thrust: "It is for man to establish the reign of liberty . . . it is necessary, for one thing, that by and through their natural differentiation men and women unequivocally affirm their brotherhood." In a word, de Beauvoir's high praise of Marx notwithstanding, the conclusion she draws from the essay of Marx as well as all her data over some 800 pages fails to grasp the reason Marx singled out the Man/Woman relationship as integral to alienation, not only under capitalism but also what he called "vulgar communism." His "new Humanism" stressed: "We should especially avoid re-establishing society as an abstraction, opposed to the individual. The individual *is the social entity*." Which is why he concluded with the sentence, " . . . communism as such is not the goal of human development, the form of human society."

Let us now reread that sentence that de Beauvoir quoted (except that I want to use a more precise translation*): "The infinite degradation in which man exists for himself is expressed in this relation to the *woman* . . . The direct, natural, necessary relationship of man to man is the *relationship of man to woman.*" Women's Liberation had to develop from an Idea whose time has come to an actual Movement before either Simone de Beauvoir or Herbert Marcuse could see the need to grapple with Marx's Promethean vision on Man/Woman relationships.

Marx's concept of the Man/Woman relationship arose with the very birth of a new continent of thought and of revolution the moment he broke from bourgeois society. Before that decade of the 1840s had ended, Marx had unfurled a new banner of revolution with the *Communist Manifesto*, where he explained how total must be the uprooting of capitalism, the abolition of private property, the abolition of the state, the bourgeois family, indeed, the whole "class culture." This was followed immediately by his becoming a participant in the 1848 Revolutions. Far from retreating when those revolutions were defeated, Marx greeted the new 1850s by calling for the "revolution in permanence." Once again, in that decade, as he now came to view other pre-capitalist societies and analyzed anew human development, he further deepened his concepts as well as aims by concretizing it as the "absolute movement of becoming."

The *Grundrisse* is the mediation, on the one hand, both to Marx's greatest theoretical work, *Capital*, and to his activity around and writings on the Paris Commune; and, on the other hand, to the *Ethnological Notebooks*. One can see, imbedded in the latter, a trail to the 1980s. At least, that is what I see; and it is for this reason that I chose as my subject the relationship of Marx's philosophy to the dialectic of women's liberation throughout the whole 40 years of his theoretic development. My emphasis on the last decade of his life—which until now has been considered hardly more than "a slow death"—is because it is precisely in that last decade that he experienced new moments, seeing new forces of revolution and thought in what we now call the Third World and the Women's Liberation Movement. The new return to and recreation of the Hegelian dialectic as he developed the *Grundrisse* was the methodology that determined all his works.

---

*There have been several translations by now of the 1844 Manuscripts. The best known are those by Martin Milligan, Erich Fromm, T. Bottomore, and Loyd Easton and Kurt Guddat. I am using my own translation, however, which is the first one that was published in English, as an appendix to my *Marxism and Freedom* (New York: Twayne Pub., 1958).

What never changed was his concept and practice of criticism of all that exists, defined as follows: "Ruthless criticism of all that exists, ruthless in the sense that the critique is neither afraid of its own results nor of conflicting with the powers that be." Which is exactly why Marx never separated criticism from revolution, and such total uprooting of all that is, sparing no bureaucracies either in production or in education, that he counterposed to the old his concept of "revolution in permanence."

And how very today-ish is his early attack on bureaucracy in education:

> Bureaucracy counts in its own eyes as the final aim of the state . . . The aims of the state are transformed into the aims of the bureaux and the aims of the bureaux into the aims of the state. Bureaucracy is a circle from which no one can escape. Its hierarchy is a hierarchy of knowledge. The apex entrusts the lower echelon with insight into the individual while the lower echelon leaves insight into the universal to the apex, and so each deceives the other.

This sharp critique of the bureaucracy in education under capitalism, like the singling out of the alienated Man/Woman relationship, was but the beginning of his critique of what is an exploitative, sexist, racist, capitalist society. It remains most relevant for our nuclear age, whether our preoccupation is that of the Third World or the very survival of civilization as we have known it.

A concentration on Marx's last decade makes it necessary for me to greatly abbreviate the two decades that followed the 1840s. The abbreviation will not, however, be at the expense of discussing one of Marx's greatest works, the *Grundrisse*, because I will consider that work together with the *Ethnological Notebooks* of Marx's last decade. Here, I mention the *Grundrisse* only to point out that it was when Marx was working on it, in 1857, that he concluded that there were more than three periods of human development—slavery, feudalism, and capitalism. He saw a whole new era of human development which he then called "Asiatic mode of production." "Asiatic" did not mean only "Oriental." He was talking about a primitive communal form of development in the West as well as in the East, whether it was among the Celts or in Russia. For anthropologists of our era to disregard Marx's sensitivity to that "Asiatic mode of production" in the 1850s beginning with the Taiping Revolution, and act as if he was totally Euro-centered then, is on the level of their disregard of his concept of the Man/Woman relationship in 1844.

II

Indeed, what I do wish to single out from the 1850s are two events, both of which relate precisely to women. The first was the 1853–54 strike in Preston, England, where no less than 15,000 workers were on strike against the despotic conditions of labor, about which Marx wrote in great detail for the *New York Tribune*, paying special attention to the conditions of the women workers. The second was the support he gave to Lady Bulwer-Lytton, the author of a novel, *Cheveley, or the Man of Honour*, who, in 1858, had dared not only to differ with the views of her conservative, aristocratic-politician husband, but to wish to make her views public. Because she dared to leave the hustings and attempted to rent a lecture hall for her views, her husband and son had her thrown into a lunatic asylum! In his article, "Imprisonment of Lady Bulwer-Lytton," Marx defended her and attacked not only the Tory press for its sexism, but also "the Radical press, which more or less receives its inspirations from the Manchester School."[6]

As for the articles on the Preston strike, Marx went into detail about both the special exploitation women were subjected to and the fact that even these monstrous conditions did not limit women to fighting those exploitative conditions of labor but challenged the educational system. Marx's Chartist activities and his studies, not only for his books but for agitational writings on behalf of labor, were never written as if only male workers were involved. Quite the contrary. And, in writing: "The factory operatives seem resolved to take the education movement out of the hands of the Manchester humbugs," Marx hit out against child labor and the extremities to which capitalists resorted. He cited the case of "a little girl of nine years of age (who) fell on the floor asleep with exhaustion, during the 60 hours; she *was roused and cried, but was forced to resume work!!*" (Emphasis is Marx's.)[7]

Marx never separated his theoretic works from his actual activities, and it is the activities of the workers in particular that he followed most carefully both in the "blue books" of the factory inspectors and what was actually happening that did reach the press. In April 1856, he summarized the whole question of capitalism and its technology in his speech at the anniversary of the Chartists' paper: "All of our inventions and progress seem to result in endowing material forces with intellectual life, and in stultifying human life into a material force."

The battle of ideas Marx was engaged in was so inseparable from both class and all freedom struggles (what Marx called "history and its process") that he hailed John Brown's attack on Harper's Ferry in

1860 as signalling not only the beginning of the end of slavery, but of a whole new world epoch. It is impossible in this age to deny the facts. The Civil War in the U.S. did break out the following year; the intensification of the class struggle in Great Britain reaching out for international labor solidarity affected the outcome of the Civil War in the U.S. in a revolutionary way; the 1863 uprising in Poland against Tsarist Russia, followed by the intense class struggles in France with its labor leaders coming to London, did culminate in the founding of the First International, with Marx as its intellectual leader.

What ideologues do deny, and even some post-Marx Marxists question, is that these objective events (and Marx's activities related to them) led Marx to break with the very concept of theory. How otherwise to account for the total restructuring of *Grundrisse* as *Capital*? After all, *Grundrisse* (and the correspondence around it) reveals that Marx was so glad about his re-encounter with Hegel's dialectic that he credited it with helping him work out the "method of presentation" of all those massive economic studies. Yet, as great as was the change when Marx decided to prepare part of *Grundrisse* for publication in 1859 as *Contribution to the Critique of Political Economy*, he began it, not with Money or Value, but wrote a whole new first chapter on the Commodity. It was, indeed, a great innovation, which would be retained as a new beginning for all drafts and for the finally edited *Capital*. Nevertheless, that wasn't all that determined the content and structure of *Capital*. What did determine the totality of the restructuring was Marx's decision to put away both the *Grundrisse* and the *Critique* and start "*ab novo.*"

His *re*-creation of the Hegelian dialectic *in the historic framework of the turbulent 1860s is what led to his break with the very concept of theory.* This becomes clear not simply from his 1877 "confession," but from the actuality of what *is Capital*; but here is his "confession" as he put it in a letter to Schott, November 3, 1877: "Confidentially speaking, I in fact began 'Capital' in just the reverse (starting with the third, the historic part) of the order in which it is presented to the public, except that the first volume, the one begun last, was immediately prepared for publication while the two others remained in that primitive state characteristic of all research at the outset."

Marx's battle of ideas with bourgeois theoreticians had so expanded at the beginning of the 1860s that the manuscript numbered nearly 1,000 pages. This "History of Theory" made up three books and we know it as *Theories of Surplus Value* (*Capital*, Vol. IV). But what is most historic and crucial about these magnificent, profound studies is that

Marx relegated them to the very end of his three volumes of *Capital*. Instead of continuing with his critique of classical political economy "on its own," what Marx did was to turn to what the workers were doing and saying at the point of production.

The first great innovation Marx introduced, as he was preparing the first volume for the printer, was an addition to the very first chapter on "The Commodity" of the section, "Fetishism of Commodities." To this day, none—either Marxist or non-Marxist—question the *today-ness*, as well as the uniquely Marxian unity of theory and practice, that characterizes Marx's historical materialist view of human development through the ages and the different types of societies. How, then, can those critics still hold on to the contention that Marx was totally "Euro-centered"; that this, indeed, was so-called "classical Marxism"; that Marx, "the economist," failed to grasp "the Asiatic mode of production" as totally different from what he allegedly made into a universal—West European economic development? Wouldn't it be more correct (even when these critics did not yet know of the *Grundrisse*, much less the *Ethnological Notebooks*) to take serious note of Marx's brief view of pre-capitalist societies right in that first chapter of *Capital*. Marx not only specified the existence of primitive communal forms "among Romans, Teutons, and Celts," but held that a "more exhaustive study of Asiatic . . . forms of common property would show how, from the different forms of primitive common property, different forms of its dissolution have been developed."[8] Clearly, that is exactly what Marx himself had embarked upon; and, still, few study seriously his *Ethnological Notebooks*.

One great economist, Joseph Schumpeter, who was most impressed with the profundity of Marx's critique of classical political economy and didn't shy away from acknowledging that economists owe much to Marx's analysis of the economic laws of capitalist development, was, nevertheless, so antagonistic to philosophy that he held it was impossible to have a truly genuine economic argument with him, because, as philosopher, he was forever "transforming historic narrative into historic reason." That *is* the dialectic of Marx's seeing, not merely the statistics he had amassed, but the live men and women reshaping history. Nowhere is this more true than concerning the so-called "Woman Question." Having turned away from further arguments with theoreticians to follow instead the happenings at the point of production and their political ramifications on the historic scene, Marx came up with the second great innovation in *Capital*—his chapter on "The Working-Day."

That chapter had never appeared in Marx's theoretical works before—be it the *Grundrisse* or *Critique of Political Economy* or *History of Theory*. Although, as a revolutionary activist, Marx had always been involved in the struggle for the shortening of the working day, it was only when his analysis covered it in such detail (76 pages, to be exact) that Marx devoted that much space to women in the process of production and arrived at very new conclusions on new forms of revolt. Where bourgeois theoreticians held that Marx, in detailing the onerous conditions of labor (and especially the degrading form of female labor), was writing not theory but a "sob story," Marx, in digging into those factory inspectors' "blue books" which the ideologues dismissed, did more than single out the inhuman attitude to women when he wrote: "In England women are still occasionally used instead of horses for hauling canal boats . . ." Marx now concluded that the simple worker's question, When does my day begin and when does it end?, was a greater philosophy of freedom than was the bourgeois Declaration of the Rights of Man that Marx now designated as "the pompous catalogue of the 'inalienable rights of man'."

Even were one opposed to Marx's description of the capitalists' "were-wolf hunger" for ever greater amounts of unpaid labor and looked only at the machine and at Marx's description of that instrumentality as a "mechanical monster" with its "demon power" organized into a whole system to which, Marx said, "motion is communicated by the transmitting mechanism from a central automation . . ."—wouldn't the today-ness of it strike our age of robotics? It certainly struck the miners on General Strike against the first appearance of automation in 1950. They thought that description was written, not by a mid-19th century man, but by someone who must have been right there in the mines with them and the continuous miner, that they called "a man killer."

Marx didn't separate his "economics" in *Capital* from its social and political ramifications, and thus he saw one and only "one positive feature"*—allowing women to go "outside of the domestic sphere." However, he warned at once against factory labor "in its brutal capitalistic form" which is nothing other than a "pestiferous source of corruption and slavery." But the collective labor of men and women, under different historic conditions, "creates a new economic foundation for a higher form of the family and of the relation between the sexes."

---

*All quotes from *Capital* in this and the following paragraph are found on p. 536, Kerr edition.

Marx continued: "It is, of course, just as absurd to hold the Teutonic-Christian form of the family to be absolute as it would be to apply that character to the ancient Roman, the ancient Greek, or the Eastern forms . . ." Marx ends by pointing to the fact that other historic conditions where both sexes work collectively could "become a source of human development."

That, of course, is not what capitalism aims at, and therefore Marx intensifies his attack as he lashes out also against the whole bureaucratic structure, not just in the state, but in the factory. There the despotic plan of capital has a form all its own: the *hierarchic structure of control over social labor*, which he further concretizes as requiring a whole army of foremen, managers and superintendents. This planned despotism, Marx points out, arises out of the *antagonistic* relation of labor and capital with its bureaucracy, which Marx likens to the military, demanding "barrack discipline" at the point of production. That is why Marx calls the whole relationship of subject to object, machines to living labor, "perverse." He has concretized what the early Marx had warned would be the result of the division between mental and manual labor: "To have one basis for life and another for science is *a priori* a lie."

Marx, the activist philosopher of revolution, was completing Volume I of *Capital* in the same period when he was most active in the First International:

(1) It is that organization that records, on July 19, 1867, that Marx proposed to the General Council that at its forthcoming Congress a discussion be held on the practical ways the International could "fulfil its function of a common center of action for the working classes, male and female, in their struggle tending to their complete emancipation from the domination of capital."

(2) On December 12, 1868 Marx wrote Kugelmann: "Great progress was evident in the last Congress of the American 'Labor Union' in that, among other things, it treated working women with complete equality . . . Anybody who knows anything of history knows that great social changes are impossible without the feminine ferment."

(3) Marx again called Dr. Kugelmann's attention to the fact that, of course, the First International was not only practicing equality where women were concerned, but had just elected Mme. Harriet Law into the General Council.

Marx's sensitivity to women both as revolutionary force and reason held true in his individual relations as well as organizational relations—and on an international level. It took all the way to the end of World War II before women's revolutionary activities in the Resistance Movement finally inspired one woman Marxist to undertake a study of women in the Paris Commune. Edith Thomas' work, *Women Incendiaries*, is the first to give us a full view of women in the greatest revolution of Marx's time—the Paris Commune. It is there we learn of Marx's role—for it was he who had advised Elizabeth Dmitrieva to go to Paris before the outbreak of the Civil War—and it was she who organized the famed *Union des Femmes pour la Défense de Paris et les Soins aux Blessés*, the independent women's section of the First International. Moreover, the relationship between Marx and Dmitrieva had developed earlier when she was sending Marx material on Russian agriculture, which was also her preoccupation.

III

"The weak points in the abstract materialism of natural science, a materialism that excludes history and its process," Marx wrote in *Capital* (Vol. I, p. 406n), "are at once evident from the abstract and ideological conceptions of its spokesmen, whenever they venture beyond the bounds of their own specialty." As we can see from this, Marx's turn, in his last decade, to the study of empiric anthropology was made under no illusion that he would there find other historical materialists who would be dialectically analyzing the new findings on pre-capitalist societies, a question he had posed to himself as he was working on the *Grundrisse* and asked himself what preceded capitalism, and concluded from his studies that human development was an "absolute movement of becoming." Marx's ever-continuing confrontation with "history and its process," as much as his Promethean vision, disclosed not only how different were his views from bourgeois theoreticians but how his views on anthropology differed from those of his very closest collaborator, Frederick Engels.

With hindsight, it is not difficult to see that Engels did not rigorously follow what Marx had asked him to do—to make sure that all further editions and translations of Volume I of *Capital* followed the French edition. Whether he was in any way responsible, with his overemphasis on the materialist aspects, the point is that it was not only the Populist, Mikhailovsky, who tried to attribute to Marx the making of "The Historical Tendency of Capitalist Accumulation" into a universal for all human development. As we showed, Marx had written a very sharp critique of Mikhailovsky's article. Post-Marx Marxists, however, continued to express similar views to Mikhailovsky's and to base themselves on Engels' editions of Volume I of *Capital*.

What mainly concerns us here is the superficial (if not outright chauvinist) attitude of post-Marx Marxists to the last decade of Marx's life. Especially shocking is the attitude of Ryazanov, who first discovered the *Ethnological Notebooks* and, without reading them, declared them to be "inexcusable pedantry." What was more damaging, however, to future generations of Marxists was the very first book that Engels wrote after Marx's death, *The Origin of the Family, Private Property and the State*, presenting it as a "bequest" from Marx. But the simple truth tells a different story. It is true that Marx had asked Engels to be sure to read *Ancient Society*, which had just come off the press and interested him greatly. We have Engels' word for it, however, that he was too busy with other matters to read it and got it only after Marx's death when he found Marx's notes on it. It is not clear whether Engels had by then found in those unpublished manuscripts of Marx either the *Grundrisse* or much of what we now know as the *Ethnological Notebooks*, except the notes on Morgan and perhaps Kovalevsky. Because he presented this as a "bequest" from Marx, we were all raised on this concept of women's liberation as if it were, indeed, a work of Engels and Marx. Now that we finally have the transcription of the *Ethnological Notebooks*—and also have Marx's commentaries on Kovalevsky and correspondence on Maurer, as well as the *Grundrisse*—it shouldn't be difficult to disentangle Marx's views on women and dialectics from those of Engels.

It is true that Engels was Marx's closest collaborator, whom he had entrusted to "make something out of" the massive material he had accumulated for Volumes II and III of *Capital*, but did not live to edit. What Marx had also entrusted him with was to make sure that the French edition of Volume I, which is the only definitive edition Marx himself edited, should be the one used for all other editions.[9] What is most relevant to us now is what exactly Engels had done on that, since the most important changes Marx had introduced there concerned the accumulation of capital. They have become crucial since the emergence of a Third World.

So little attention had been paid to that little word, "so-called," as used for Part VIII ("The So-Called Primitive Accumulation of Capital"), that Marx evidently felt that, in order to stress both the concentration and centralization of capital and the dialectical development of Part VII ("The Accumulation of Capital"), he should subordinate Part VIII to that Part VII, thereby showing that the so-called primitive accumulation wasn't at all limited to the beginnings of capital. The key to the ramifications of the concentration and centralization of capital, and its extension to what we now call imperialism, was one of the most significant paragraphs in that French edition. Unfortunately, that is precisely the paragraph Engels omitted as he edited the English edition. It is the one which stresses the creation of a world market when capitalism reaches its highest technological stage. It is at that point, says Marx, that capitalism "successively annexed extensive areas of the New World, Asia, and Australia."[10]

When we come to Engels' *The Origin of the Family* it is necessary to keep in mind that it wasn't only a quantitative difference between what Engels quoted from Marx's "Abstract"—some few pages—and the actual excerpts and commentary that Marx had made, which amounted to some 98 pages . . .

What was a great deal more important in tracing historic development and seeing other human relations was that it allowed for seeing new paths to revolution and the multidimensionality of human development. For example, as early as the *Grundrisse* (but then, Engels did not know the *Grundrisse*), Marx called attention to the "dignity" of the guild, commenting: "Here labor itself is still half the expression of artistic creation, half its own reward. Labor still belongs to a man."

What was crucial to Marx in seeing the great freedom of the Iroquois women was to show how great was the freedom the women had before American civilization destroyed the Indians. Indeed, first, it was true throughout the world that "civilized" nations took away the freedom of the women, as was true when British imperialism deprived the Irish women of many of their freedoms when they conquered Ireland. Marx's hatred of capitalism as he studied pre-capitalist societies grew more intense . . .

Secondly, and that is inseparable from the first, was the resistance of the women, the "feminine ferment" Marx saw in every revolution. Thus Marx criticized Morgan on some of his statements about ancient Greece and the degraded status of women. Marx held that the Greek goddesses on Olympus were not just statues, but expressed myths of past glories that may, in fact, have reflected a previous stage, and/or expressed a desire for a very different future . . .

If I may divert for a moment, I'd like to cite the fact that in my national lecture tour this year on the Marx Centenary, I found the greatest interest in that subject when I addressed the Third World Women's Conference held in Urbana, Illinois from April 9 to 13. I was especially impressed with the fact that there seemed to be no separation in their minds between the question of Third World and the question of women's liberation. As impressive, also, was the audience at my lecture in Salt Lake City, where I found that a woman anthropologist, Patricia Albers, had just co-edited with Beatrice Medicine *The Hidden Half: Studies of Plains Indian Women* (Washington, D.C.: University Press of America, 1983). In her introductory essay, Albers points out that the views of the Plains Indian women as "chattel, enslaved as beasts of burden" in which the creativity and struggle of these women is ignored, "tell us more about the attitudes of the Euro-Americans who studied Plains Indians than about the actual conditions under which these people lived."

One of the most important differences between Marx and Engels is that Marx drew no such unbridgeable gulf between the primitive and the civilized as Engels did. The pivotal point, to Marx, always was "the historical environment in which it occurs." Instead of seeing human development unilinearly, he pointed to the variety of paths which led from the primitive commune to a different world—never, however, without a revolution. Thus, when, in his last year, his trip to Algiers led him to become so excited with the Arabs that he praised not only their resistance to authority but even their "elegant and graceful dress," he ended his description of the experience: "Nevertheless, they will go to the devil without a revolutionary movement." As Paul Lafargue reported the end of Marx's trip: "Marx has come back with his head full of Africa and the Arabs."[11]

The new moments he was experiencing as he intensified his studies of pre-capitalist society, on women, on the primitive commune, on the peasantry, illuminate Marx's works as a totality. Thus it isn't a question of a mere return to the concept of women which he first expressed in the *1844 Manuscripts*, nor, as some anthropologists would have it, simply a move from a philosophic to an empiric anthropology. Rather, as a revolutionary, Marx's hostility to capitalism's colonialism was intensifying to such a degree that his emphasis was on how deep must be its uprooting. His latest studies enabled Marx to see the possibility of new human relations, not as they might come through a mere "updating" of primitive communism's equality of the sexes, as among the Iroquois, but as Marx sensed they would burst forth from a new type of revolution.

The economist, Schumpeter, was not the only one who saw Marx turning historic narrative into historic reason. The great anthropologist, Sir Raymond Firth, who is certainly no Marxist, focuses on the fact that *Capital* is not so much an economic work as "a dramatic history designed to involve its readers in the events described."[12] I heartily agree with Professor Diamond's editorial in the first issue of

Dialectical Anthropology in 1975: "The Marxist tradition can be taken as an anthropology which was aborted by the rise of academic social science, and including academic Marxists, and the stultifying division of intellectual labor involved in the very definition of a civilized academic structure, whether right, left, or center." Marx, of course, was not limiting his critique to "stultifying division of intellectual labor," but to the division between mental and manual labor. However, he never underestimated the creativity of hard intellectual labor once the intellectual related himself to the labor movement. What post-Marx Marxists have failed to do with his legacy and their near disregard of his *Ethnological Notebooks* is no reason for us not to do the hard labor required in hearing Marx think.

Marx's historic originality in internalizing new data was certainly worlds apart from Engels' being overwhelmed by it. And in each case he saw economic crises as "epochs of social revolution." The Taiping Revolution led him to an interest in pre-capitalist society. Not only did the *Grundrisse*, the impulse for which has always been attributed to the British economic crisis in 1857, have that magnificent part on pre-capitalist societies; but Marx remembered the Taiping Revolution in *Capital* itself.

In the 1860s, it was not only the Civil War in the United States which ended slavery and opened new doors of development, but all the actual struggles of women were seen at their highest point in the greatest revolution of Marx's day—the Paris Commune. Marx's new studies in the 1870s until his death meant a return to anthropology, not as concept alone, nor as empiric studies in and for themselves, but as a movement of "absolute becoming" through his philosophy of "revolution in permanence."

NOTES

1. In a letter from Marx to Engels in 1856, he commented on the attitude of the journalist who had written about them: "What is so very strange is that he treats the two of us as a singular, '*Marx and Engels says*', etc."
2. See Mikhail Vitkin, *Vostok v Philosophico-Historicheskoi Kontseptsii K. Marksa y F. Engelsa* (Moscow: 1972). Those who do not read Russian can get the essence of his view in several articles which have appeared in English, among which are: "The Problem of the Universality of Social Relations in Classical Marxism," *Studies in Soviet Thought* 20 (1979); "The Asiatic Mode of Production," *Philosophy and Social Criticism*, Vol. 8 (1) 1981; and "Marx Between West and East," *Studies in Soviet Thought* 23 (1982).
3. Marx's "revolution in permanence" is not to be confused with Trotsky's theory of permanent revolution, which had always subordinated the peasantry as any sort of vanguard revolutionary force; indeed, not even granting them a "national consciousness."
4. Marx's November 1877 letter to the editor of the Russian journal which had printed

Mikhailovsky's critique is included in Marx-Engels *Selected Correspondence*, Moscow, 1955.

5. The 1932 essay by Marcuse, "The Foundation of Historical Materialism," was translated and included in *Studies in Critical Philosophy* (London: New Left Books, 1972).

6. See Marx's Aug. 4, 1858 article in the *New York Daily Tribune*, "Imprisonment of Lady Bulwer-Lytton," in Saul K. Padover, ed., *The Karl Marx Library Vol. VI: On Education, Women, and Children* (New York: McGraw-Hill Book Co., 1975), pp. 76–80.

7. This article is included in Karl Marx and Frederick Engels, *Collected Works*, Vol. 12, pp. 460–463.

8. *Capital*, Vol. I, p. 89, ftn. 1, Kerr edition

9. For a critical discussion see Kevin Anderson, "The 'Unknown' Marx's *Capital*, Vol. I: The French Edition of 1872–75, 100 Years Later," *Review of Radical Political Economics*, 15:4 (1983).

10. For the full paragraph which Engels left out, see my *Rosa Luxemburg, Women's Liberation and Marx's Philosophy of Revolution* (New Jersey: Humanities Press, 1982), p. 148.

11. These letters are included in Saul K. Padover, *Karl Marx: An Intimate Biography* (New York: McGraw-Hill, 1978).

12. See Raymond Firth, "The Sceptical Anthropologist? Social Anthropology and Marxist Views on Society," in *Marxist Analyses and Social Anthropology* (London: Malaby Press, 1975).

SECTION II:
The Challenge from Today's Global Crises

CHAPTER 24

Marx's and Engels' Studies Contrasted: Relationship of Philosophy and Revolution to Women's Liberation*

1. WHY A CENTURY TO PUBLISH MARX?

Because Marx had discovered a new continent of thought as well as revolution, and because both concept and fact have ever been rigorously tied together in Marx's Marxism, his works carry a special urgency for our age. More relevant than the ceaseless question of private vs. collective (or state property that calls itself Communism) is Marx's articulation of Man/Woman as the fundamental relationship, at the very moment (1844) when he first laid the philosophic foundation for what became known as Historical Materialism. The new continent of thought Marx discovered soon issued its indictment of the past—"The history of all hitherto existing society is the history of class struggles"—and its call for a new world, new human relations, a classless society.

What has an imperativeness for today is the fact that, at the very end of his life (1880–1882)—after the French edition of his greatest theoretical work, *Capital*, which was published after the defeat of the greatest revolution he had witnessed, the Paris Commune—Marx returned to the pivotal Man/Woman relationship, as, at one and the same time, he excerpted Lewis H. Morgan's *Ancient Society*[1] and wrote to Vera Zasulitch about the needed Russian Revolution.

It has taken nothing short of a series of revolutions to bring out the unpublished writings of Marx.[2] The *1844 Economic-Philosophic Manuscripts* were not published until after the Russian Revolution. The

---

*The first draft chapter of *Rosa Luxemburg, Women's Liberation, and Marx's Philosophy of Revolution* was printed in *News & Letters*, January-February 1979. It is important to note that, in the finished work, the material in this draft chapter does not appear in the first chapter but is included in a further developed form in the final chapter: "The Last Writings of Marx Point a Trail to the 1980s."

1857-58 *Grundrisse* was not published until after the Chinese Revolution. Unfortunately, Women's Liberationists of the mid-1960s to mid-1970s exercised no revolutionary prod to wrest Marx's notes on anthropology from the Archives, much less dialectically work out, on that ground, all the new from the ongoing Movement. Quite the contrary. The Women's Liberation Movement, which *had* helped create a new interest in Engels' *The Origin of the Family, Private Property and the State*, only served to provide new loopholes for Marxists, "orthodox" and so-called independent alike, to rush in and try to have *that* work be the ground, the direction the Movement would take.

Though there had always been a Party, and, indeed, an International (the Second) that laid claim to the heritage of Marx, the truth is that it took the Russian Revolution of November 1917 to prod even Marxist scholars to discover the now famous *1844 Economic-Philosophic Manuscripts*. And once the early workers' state became transformed into its opposite—a state-capitalist society—these continued to gather dust until the 1956 Hungarian Revolution brought them on to the historic stage.

To bring about a serious study of the next unpublished work, the *Grundrisse*,[3] in the 1950s, it took nothing short of the Chinese Revolution of 1949. It took still another decade before even the single most discussed chapter of that work—"Forms Which Precede Capitalist Production"—was published in English as *Pre-Capitalist Economic Formations*. Because, however, the discussion was focused mainly on feudalism, or, rather, the transition from feudalism to capitalism, many lacunæ gaped open as to its relationship to Engels' *The Origin of the Family*, with all Marxists, Eric Hobsbawm included, claiming: "This was a work which Marx wanted to write, and for which he had prepared voluminous notes, on which Engels based himself so far as possible."[4] Was that really so?

The year which finally saw the publication of Lawrence Krader's transcription of Marx's *Ethnological Notebooks*, 1972, was the year also when Eleanor Burke Leacock wrote a new Introduction "updating" Engels' work. She perpetuated the myth that *The Origin of the Family* is a product of Marx as well as Engels.[5] In 1974, Charnie Guettel, in her pamphlet *Marxism and Feminism*, makes Leacock's Introduction "mandatory reading for any serious Marxist."[6]

1972 is also the year that saw the publication of a most serious independent work on the history of women's resistance from the 17th century to the present, *Women, Resistance and Revolution*, by Sheila Rowbotham, who likewise not only acts as if Marx and Engels were one, but singles out Hal Draper's "Marx and Engels on Women's Liberation" thusly: "This is a very useful summary of what Marx and Engels wrote about women."[7] While she is independent enough of Marx to call Marx and Engels "a couple of bourgeois men in the 19th century,"[8] she has but one criticism of Draper's "summary": "It doesn't really point out problems and inadequacies of what they wrote."

Hal Draper, the author of the article Rowbotham recommends was then (1970) working on a book pretentiously[9] entitled *Karl Marx's Theory of Revolution*. It is first now (1978) seeing the light of day and still not in toto. Clearly, however, eight years back, Draper was so very anxious to bring his views to bear on the Women's Liberation Movement, subjected to "less-than-knowledgeable summaries that have seen the light recently," that he chose that chapter for separate publication.[10] Neither then, nor now, has he shown any knowledge of the finally available *Ethnological Notebooks of Karl Marx*. The pretentious scholar who so heavily roots himself in Engels' *The Origin of the Family*—not only in the chapter on "Women's Liberation" but throughout his projected six-volume work—should surely have known about these Notebooks, and I'm not referring only to 1972, when they were finally transcribed in their original English, but to the first mention of them in the early 1920s when Ryazanov discovered them and had them photographed.[11] In 1941, the Marx-Engels Institute published a Russian translation.[12] And therein lies a tale.

It is true that Engels did think he was carrying out a "bequest" of Marx in writing *The Origin of the Family* . . . But Engels was not Marx, as he, himself, was the first to admit, and *The Origin of the Family* was *his* version, in which the select quotations from Marx gave the impression that he was reproducing Marx's "Abstract" . . .

Far from that being true, we now know that not only is the "Abstract"—that is to say, Marx's actual Notebook on Morgan—148 pages long, but also that it is not the whole of Marx's Notebooks on anthropology. The whole is 254 pages—and even that is not the whole.[13] It will be sufficient to focus first on a fairly minor matter—how important even a mere excerpt is in Marx's hands—through the way in which he emphasized certain words that were not emphasized in Morgan. Here is one excerpt on women of the Iroquois:

> The *women allowed to express their wishes and opinions through an orator of their own election. Decision* given by the Council. *Unanimity was a fundamental law of its action among the Iroquois. Military questions* usually left to the *action of the voluntary principle.*[14]

Secondly, and this is the critical point, the Russians took liberties when they, in 1941, did translate the Marx text on Morgan. Engels, naturally, cannot be blamed for this mistranslation. Nor can the Russians excuse themselves on the basis that the inspiration for using the words "private" and "hallowed" came from Engels. Here is how Marx excerpted a part of Morgan:

> When *field culture* bewiesen hatte, dass d[ie] ganze Oberflæche der Erde could be made the subject of property owned by individuals in severalty u[nd] [das] Familienhaupt became the natural center of accumulation, the new property career of mankind inaugurated, fully done before the close of the Later Period of Barbarism, eubte einen grossen Einfluss auf [the] human mind, reif new elements of character wach... [*Ethnological Notebooks*, pp. 135–136]

Here is how the Russian translation reads:

> When field agriculture had demonstrated that the whole surface of the earth could be made the *object* of property of separate individuals and the head of the family became the natural center of accumulation of wealth, mankind entered the new *hallowed path of private property*. It was already fully done before the later period of barbarism came to an end. *Private* property exercised a powerful influence on the human mind, awakening new elements of character... [*Arkhiv Marksa y Engelsa*, 9:52. Emphasis is mine to stress what was neither in Morgan nor in Marx's excerpt.]

Here is the original Morgan excerpt:

> When field agriculture had demonstrated that the whole surface of the earth could be made the subject of property owned by individuals in severalty, and it was found that the head of the family became the natural center of accumulation, the new property career of mankind was inaugurated. It was fully done before the close of the Later Period of barbarism. A little reflection must convince any one of the powerful influence property would now begin to exercise upon the human mind, and of the great awakening of new elements of character it was calculated to produce.

Now, the Russians have very concrete, *class*—state-capitalist class— interests that inspire them to translate "the career of property" as "private property" and repeat the word twice. But why should independent Marxists who are not statist-Communists likewise narrow the subject to collective vs. private property, when Marx's point is that the "property career" i.e., accumulation of wealth, is that which contains the antagonisms of the development of patriarchy and later class divisions?

2. HAL DRAPER MISCONTRUES

Hal Draper no sooner opens his chapter on women's liberation than he at once starts sniping at today's Women's Liberationists' "social psychology and attitude (like 'male chauvinism')," contrasting it to the view of "Marx and Engels" who, he claims, rooted the "Woman Question" in the "primordial division of labor" between the sexes, and warning us that since that preceded "capitalism, or the state, or the division between town and country, or even private property . . . *this* division of labor will be most resistant to uprooting" (p. 20, col. 2).

To help us in this tortuous task, it would seem he would at once plunge into Marx's whole new continent of thought. No. Draper, instead, chooses to roll Marx's views back to his "pre-socialist" days. This at once makes it clear that the "Woman Question" is not the only theme of which Draper is oppressively aware; the other apparition is Hegel. He blames Marx for casting his views "in typically Hegelian-idealist terms" (p. 21, col. 1). By no accident, what then manifests itself is that these two preoccupations, in turn, take second place to the overwhelming drive to do *nothing short of transforming into opposite Marx's concept of that most fundamental relationship of Man/Woman as measure of just how deep a revolution is needed to uproot this exploitative alienating social order.*

Bent on that goal, Draper begins his task by trying to reduce Marx's concept to that of Fourier, frothing at the mouth about the first "lucubrations of this newfledged socialist, his 'Paris manuscripts'." He is talking about the epochal Humanist Essays of Marx, holding that they are a product of the fact that Marx's view that the Man/Woman relationship is a measure of humanity's development is only due to the fact that Marx "enthusiastically" adopted Fourier's view.[15]

So anxious is Draper to force Marx's Promethean concept of the Man/Woman relationship into the Procrustean attitude of Draper's view of Fourier that he embarks on yet another bold leap downward to his *reductio ad absurdum* thesis by skipping the years between 1844 and 1868, though he is still dealing with the first section, "Marx's Early Views (1842–1846)." Obviously not all that confident that he has succeeded in obfuscating the year before Marx broke with bourgeois society (1842) with the year after (1844), as he presents the years 1842 to 1846 as a single unit, Draper now decides to devise a different scenario in jumping to 1868. First he refers to Engels in *Anti-Dühring* (1878) as again playing "homage to Fourier."[16] Then Draper divines that Marx is also paying homage to Fourier in 1868. Proof? It takes strange ears to hear it in Marx's letter to Kugelmann (Dec. 12, 1868): "Great progress was evident in the last Congress of the American 'Labour Union' in that, among other things, it treated working women with complete equality... Anybody who knows anything of history knows that great social changes are impossible without the feminine ferment. Social progress can be measured exactly by the social position of the fair sex (the ugly ones included)."

If you failed to hear that "echo" of enthusiasm for Fourier in Marx's 1868 letter, you are obviously not as adept as Draper in "the exercise in excavation."[17] To hear it where it isn't, you need the presumptuousness of Draper's divinations that Marx, "perhaps without thinking of the source" (p. 21, col. 2), nevertheless achieved that "echo."

Please remember that Draper is not at this point writing about "the lucubrations of the newfledged socialist." No, the Marx he is talking about here is the Marx who, the year before, finally published his greatest theoretical work, *Capital*. Marx had devoted no less than 80 pages of *Capital* to the struggles for the shortening of the working day, and the bulk of that chapter dealt with the oppression of women and children.[18] Now Marx sees something happening across the ocean on the subject, and he calls Dr. Kugelmann's attention to the women being invited to join the First International. That letter does have another sentence Draper chose to leave for later. Marx was stressing that they had elected Madame Harriet Law to the highest ranking body, the General Council. Wouldn't that have been something to shout to the skies about, that in mid-19th century Victorian England, Marx organized the First International which had women not only as members but in decision-making positions?[19]

The question of sexual relations, forms of marriage, the family, are certainly pivotal, and even if one, like Draper, wishes he could skip over the *1844 Economic-Philosophic Manuscripts*, especially so on the question of that fundamental relationship of Man/Woman, there nevertheless has been plenty of other evidence about Marx's disgust with bourgeois monogamy and its double standard, all of which needed total uprooting in any new society. After all, the very next year, 1845, there was the joint work of Marx and Engels, *The German Ideology*, which is recognized as the first statement of Historical Materialism, and which Draper quotes at length on these questions. And in that famous year, there is Marx's *Theses on Feuerbach* that again Draper quotes, even calling attention to the fact that where Marx wrote that "the family" had to be "destroyed in theory and in practice," Engels had edited it to read that the family "must be criticised in theory and revolutionized in practice." Nor did one have to search for heretofore unpublished documents, since the most famous of all of Marx's works—the *Communist Manifesto*—made no bones about the fact that it was "self-evident" that with the "abolition of private property" would come "the abolition of the family."

Whether it's out of Draper's sheer ignorance of Marx's Notebooks (he refers only to an "Abstract" that Engels supposedly reproduced more or less in full), or because the erudite Draper decided to invent new categories of his own, one thing his footnote to Kautsky does disclose is the smug attitude of Draper on Women's Liberation. He clings to Engels' designation about "*the world historic defeat of the female sex*," which, in turn, he is always relating, with great emphasis, to the "primordial division of labor between the sexes." And, of course, both are deeply rooted in the transition from matriarchy, or at least matrilineal descent, to patriarchy. No matter how hard Draper tries to insinuate that "the world historic defeat of the female sex" is a view that Marx shares with Engels, *that is no expression of Marx's*. What is true of both Marx and Engels is that they were constantly driving at the "etymology" of the word, family. Far from the word bearing a reference to a married couple and their children, it was the word for slaves. *Famulus* meant domestic slave, *familia* referred to the total number of slaves one man owned. (See *The Origin of the Family*, p. 121.) And Marx's stress is on the *social* and not only the "sexual division of labor."

Of course, Marx strongly opposed patriarchy, calling for the "abolition" of the patriarchal family. He held that: "The modern family contains in embryo not only slavery (*servitus*) but serfdom also, since from the very beginning it is connected with agricultural service. It contains within itself, *in miniature*, all the antagonisms which later develop on a wide scale within society and its state."[20] And "all the antagonisms" extended from "ranks" that begin in communal life and lead to the division between chieftain and the masses, class divisions in embryo, "*in miniature*."

It is not true, as Draper would have it, that Engels devoted "one" chapter to "The Family," so entitled; in truth, very nearly one-third of the book is devoted to that subject. Engels appears to have a unilinear instead of a multilinear attitude to the question of the development of Man/Woman.

Marx, on the contrary, showed that the elements of oppression in general, and of woman in particular, arose from *within* primitive communism, and not only related to change from "matriarchy," but beginning with establishment of ranks—relationship of chief to mass—and the economic interests that accompanied it. Indeed, in Volume 3 of *Capital*, as Marx probed in his chapter, "Genesis of Capitalist Ground Rent," "the economic conditions at the basis" of class "individuality," you can see the actual dialectical foundation for his stress, in the Notebooks on anthropology, on property as the material base for changing social relations. He was not using Morgan's phrase, "career of property," as if it were a synonym for historical materialism.

Engels' uncritical acclaim of Morgan notwithstanding, Morgan had not "discovered afresh in America the materialist conception of history discovered by Marx forty years ago."[21]

Marx emphasized Morgan's great contribution on the theory of the gens and its early egalitarian society, but he certainly didn't tie it, alone, to the precedence of matriarchy over patriarchy as did Engels in the Preface to the Fourth Edition, 1891: "This rediscovery of the primitive matriarchal gens as the earlier stage of the patriarchal gens of civilized peoples has the same importance for anthropology as Darwin's theory of evolution has for biology and Marx's theory of surplus value for political economy."

Marx didn't take issue with Morgan's findings about the Iroquois society and especially singled out the role of women in it. But he did not stop there. He called attention to other societies and other analyses, and brought new illumination to the writings of Plutarch with his own commentaries in his *Ethnological Notebooks*:

> The expression by Plutarch, that 'the lowly and poor readily followed the bidding of Theseus' and the statement from Aristotle cited by him, that Theseus 'was inclined toward the people' appear, however, despite Morgan, to indicate that the chiefs of the gentes, etc., already entered into conflict of interest with the mass of the gentes, which is inevitably connected with the monogamous family through private property in houses, lands, herds.[22]

Then, Marx demonstrates that, long before the dissolution of the primitive commune, there emerged the question of ranks *within* the egalitarian commune. It was the beginning of a transformation into opposite—gens into caste. That is to say, within the egalitarian communal form arose the elements of its opposite—caste, aristocracy, different material interests. Moreover, these weren't successive stages, but coextensive with the communal form. As Marx observed of the period when they began changing the names of the children to assure paternal rather than maternal rights (a paragraph Engels did reproduce in *The Origin of the Family*): "Innate casuistry! To change things by changing their names! And to find loopholes for violating tradition while maintaining tradition, when direct interest supplied sufficient impulse."

In a word, though Marx surely connects the monogamous family with private property, what is pivotal to him is the antagonistic relationship between the Chief and the masses.

Marx's historic originality in internalizing new data, whether that be in anthropology or "pure" science, was a never-ending confrontation with what Marx called "history and its process."[23] That was concrete. That was ever-changing. And that ever-changing concrete was inexorably bound to the universal, because, precisely because, the determining concrete was the ever-developing Subject—self-developing men and women.

The whole question of transitions is what is at stake between Marx's and Engels' views. Marx is showing that it is *during* the transition period that you see the duality, the beginnings of antagonisms, whereas Engels always seems to have it only at the end, as if class society came in very nearly full blown *after* the communal form was destroyed and private property was established. *Moreover, where, to Marx, the dialectical development from one stage to another is related to new revolutionary upsurge, Engels sees it as a unilateral development.*

In the 1850s, for example, what inspired Marx to return to the study of pre-capitalist formations and gave new appreciation of ancient society and its craftsmen was the Taiping Revolution.[24] It opened so many new doors on "history and its process" that "materialistically" a stage of production wasn't just a stage of production—be it the Western or the Asiatic mode of production—but a question of revolutionary relations. Whether that concerned the communal form or the despotic form of property, the development of the individual to society and to the state was crucial. It was no accident, on the other hand, that Engels, who certainly agreed with Marx's singling out the Asiatic mode of production, nevertheless happened to skip over the question of the Oriental commune in *his* analysis of primitive communism in *The Origin of the Family*.

Hal Draper, on the other hand, not only continues to act as though Engels' *The Origin of the Family* was written also by Marx, but as if he, Draper, is speaking for them, as he reaches the last part of his chapter, entitled "Problems of Women's Liberation." Thus, in returning to Marx's Dec. 12, 1868 letter to Kugelmann, this time citing that the First International had elected "Madame Law to be a member of the General Council," Draper presents that fact with the same attitude that he has towards the statement of Engels that became such a favorite of Clara Zetkin and the whole Social Democratic women's movement: "In the family, he [man] is the bourgeois; the wife represents the proletariat." Draper's comment is that that was meant "as a strong metaphor, of course" (p. 24, col. 2).

No wonder that the stress, as he goes to the actual women's movement, is on Engels' and Bebel's role in encouraging the establishment of women's organizations with their own "autonomous leadership" (p. 27, col. 1), rather than the women's autonomous leadership itself. No wonder Clara Zetkin rates hardly more than a couple of paragraphs, and whereas he does say she was the head of the movement, whose organ, *Gleichheit*, reached a circulation of 100,000, he acts as if all they discussed was the "Woman Question." Not a word comes into it about the fact that women played the greatest revolutionary role in opposing the First World War.

Why should Eleanor Marx, who is finally recognized "as a revolutionary organizer and agitator" as well as "extraordinarily effective political activist" be listed only as "the ablest woman trade union organizer in the *New Unionism*," when, in fact, it wasn't only "as a woman" that she was a great organizer. She was the one who took seriously Marx's urging, after the fall of the Paris Commune, that revolutionaries should go "lower and deeper"[25] into the proletariat, away from the skilled toward the unskilled and the most exploited, not to mention the newly arrived peasants and the doubly exploited Jew of London's East End. Draper does give her credit for playing "an active role in the building of the new-type Gas Workers' and General Laborers Union" (p. 27, col. 1) and says she "co-authored a pamphlet for England on *The Woman Question*." But he doesn't single this out as something significantly new both for her, and the Movement.*

Most important and relevant for our age, however, is not what Engels wrote in 1884, much less whether there was or wasn't a matriarchal stage. Nor is it the "Woman Question" as Bebel saw it at the beginning of the 20th century, though both men's writings had a great influence on the development of the socialist women's movement, which was likewise way ahead of the times, not just theoretically, but in the actual mass organization of working women. What is cogent today is whether the ground laid helps or doesn't help today's Women's Liberation Movement. Draper's doesn't.

Even without knowing (or perhaps just not caring) about Edith Thomas' *The Women Incendiaries*,[26] there was no way of his not knowing

---

*Contrast this to what has since been developed by a young woman revolutionary, Terry Moon, in an essay on "Eleanor Marx in Chicago," published by *News & Letters* for International Women's Day, March 1984.

about the most famous woman revolutionary, Louise Michel, and about the young woman Marx advised to go to Paris, Elizabeth Dmitrieva, to organize a women's section of the International. What was necessary, to make the women's participation in the Paris Commune, as both force and reason, come alive, required more space than the single paragraph Draper devoted to it. Let us see what he does when he finally reaches the culmination of his subject with the thunderous "Social Revolution Comes First."

It focuses on *counter*revolution, with the apex of the whole—the very, very final sentence—narrowing the question to the "division of labor between the sexes": "But in the last analysis the historic forms of the division of labor between the sexes could be uprooted for good and all only by as profound an upheaval as it had originally taken to impose 'the world-historic defeat of the female sex' of which Engels had written."

The nonsense of talking about the "division of labor between the sexes" as if that "primordial" state is the burning question of the day, when even for the primitive stage it was part of the *social* division of labor, is not only forgetting what was at stake, but what *is* pivotal and underlies all class societies—the division between mental and manual labor. There is not a whiff of *that Great Divide*, and that is of the essence for our age.

Is the totality of that "primordial" counterrevolution the ground for Women's Liberation today? And can we possibly disregard Draper's cynicism as he feels compelled to add, parenthetically, of course, that the totality of the change needed in the Man/Woman relationship holds under "all" circumstances: "(That would be so even without the Pill.)"? Does he consider it mod to keep stressing, when he refers to "the world-historic defeat of the female sex," that it "cannot be changed basically simply by ideological (including psychiatric) exhortation" (p. 24, col. 2)? What idiocy, first to reduce today's fight for total liberation to the merely "ideological," and then further to reduce ideology to "psychiatric exhortation"!

3. MARX'S NOTEBOOKS: THEN AND NOW

Marx died before he could write up his Notebooks on anthropology either as a separate work, or as part of Volume 3 of *Capital*. There is no way for us to know what Marx intended to do with this intensive study, much less the concrete manner in which he would have dialectically related the external to the internal factors in the dissolution of the primitive commune. What is clear, however, is that the decline of the primitive commune was not due just to external factors, nor due only to "*the world historic defeat of the female sex.*" (That was Engels' phrase, not Marx's.) Just as there was conquest, even when the commune was at its height, and the beginning of slavery when one tribe defeated another, so there was the beginning of commodity exchange between the communes as well as emergence of conflict within the commune, within the family, and not only between the family and the gens. All these conflicts coalesced during the dissolution, which is why Marx's Notebooks keep stressing the duality in primitive communism.

Take, for example, the question of the division of labor. Though, in 1845, in *The German Ideology*, he called attention to the fact that the first division of labor was sexual, he now stresses the two-fold nature in the division of labor: (1) physiological as well as inter-tribal conflict; (2) the *social* division of labor based both on exchange of surplus products between communities and on the mode of labor. As the family develops as an *economic unit* and gets separated out of the gens, the focus changes again to the different material interests that are developing both internally and externally, including development of technology and agriculture. Which was why, in the paragraph that Engels did quote in *The Origin of the Family*, Marx emphasized that not only slavery, but also serfdom was latent in the family, indeed, that all conflicts that were developing in the transition to class society were present in the family "*in miniature.*"

Finally, what Marx called "the excrescence of the state" in class-divided society—and he uses that in his reference to a period during the dissolution of the commune—is introduced into the question of transition from primitive communism to a political society. The point at all times is to stress a differentiation in the family, both when that is part of the gens and as it evolves out of the gens into another social form, at which point Marx again differentiates between the family that is in a society that already has a state and the family before the state emerged. The point at all times is to have a critical attitude both to biologism and uncritical evolutionism.

It was by no means simple, unitary development, and it cannot under any circumstances be attributed to a single cause like patriarchy winning over matriarchy and establishing thereby nothing less than some sort of "world historic defeat of the female sex." Marx, by taking as the point of departure not the *counter*-revolution, but new stages of revolution, was enabled to see, even in the Asiatic mode of production, the great resistance to Western imperial encroachments, contrasting China to India, where British imperialism won.

Throughout Marx's Notebooks, his attack on colonialism, racism, as well as discrimination against women, is relentless, as he refers to the British historians, jurists, anthropologists, and lawyers as "blockheads" who definitely didn't appreciate what discoveries were being made and therefore often skipped over whole historic periods of humanity. Listen to the criticisms included in Marx's Notebooks on Maine: "Herr Maine als blockheaded Englishman geht nicht von gens aus, sondern von Patriarch, der spæter Chief wird etc."[27] And a little later: "Nach dem *Ancient Irish Law* women had some power of *dealing with their own property without the consent of their husbands*, and this was one of the institutions *expressly declared by the English blockheaded Judges to be illegal at the beginning of the 17th century.*"[28]

As against Engels, who was so overwhelmed with all the new data on forms of marriage and the development of a family, in and out of the gens, that it very nearly subsumed the question of property, i.e., economics, Marx, in assembling new data, never fails to criticize the major writers he is excerpting. He does this, not just "politically," i.e., calling attention to the fact that they are bourgeois writers, but calling attention to the fact that their method is empiric, and nowhere is empiricism as method as vacuous as when gathering new facts. What Marx was doing, instead, was following the empiric facts dialectically, relating them not only to other historic facts, but tracing the development of each fact, its petrifaction and transformation into opposite, caste. Which is why he kept his eye on the differences in rank in the gens, emergence of conflict within it, both in changing material interests and in relations between Chief and ranks. And yet, Marx drew no such unbridgeable gulf between primitive and civilized as Engels had. As he was to write to Zasulitch, in the year he was working most intensively on Morgan's *Ancient Society*, the pivotal point was that everything "depends on the historical environment in which it occurs."

While there was no difference between Marx and Engels on such a conclusion—indeed, the expression "Historical Materialism" was Engels', not Marx's—the relationship of concrete to universal always remains, with Engels, in two totally separate compartments. Put differently, "knowing" Historical Materialism, and having that always at the back of his mind, and recognizing Marx as "genius" whereas he and the others were "at best, talented," did not impart to Engels' writings *after Marx's death*, the totality of Marx's new continent of thought. Engels' *The Origin of the Family*, as his first major work after the death of Marx, proves that fact most glaringly today, because Women's Liberation is an Idea whose time has come, and for that, *The Origin of the Family* sheds little direction.

As Marx, in the last years of his life, was turning to anthropology, it was neither as the philosophic anthropology which ran through his 1844 Essays, nor just as the latest empiric data in the 1880s. Rather, whether it's a question of the description of the equality of women during primitive communism or the question of Morgan's theory of the gens, what Marx was focusing on was the self-development of humanity from primitive communism to the period in which he lived, through revolutionary praxis. That is what kept him enthralled as he dug deep into the latest in anthropology, in early history, technology, and agriculture, craftsmanship and primitive human relations. Truly, we see here that *no greater empiricist ever lived than the great dialectician, Karl Marx*. And Marx wasn't hurrying to make easy generalizations, such as Engels' on the future being just a "higher stage" than primitive communism. No, Marx envisioned a totally new man, a totally new woman, a totally new life form (and by no means only for marriage): in a word, a totally new society.

Suddenly, Marx found it difficult to answer a simple question from Vera Zasulitch on the future of the Russian commune, in the manner in which it was debated between the Narodniks and the Marxists—that is to say, whether it could lead to communism without needing to go through capitalism and evidently without a revolution! He wrote no less than four different versions of his answer, the first of which was fully ten pages long. From that first draft until the very much abbreviated one that he finally sent, what is clear is that his preoccupation is not "the commune" but the "needed Russian Revolution": "In order to save the Russian commune a revolution is needed."[29]

The second draft manifests also what he had developed with the Asiatic mode of production: "The archaic or primary formation of our globe contains a number of strata of different ages, one superimposed on the other . . . [isolation] permits the emergence of a central despotism above the communities . . . I now come to the crux of the question. We cannot overlook the fact that the archaic type to which the Russian commune belongs, conceals an internal dualism."[30]

The third draft, which in part was quoted above on the question of the historical environment being the crucial point, was a conclusion Marx reached as he emphasized "the dualism within it [the commune] permits of an alternative: either the property element in it will overcome the collective element, or the other way "

This is always the key to the whole. We must remember that just as, in 1844, Marx was projecting not just the overthrow of the old but stressing that a new society must change human relationships totally, actually as well as philosophically, so, once the 1848 Revolutions were defeated, Marx developed a new concept—the "revolution in permanence." In a word, it was in the 1850 Address to the Communist League that Marx first projected both the deepening of the concrete revolution as well as the world revolution, the interrelatedness of both.

As we saw, it was the Taiping Revolution in the 1850s which led, at one and the same time, to his probing of pre-capitalist forms of society and seeing the Chinese Revolution as "encouraging" the West European proletariat, which was quiescent at the moment, to revolt. The *Grundrisse*, which contained that most brilliant chapter on pre-capitalist formations, also contained the projection of a totally new society wherein man, wrote Marx, "does not seek to remain something formed by the past, but is in the absolute movement of becoming."

And here—*after* the great "scientific-economic" work, *Capital* (which, however, likewise, projected "human power is its own end"[31]); *after* the defeat of the Paris Commune; and *after* four full decades from the start of Marx's discovery of a whole new continent of thought, first articulated in 1844—we see that Marx returns to probe "the origin" of humanity, *not* for purposes of discovering "new" origins but for perceiving new revolutionary forces, *their* reason, or as Marx called it in emphasizing a sentence of Morgan, "powers of the mind." How total, continuous, global must the concept of revolution be now? One culminating point in this intensive study of primitive communism and in the answer to Vera Zasulitch[32] can be seen in the Introduction Marx and Engels wrote for the Russian edition of the *Communist Manifesto*, which, without changing a word in the Manifesto itself,[33] projected the idea that Russia could be the first to have proletarian revolution: "If the Russian Revolution becomes the signal for a proletarian revolution in the West, so that both complement each other, the present Russian common ownership of land may serve as the starting point for a communist development."

The Introduction was dated January 1882. Marx continued his work in ethnological studies for the rest of the year. The last writer he excerpted—Lubbock—was studied but four months before his death. He did not abate his criticism of either the writers or their reports. Thus, in excerpting Lubbock's statement, "Among many of the lower races relationship through females is the prevalent custom . . . " and noting that Lubbock still continues to talk of "a man's heirs," Marx contemptuously noted "but then they are not the man's heirs; these civilized asses cannot free themselves of their own conventionalities."[34]

How can anyone consider that what Engels was writing in *The Origin of the Family* was the equivalent of Marx's accumulated depth and breadth of thought and revolutionary experience? The dialectic of all the developments, subjective and objective, in Marx's day (1843–1883) has a great deal to tell us, but we will not get it from Draper's "summation" of what "Marx and Engels" wrote on women's liberation, or from the socialist women who accept that summation.

I began this chapter by focusing on the fact that, though Marx's discovery of a new continent of thought signalled, as well, an epoch of revolution, it nevertheless took a whole series of revolutions to bring out his unpublished works. The fact that the mid-1960s also gave birth to a new Women's Liberation Movement, as both force and reason, makes it necessary to study the finally published notebooks of Marx on Morgan, Maine, Phear, and Lubbock.[35] As theoretic preparation for the American Revolution, it is of more than passing interest that what preoccupied Marx in his last years was a study by an American anthropologist, Morgan, centering on the Iroquois Confederacy. Of course, each generation of Marxists must work out its own problems. But Marx's philosophy of revolution is so total a concept that it cannot be just heritage. Rather, it is the type of past that is proof of the continuity of Marx's philosophy for our age. We will continue to grapple with it throughout this projected work, *Rosa Luxemburg, Today's Women's Liberation Movement and Marx's Philosophy of Revolution.*

NOTES

1. In 1972, Marx's Notebooks, under the title *The Ethnological Notebooks of Karl Marx* (Assen, The Netherlands: Van Gorcum, 1972), were finally transcribed by Lawrence Krader and painstakingly footnoted, with quite a profound, 90 page Introduction. It is necessary to emphasize the word, transcribed. It is not a translation. The Notebooks were written by Marx in English but include many phrases and full sentences in French, German, Latin, and Greek.

2. Not all have been brought out even now! There is no dearth of scholars who are happy to jump at such an excuse in order not to grapple seriously with that which is available, especially on *Capital*. See Ernest Mandel's Introduction to the Pelican edition of vol. 1 of Karl Marx's *Capital* (Middlesex: Penguin Books, 1976; New York: Vintage Books, 1977), p. 29 and again p. 944. And see my critique of Mandel, "Today's Epigones Who Try to Truncate Marx's *Capital*," in my *Marx's Capital and Today's Global Crisis* (Detroit: News & Letters, 1978).

3. The *Grundrisse* was not published in full in English until 1973, when the Pelican Marx Library published it in London. (London: Penguin Books; New York: Vintage Books).

4. Karl Marx, *Pre-Capitalist Economic Formations*, with an Introduction by Eric J. Hobsbawm (New York: International Publishers, 1965), p. 51, n. 2. There is no indication anywhere that Hobsbawm had seen these "voluminous notes," which dealt with Morgan, Phear, Maine, and Lubbock.

5. Frederick Engels, *The Origin of the Family, Private Property and the State* (New York: International Publishers, 1972, 1975. All pagination is to this edition.) In her 66 page Introduction, Leacock writes: "The book was written after Marx's death, but was drawn from Marx's as well as Engels' own notes" (p. 7). Neither the 1972 nor 1975 edition has any reference to *The Ethnological Notebooks*, nor does Leacock show any awareness of the fact that Marx's notes on Morgan had been available in Russia since 1941.

6. Charnie Guettel, *Marxism and Feminism* (Toronto: The Women's Press, 1974): "Leacock's introduction is the most valuable current study of Engels available and mandatory reading for any serious Marxist" (p. 14, n. 8).

As for Evelyn Reed's *Woman's Evolution* (New York: Pathfinder Press, 1975)—the pretentious "product of over 20 years of research," glorifying a "matriarchal age" "comprising more than 99 percent of human existence"—its emptiness of any revolutionary socialism is seen in the studied elimination of any and all reference to Marx. This is further emphasized by the fact that none of Marx's works are listed in the bibliography. Consider the fact that Evelyn Reed's subject is "woman's evolution," and both Morgan's and Engels' studies do play an acknowledged, important part in her analysis, but there is not one word about *The Ethnological Notebooks of Karl Marx*. Whether that is out of sheer ignorance or out of studied omission, one must question what is her purpose. A little bit of dialectics, of course, would have gone a long way to soften her complaint that the "wealth of data on the question of anthropology and archeology has not been matched by an equivalent expansion in theoretical insight" (p. xvi). Evelyn Reed explains her methodology to be "evolutionary and materialist." All one can say about that is that it certainly isn't revolutionary or historical.

7. Sheila Rowbotham, *Women's Liberation and Revolution* (Bristol, England: Falling Wall Press, March 1972, expanded in 1973), p. 6. This is the "extensive, descriptive bibliography" to which Rowbotham refers in *Women, Resistance and Revolution*.

8. Sheila Rowbotham, *Women, Resistance and Revolution* (New York: Vintage Books Edition, 1974), p. 62.

9. Draper explains his goal to have been "a full and definitive treatment of Marx's political theory, policies, and practice," but since that is "unattainable," since politics has come to have a narrow meaning, and since there is a need to go "beyond the indispensable 'grand theory' ... It is to bend the stick the other way that this work is titled *Karl Marx's Theory of Revolution* rather than *Political Theory*, which might be interpreted too narrowly." See Hal Draper, *Karl Marx's Theory of Revolution* (New York and London: Monthly Review Press, 1977), pp. 11,12.

10. Hal Draper, "Marx and Engels on Women's Liberation," *International Socialism*, July/August 1970. All pagination in the text is to this article.

11. See "New data about the literary legacy of Marx and Engels (report of Comrade Ryazanov made to the Socialist Academy on Nov. 20, 1923)," in *Bulletin of Socialist Academy*, book 6, October-December 1923 (Moscow and Petrograd: State Pub. House, 1923).

12. *Arkhiv Marksa y Engelsa*, vol. 9, 1941 (Leningrad).

13. Marx's notes on Kovalevsky, which the Russians published in 1958, were reproduced by Lawrence Krader in *The Asiatic Mode of Production* (Assen, The Netherlands: Van Gorcum, 1975), available from Humanities Press.

14. *The Ethnological Notebooks*, p. 162. In the edition of *Ancient Society* I am using (Chicago: Charles H. Kerr Pub. Co., 1907, the reproduction of the original 1877 edition), this appears on p. 118. Not only is there no underlining in Morgan, but in Marx the role of the women is not limited by "even," nor is the word "decision" limited by a "but" as in Morgan: "Even the women were allowed to express their wishes and opinions through an orator of their own selection. But the decision was made by the council ..."

15. Contrast this to Simone de Beauvoir's *The Second Sex*, where she shows that Fourier "confused the emancipation of women with the rehabilitation of the flesh, demanding for every individual the right to yield to the call of passion and wishing to replace marriage

with love; he considered woman not as a person but only in her amorous function" (New York: Bantam edition, 1961), p. 103. As total opposite to Fourierism, the penultimate paragraph of de Beauvoir's entire work is that very paragraph from Marx on the Man/Woman relationship.

16. What is especially telling about all these references to Fourier and the homage paid to him is that the bulk of the quotations are from *The Holy Family*. This happens to be the work where Marx and Engels defended Flora Tristan's "Union Ouvrière" as against the bourgeois philistine, Eugene Sue, who attacked her in his best-selling novel, *The Mysteries of Paris*. There is not a single reference to that in Draper's article, although one would think that anyone writing on Women's Liberation in 1970 would know that that would hold great interest for the movement.

17. The phrase Draper uses here is what appears in his *Karl Marx's Theory of Revolution* as *the* method that will govern the whole work. See pp. 20–23 of that work.

18. See the section on "The Working Day and the Break with the Concept of Theory" in my *Marxism and Freedom* (New York: Bookman, 1958; fourth edition, London: Pluto Press, 1975).

19. In the U.S., the first national trade union organization, the National Labor Union, joined the First International and elected many women to decision-making positions. Two of the best known were Kate Mullaney, president of the Troy Collar Laundry Workers, who was appointed assistant secretary and national organizer for women, and Augusta Lewis, a leader in the typographical union. See Joyce Maupin's *Working Women and Their Organizations* and *Labor Heroines*, both published in 1974 by Union WAGE, Berkeley, California.

20. Quoted by Engels in *The Origin of the Family*, pp. 121–122. Incidentally, and not so incidentally, Engels omitted the sentence that preceded this paragraph. It reads: "Fourier characterizes the Epoch of Civilization by Monogamy and private Property in land" (*The Ethnological Notebooks*, p. 120). From the manner in which Engels had worked the omitted single sentence into an entire paragraph that he placed prominently in a note at the very end of his work (p. 236) on how we find already in Fourier "the profound recognition that in all societies which are imperfect and split into antagonisms, single families (les familles incoherentes) are the economic unit," Draper would have learned a great deal about the difference between Marx and Engels on the "acceptance" of Fourier.

21. Engels' Preface to the First Edition of *The Origin of the Family*.

22. I'm using Krader's translation in his article, "The Works of Marx and Engels in Ethnology Compared," *International Review of Social History*, Vol. XVIII, Part 2, 1973. This is really an extension of his magnificent transcription and editing of Marx's *Ethnological Notebooks*, and I am greatly indebted to the seminal Introduction he wrote for it.

23. *Capital*, Volume 1 (Chicago: Charles H. Kerr, 1909; reprinted New York: International Publishers, 1967), p. 406, n. 2: "The weak points in the abstract materialism of natural science, a materialism that excludes history and its process, are at once evident from the abstract and ideological conceptions of its spokesmen, whenever they venture beyond the bounds of their own specialty." See also Chapter 2, "A New Continent of Thought," in my *Philosophy and Revolution* (New York: Dell, 1973).

24. It is not clear whether Engels knew Marx's *Grundrisse*, but he did know the articles in *The New York Tribune* on the Taiping Revolution.

25. It took World War I before Lenin found that phrase of Marx, made to the 1871 Congress of the International Workingmen's Association, and first then made a category of it. See Chapter X, "The Collapse of the Second International and the Break in Lenin's Thought," in *Marxism and Freedom*.

26. Draper published, edited and wrote a Foreword to a whole book, *Karl Marx and Friedrich Engels: Writings on the Paris Commune* (New York: Monthly Review Press, 1971), which likewise failed to take into account any of the material on what actually happened, uncovered by this magnificent book, *The Women Incendiaries*, written by Edith Thomas and published in France in 1963, and in New York in 1966 (New York: George Braziller, 1966).

27. *The Ethnological Notebooks*, p. 292: "Mr. Maine, as a blockheaded Englishman, doesn't proceed from *gens*, but rather from Patriarch, which later becomes Chief, etc."
28. *Ibid*, p. 323. It should be noted also that Marx had an extensive library on matriarchal laws.
29. The 1970 edition of the three volume *Karl Marx and Frederick Engels: Selected Works* (Moscow: Progress Publishers) finally published the first draft of Marx's reply, pp. 152–163. Peculiarly enough, the explanatory note (p. 522, n. 113) refers to the fact that Marx was working on the third volume of *Capital* at this time, without referring to the fact that he was then studying Morgan's *Ancient Society*, though Marx himself refers to it and they have to footnote the actual title of Morgan's book.
30. Excerpts from the second and third drafts are included in *Pre-Capitalist Economic Formations*. All four drafts are included in full in *Arkhiv Marksa y Engelsa*, vol. 1. They are also included in the Russian *Collected Works of Marx and Engels*, vol. 19. Actually, Marx wrote all the drafts in French.
31. *Capital*, volume 3 (Chicago: Charles H. Kerr, 1909; reprinted New York: International Publishers, 1967), p. 954. One erudite anthropologist, who is certainly no Marxist, Sir Raymond Firth, also focuses on the fact that *Capital* is not so much an economic work as "a dramatic history designed to involve its readers in the events described." See "The Sceptical Anthropologist? Social Anthropology and Marxist Views of Society," by Raymond Firth in *Marxist Analyses and Social Anthropology* (London: Malaby Press, 1975).
32. Her letter to Marx is included in *The Russian Menace to Europe*, edited by Paul W. Blackstock and Bert F. Hoselitz (Glencoe, Illinois: Free Press, 1952), but the liberties they take by trying to create a one page composite of the four drafts of Marx's answer leave a great deal to be desired.
33. In that 1882 Introduction, signed by both Marx and Engels, Marx saw no reason for making any changes, although he was then intensively studying primitive communism, something they knew little about in 1847 when the Manifesto was first written. Engels, on the other hand, in the 1888 English edition, felt called upon to offer a demurrer to the epoch-making statement: "All history is a history of class struggles." He claimed in a footnote that this meant all *"written"* history, but that since the publication of Morgan's *Ancient Society*, much more had been learned about primitive communism. To this writer, Engels thereby modified the dialectic structure of Marx's historic call to revolution.
34. *The Ethnological Notebooks*, p. 340.
35. Marx's *Ethnological Notebooks* include his studies of Lewis Henry Morgan's *Ancient Society*, John Budd Phear's *The Aryan Village*, Henry Sumner Maine's *Lectures on the Early History of Institutions*, and John Lubbock's *The Origin of Civilization*.

CHAPTER 25

Selected Letters on the process of writing Rosa Luxemburg, Women's Liberation, and Marx's Philosophy of Revolution

August 9, 1978

"The revolution is magnificent, and everything else is bilge."
—Rosa Luxemburg

Dear Sisters:
Because the dialectic never fails to reveal facets one has never thought of at the start of writing, I hesitate to write to you something on Rosa Luxemburg when the work on it *as a book* has not yet begun. But because the urgency of the very idea of a philosophy of revolution—Marx's—compels confrontation, no matter how dissatisfied I may be with my articulation of this topic when I have not worked out what is in my head, I will be brave enunciating it.

Take the quotation at the top. No doubt some of today's women theorists who refuse to grapple with Rosa's theories on the ground that she didn't write on Women's Liberation are using that magnificent quotation as "proof" of her playing down women's uniqueness, as if revolution and women were opposites! The truth is that no greater proof could be given of how *total* was her concept of revolution as the way, the only way, of uprooting exploitative, racist, sexist society.

Just recently I found a letter that Rosa had written to Diefenbach from prison on, of all things, a review of a performance of Shakespeare's *As You Like It*. She was so enamored with the review by a Dr. Morganstern that she quoted it at length: " 'This is by no means the only case where Shakespeare draws this type of assured young woman: in his work, one encounters several of this sort. We do not know whether he ever met a woman like Rosalyn, Beatrice, or Portia, or whether he had models to work from, or whether he created pictures from his longing. But this we definitely know. From these characters, there speaks his own belief of woman. His conviction is that woman can be so magnificent because of her special nature. At least for a time in his life he extolled woman as few poets did. In woman he saw a force of nature working which culture could never harm...' " Then Rosa comments: "Isn't this a fine analysis? If you knew what an insipid, dried up, queer fish Dr. Morganstern is in private! But his psychological penetration is what I would wish for the future creator of the German essay."

Although this has nothing to do with theories of revolution and very little to do with women's "role"—nor even the question of women's suffrage for which Rosa did fight and did write about, although you wouldn't think so from women's theorists' disregard of her—I wished to call attention to it. This is *not* because it is one of the rare things in which she did speak of women, since the women it speaks about are not those working class women and socialist women with whom she worked. Rather, it is about women as characters in literature by one genius of a dramatist who certainly was no "proletarian revolutionary," and the reviewer she quotes whom she considers "insipid." Why, then, did she pay attention to it, and why did I single it out? It has to do with the multidimensionality of Rosa Luxemburg, both as revolutionary and as human being, that she is concerned, in writing from prison to a young socialist, that he be concerned that "the future creator of the German essay" have "deep psychological penetration" of women as "magnificent"!

In a word, when she writes of revolution which is "magnificent, and everything else is bilge," it doesn't mean the downplaying of women. Rather, it is the totality she aspires for "future." The point, especially for us today, is not any counter-position of revolution and woman. Quite the contrary. The real point—and that's why I have changed the title of the projected book on Rosa Luxemburg and the relationship to Marx's theories, from Marx's theory of revolution to Marx's *philosophy* of revolution—is that so long as we only talk of theory, we are talking only of the immediate task of revolution, that is to say, the overthrow of capitalism. But when we talk of a philosophy of revolution, we do not mean only the overthrow of capitalism, but the creation of a new society. *Only when we have that in mind can the revolution be truly total.*

At the same time, what is most comprehensive in the projected work is that the very "taking up" of Marx's philosophy of revolution means that we have the opportunity of considering a very specific revolution, 1905, in which all three great revolutionaries—Luxemburg, Lenin,

Trotsky—were active. Each singled out what he/she considered the greatest achievement of that revolution and then built on that as preparation for the future revolution. It is this *building on* that we wish to break down for our age.

There is no doubt that Rosa was so enamored of the proletariat as revolutionary that she seems to subsume the woman in her concept of revolutionary. But there is equally no doubt whatsoever that she both worked closely with Clara Zetkin in all aspects of the women's movement, from suffrage to anti-imperialism. And indeed, the majority in such crucial industrial centers like Hamburg were adherents of her theories and activities in the anti-war movement. There is further no doubt that the letters she wrote to women, again especially from prison, were of such profound nature that they reveal her whole philosophy. Take the letter I have often quoted, to Mathilde Wurm:

> I swear to you, let me once get out of prison and I shall hunt and disperse your company of singing toads with trumpets, whips and bloodhounds—I want to say like Penthesilea, but then, by God, you [all?-rd] are no Achilles. Had enough of my New Year's greeting? Then see to it that you remain a human being ... to be human means throwing one's life "on the scales of destiny" if need be ...

That's the point, the whole point.

Marx's 1844 Essays were unknown to Rosa Luxemburg. But there is no doubt of the fact, the profound fact, that Marx's whole new continent of thought that began with revolution—so total and deep a revolution as to begin with the Man/Woman relationship as the most basic one of all that needed *total* reorganization—was also Rosa's concept. When Marx stressed that that relationship needed uprooting in all class societies (indeed, I am ready to say in *all previous societies*), it is proof of how total was Marx's concept of tearing society up at its roots. So totally new was his philosophy of revolution on *that* relationship that even under primitive communism, which he much admired when discovered by Morgan in the communal life among the Iroquois—*Ancient Society*—Marx sensed women's enslavement. He was certainly impressed with the communal life and with how much greater was woman's role there than under capitalism. Nevertheless, much more was needed in the creation of a new Man/Woman than "modernization". Marx is the one whose extensive notes Engels used the year after Marx died for his *The Origin of the Family, Private Property and the State*. But, where Engels only glorified primitive communism, as if all it needed were a sort of "updating," Marx, the genius who discovered a whole new continent of thought in developing his philosophy of revolution, sensed in the family structure nothing short of elements of "slavery," of "serfdom."

(This is not the place to develop the difference between Marx and Engels and why one—Marx—is the genius who discovered a whole new continent of thought while the other—Engels—no matter how talented and how close a collaborator of Marx, was not that founder. But here, since it is also grounded on the Man/Woman relationship, the women can reach something totally new if they work it out multidimensionally and dialectically.)

Rosa's whole life as a revolutionary, as a theoretician, as a multidimensional woman, was so preoccupied with the spontaneity of revolution that, not only as against "the educated" but also revolutionary theoreticians who thought they needed "to teach" revolution to the masses, she focused instead on the great truth that, as she put it, "revolution cannot be schoolmastered." Neither on the revolution's nor on spontaneity's "magnificence" was it a question of "throwing out" the need for theory. There may have been a playing down of "philosophy" as if that were "abstract," but never any playing down of theory of revolution.

What concerns us now is to see what impulses we can "catch" in the newest development of the Women's Liberation Movement of today, women who would feel emboldened to become collaborators with us in the writing, in the activities, to, at one and the same time, develop what is most immediate (be it ERA or a strike, or any single case) and, at the same time, dig so deeply both in their experiences and in our theories as to find common ground for universal as well as individual self-development . . .

There surely is some time in everyone's life when one wants to reach for something of the future. I do not doubt that in the present historic stage women *want* to reach for that total uprooting of this sexist, racist, exploitative society. Let's begin there.

Yours,
Raya

October 15, 1978

Dear Sisters:

Two seemingly opposite universals—"one, not two" and a *total* uprooting—have become especially alive for me, as I am at the very first stages of the work on Rosa Luxemburg and Marx's Philosophy of Revolution. It is Engels' *The Origin of the Family* upon which not only the Stalinist-Trotskyist "Left" still rely very heavily, but from which the latest pretentious six-volume work-to-be of Hal Draper, *Marx's Theory of Revolution*, never departs. On the contrary: Draper is so busy *not* separating in any respect whatever Engels from Marx, that he writes of them as one. Nowhere is this more striking than in his chapter entitled "Marx and Engels on Women's Liberation."

(According to his projection of the work in the only two books so far available to the public, that chapter is supposed to be in Part III of Volume II, which deals with "Mixed-Class Elements and Movements" and includes the "Women's Rights Movements." So anxious was Draper to intervene in the Women's Liberation Movement that he singles out that chapter, called "Marx and Engels on Women's Liberation," and had it published in *International Socialism* in 1970.)

I want to limit myself here to just one reference. Footnote 29 states: "Marx, 'Abstract of Morgan's *Ancient Society*', quoted by Engels' *Origin of the Family*." Since I knew that Engels quoted only a few paragraphs of Marx's "Abstract," I became curious. Sure enough I found that, though Engels himself gave the impression that he was giving the essence of Marx's Notes, he did no such thing.

What Marx's Notes turn out to be are no less than 254 pages. Moreover, although he thought that Morgan's work was quite important and asked Engels to read it, he by no means agreed with Engels that it was "epochal." Secondly, the Notes are not only on Morgan's work, but also on the latest works in anthropology by John Budd Phear (*The Aryan Village*), Henry Sumner Maine (*Letters on the Early History of Institutions*), and John Lubbock (*The Origin of Civilization*). And as if all that were not enough, he had checked on all of Morgan's references to Greek literature as well as comparing what Morgan had done that was new and how it related to works by other anthropologists. (The bibliography itself is five pages of bibliographic notes by Marx).

Above all, these Notes that Marx never got to develop in full, and on which he worked in the last years of his life, can under no circumstances be separated either from the new works on the Orient that Marx included in his 1857–58 *Grundrisse*, nor from the 1881 four different drafts of the letter in answer to Vera Zasulitch on the prospects of revolution in Russia and its relationship to "the village commune." In a word, what we have here, if anything at all was needed on the question, is the ocean*s* that separate the genius Marx from the "second-in-command," Engels. No one should read Engels' *The Origin of the Family* without also studying Marx's Notebooks, which are now available in a magnificently edited work entitled *The Ethnological Notebooks of Karl Marx*, edited by Lawrence Krader. By editing I do not mean that Krader took any liberties with Marx's notes, but that he has a very profound and comprehensive Introduction of some 85 pages, as well as notes to both his own Introduction and to Marx's Notebooks of 67 pages, as well as a bibliography. The book as a whole totals 454 pages and is issued by a Dutch publisher, Van Gorcum, Assen, 1972. Most of these Notebooks are in *English*. Of course, you need to know half a dozen other languages since a sentence may start in English, continue in German, French, Greek, or Latin before he returns back to finish the sentence in English. The point is that Krader did not "translate"—he *transcribed* from the original handwritten notebooks, available at the International Institute of Social History in the Netherlands.

Now then, the total uprooting that Marx's, *and only Marx's*, philosophy of revolution projected at the very start of his new continent of thought—the 1844 Manuscripts which first raised the question of Man/Woman as the most fundamental relationship—was never let go of but constantly deepened until the very last year of his life, 1883. It is this which Draper is trying to so pervert as to call Marx's expression "rhetorical." Even this transformation into opposite was done not only for the purposes of reducing Marx and Engels to his own narrow vision, but in order to hit at today's Women's Liberation Movement, with its daring to point a finger at male chauvinism.

I thought you might want to be with me in the process of working out the new book rather than be confronted with its worked-out views, even if as presently expressed they are not all too clear.

Yours,
Raya

P.S. You wouldn't think that the Conference of the Association of Social Anthropologists of the Commonwealth on "New Directions in Social Anthropology," meeting at St. John's College, Oxford, would be the occasion for me to be mentioned. But at that conference, Sir Raymond Firth delivered an address on "The Skeptical Anthropologist? Social Anthropology and Marxist Views on Society" in which he says: "I have used 'transcendence' in the ordinary, secular sense of surmounting a particular in favor of a more general aim. Raya Dunayevskaya (1958: 319) discusses transcendence more technically in relation to alienation."

The essay may be found in *Marxist Analyses and Social Anthropology*, London: Malaby Press, 1975.

November 24, 1978

Dear Sisters:

... [I have heard that there is to be a meeting in New York for Eleanor Leacock and Evelyn Reed] ... I'm quite amazed that as serious an anthropologist as Leacock (not to mention that she is a Communist) should consent to debate or whatever Evelyn Reed, whose book *Woman's Evolution* is so retrogressive a venture that Bachofen's Mother Right appears "mod." I had intended to disregard that very opportunistic "analysis" which is hardly more than an attempt to be "in the forefront" of the feminists. Even Charnie Guettel's *Marxism and Feminism* isn't that vulgar in making the transition from Marxism "to" Feminism. But I've been told that Reed's book is popular among feminists, all of which goes to show how anxious we are to live in a mythology rather than history-in-the-making. In any case, I struggled through it yesterday and decided to add a footnote to the draft chapter, directly after I say that it isn't only male chauvinists like Draper who swear by Engels, but also women socialists. At that point, here is what you will read:

> As for Evelyn Reed's *Woman's Evolution*—the pretentious "product of over 20 years of research," glorifying a "matriarchal age" "comprising more than 99 percent of human existence"—its emptiness of any revolutionary socialism is seen in the studied elimination of any and all reference to Marx. This is further emphasized by the fact that none of Marx's works are listed in the bibliography. Consider the fact that Evelyn Reed's subject is "woman's evolution," and both Morgan's and Engels' studies do play an acknowledged, important part in her analysis, but there is not one word about the *Ethnological Notebooks of Karl Marx*. Whether that is out of sheer ignorance or out of studied omission, one must question what is her purpose. A little bit of dialectics, of course, would have gone a long way to soften her complaint that the "wealth of data on the question of anthropology and archeology has not been matched by an equivalent expansion in theoretical insight" (p.xvi). Evelyn Reed explains her methodology to be "evolutionary and materialist." All one can say about that is that it certainly isn't revolutionary or historical.

The point is: do we really need the matriarchy to show that, "as females," we had made history once in "savagery" period? Aren't we, beginning with Engels, acting as if a "world historic defeat" occurred with the move from matriarchy to patriarchy and we now have to wait another million years to, first, get freedom (or only abortion rights?)

before we can once again be makers of history? You mean—all this history that has been made since class society was established has been without women as creators, as reason? What happened to all those revolutions where we were supposed to be such "ferment"? And are we going to continue to "excavate" everything from savagery to Evelyn Reed without ever finding Rosa Luxemburg, not to mention the Paris Communards, those women incendiaries? Isn't it about time that women as well as men should concern themselves with the total uprooting of this society, and not consider that a question of being on Cloud Nine but *know* that this is the only way we will uproot the *pre*-history of Man/Woman and finally release the true history of humanity?

Yours,
Raya

March 10, 1979

Dear Friends:

On my way to the talk in celebration of International Women's Day, that I was to give at Wayne State University on "Rosa Luxemburg and Marx's Philosophy of Revolution," came the news of the most magnificent international event: tens of thousands of Iranian women were demonstrating against Khomeini, shouting "We fought for freedom and got unfreedom!" Naturally, I began the talk with a homage to those Iranian women's liberationists who had, with this act, initiated the second chapter of the Iranian Revolution. Thus, my very first sentence stressed the *today-ness* that this mass outpouring had placed on our topic, though it was to begin with rolling back the clock to 62 years ago, when the Russian working women transformed International Women's Day into the first of the five days that toppled the centuries-old Tsarist Empire.

The point was not only to single out great revolutionary acts, but to demonstrate that even in the first Russian Revolution of 1905, a great theoretician, Rosa Luxemburg, was as "shortchanged" about her thoughts as were the Russian working women, en masse, who were later to be played down as allegedly "unconscious" about their historic act which began the second Russian Revolution. Toward that end, I read from the still-unpublished speech of Rosa at the famous 1907 Congress of all Russian Marxist tendencies, which pointed to the fact that 1905 was but the first of a series of 20th century revolutions . . .

I spent the following day, March 9, talking with an Iranian male revolutionary, developing ideas not only of the revolution but how we must be prepared for the *counter*revolution that is sure to arise in Iran as Khomeini holds on to power and gathers not only men but some women to consent to turning back the clock to Islam's reactionary viewpoint on women—and by no means only on the question of dress; and I singled out the historic points in the development of the Russian Revolution, which moved from the February events through Lenin's April Thesis to Kornilov's July counterrevolution, and only after many laborious and bloody months arrived finally at October. In a word, we were discussing my next Political-Philosophic Letter on the Iranian Revolution.

March 10 was still a newer day when, but half an hour before the Iranian's plane left, I came up with the idea of translating into Farsi Ting Ling's "Thoughts on March 8th," which would carry also the following message of solidarity with the Iranian women of today, stretching back to 1908 on native grounds:

> In Spring 1908—when the 1906 Constitutional Revolution everyone is talking about today was still alive, and a Women's Anjumen [Soviet] was still most active, especially in Tehran—New York garment workers declared March 8 to be Women's Day. The following year, in support of the locked-out Triangle Shirtwaist Makers, the mass outpouring became known as the "Uprising of the 20,000"; that so inspired the German Working Women's movement that its leader, Clara Zetkin, proposed to the Marxist International that March 8 become an International Women's Day. Today, you—the daring women of Iran—have opened a new chapter in the Iranian Revolution of 1979. In homage to you, and to express our solidarity with your ongoing revolution, we are here translating the thoughts of still another opponent of the status quo, this time in China—Ting Ling, who opposed both Stalin and Mao (who purged the great writer), as she expressed herself creatively in *Thoughts on the Eighth of March*.

The friend who volunteered to do the translation felt that, indeed, the simple act of translation would thus express a totally new Man/Woman relationship...

Yours,
Raya

November 26, 1979

Dear Colleagues:

Offhand, it may appear that Chapter II of the Rosa Luxemburg book—"The Break with Kautsky, 1910–1911: From Mass Strike Theory to Crisis over Morocco—and Hushed-Up 'Woman Question' "—would

have nothing to do with the crisis in Iran, especially the so-called Left's tail-ending of Khomeini. But, in fact, as you, yourselves, will be able to work out, when you have a chance to read the chapter, you will gain quite an illumination of the present crisis. Let me first tell you its content:
1) Spontaneity and Organization
2) Single Revolutionary Practice vs. "Two Strategies"
3) Imperialism Raises its Ugly Head
4) Prescience about Kautsky's Opportunism, but Tone-Deafness about Leadership's Attitude to "Woman Question"

The first section is, in a fundamental sense, known to you since it deals with the most popular part of Luxemburg's heritage—The Mass Strike. But, in fact, in the context of 1910, when she restates the question of the Mass Strike, 1905–07, what comes out most clearly is that, because she considers the essence of revolution to be that Mass Strike, what she is talking about when she relates the Mass Strike to the revival of strikes in Germany is what she considers to be a pre-revolutionary situation in Germany. From that point of view, the whole question of spontaneity and organization is not just a question of strikes and trade unions, nor even the question of when a strike becomes both political and economic, but a matter of the whole role of leadership, Marxist leadership.

That concept of leadership is the nub of the dispute with Kautsky, the reason for her prescience about opportunism within the movement, and the feeling that revolution is being made into an abstraction while all sorts of deviations raise their ugly heads. The proof is that no sooner was the dispute on General Strike in 1910 concluded than the pusillanimity of the German Social-Democracy on the question of Germany's imperialist attack on Morocco came to the fore in 1911. What is missing in all this is that no political or "factional," i.e., actually organizational conclusions are drawn from this, so that Luxemburg's break with Kautsky appears very nearly "personal."

Not only that. The most fantastic letters against Luxemburg are being exchanged within the leadership. They reveal the most disgusting male chauvinism. No male opponent of the "line," not even the founder of Revisionism, was ever referred to in such scurrilous terms as "poisonous bitch." Surely, she knew about these letters and felt the acid tongues, even when they found political designations for her dissent. And yet, with very great deliberation on her part, she continued to be tone-deaf on the question. This is not the chapter where this question is dealt with in great detail, and most important of all, fully philosophically, but it does serve as the transition point to Chapter III.

The point that gave me the most trouble, as I was working on this chapter, was also double-edged. On the one hand, I was very disappointed because, originally, I had definitely thought 1910 would be the focal point of the book since it would have shown that Luxemburg had broken with Kautsky four years ahead of Lenin, that she had been a genuine vanguard in sensing the opportunism in that "Pope of Marxism," and thus . . .

In the actual confrontation with that year—and not so incidentally, I found that very nearly nothing is available in English, and everything had to be translated for the very first time—I found that when one is prescient, instead of having worked it out philosophically; if one is "ahead of the time," but has not drawn organizational conclusions, i.e., seen what is the historic significance of a *tendency*, a tendency for which one is willing to take total responsibility; and if one therefore goes to the next point on the agenda—in Luxemburg's case, *Accumulation of Capital*—then theory, too, fails. That is why I had to end the preceding paragraph with three dots; that is to say, I couldn't possibly conclude that she was "in advance" of Lenin.

On the other hand, when it comes to the question of her hatred of imperialism, of great feeling for all the peoples of all the world whom capitalism was oppressing, of the truly human warmth for the cries of the Hottentot women and children that she kept hearing from the Kalahari Desert as if they were just around the corner from her home, then you wish to lash out against the so-called "New Left," which seems to feel nothing but its own narrow sloganeering, and its all-too-willing tail endism of state powers. It is for this reason that I feel it necessary to send out a letter about Iran tomorrow.

Yours,
Raya

December 2, 1979

Dear Colleagues:

In jumping the gun on myself by disclosing to you a very difficult philosophic problem that I, myself, have not yet worked out, I do so only because the concreteness of the political crisis and *counter*revolutionary move with theocratic constitution that the Iranian masses will now be pushed to adopt, makes philosophy more *practically* urgent than any "political line."

Here is what has come up in the Rosa Luxemburg book (which more precisely should be called MARX'S PHILOSOPHY OF REVOLUTION—except that it is always the concrete, in the Hegelian sense of *total*, which must take priority and it *is* the subject of Rosa Luxemburg that is the compulsion to take a 25th look at the problem we have raised directly after *Philosophy and Revolution* appeared).

Here is the 1905–07 Revolution in Russia, reaching into Iran, Afghanistan, and China, that became *the* Great Divide between reform and revolution on the Russian scene where supposedly there are no reformists but only Mensheviks within "revolutionary" Marxism. Surely, Lenin, Luxemburg, and also Trotsky not only "side with," but most actively act out revolution. And, surely, they base themselves on Marx in the 1848 revolution, to the point that Luxemburg even projects the concept that it is not the end of the 19th century revolutions but the beginning of a whole new series of 20th century revolutions, with the Russian Revolution in the vanguard internationally (and, of course, Trotsky proclaims, even if not at the London Congress, the concept of *permanent revolution*).

AND YET, AND YET, AND YET not a single one mentioned (and they didn't mention it because it was not concrete *to them*, though they surely had read Marx's 1850 Address) Marx's declaration in 1850 that from now on—that is to say, since the 1848–49 Revolution with the bourgeoisie had proved a failure and disclosed the bourgeoisie's betrayal—revolutionary socialists must proclaim "revolution in permanence."

Not only that. Though they were all *Russians*, and though the 1882 Preface to Marx's *Communist Manifesto articulated* a possible revolution in that backward country in advance of "the West," none saw this as anything relating to them at the precise moment of 1907.

And not only that. So far as Luxemburg was concerned, in 1910 she had all the revolutionary positions not only on General Strike, but on descending imperialism, which the Morocco Incident made clear in 1911—AND YET AND YET AND YET when she broke with Kautsky, it was very nearly made "personal," not only because she did not build a faction around herself *as tendency*, but because when she was off to theory—*Accumulation of Capital*—she deviated not so much from Kautsky,

BUT FROM MARX!

All this brings me back to the point that we, and we alone, called Marx's philosophy of revolution not just economic theory or political theory or even theory of revolution except as manifestation of a NEW CONTINENT OF THOUGHT. Think of it, Internalize it. Don't let go of it for a single second just because the urgency of the moment is Iran—or whatever . . .

Now then: *If* I am to bring in the 1850 Address that was not seen by those whom I praised, when discussing 1905, as great Marxist leaders who were "making" revolution on the immediate theory; *if* I am to bring out from the "hushed up" so-called "Woman Question" not just what they didn't see but what they even failed *to look for*, so that we learned of the Ethnological Notebooks only a full century later; *if* both permanent revolution and Women's Liberation come in this early— that is, here in Chapter III, directly after 1911 is discussed in Chapter II—then how does it flow from the historic period in question? Of course, that, again, will be our contribution and should make people realize what NEW CONTINENT OF THOUGHT MARX DISCOVERED, and question why all those Marxists who swear by Marx have nevertheless wanted to carve his philosophy into so many academic or empiric fields that you never did see the WHOLE AS NEW BEGINNING...
 Yours,
 Raya

January 14, 1980
Dear Friends:
 Chapter III*, which I have just completed, is at first glance so totally different from anything else I have written or spoken about Luxemburg that I consider it important to call it to your attention. First is the question of the title: "Luxemburg's Interregnum on the Way to New Theory; and Excursus on Why a Century to Publish Marx's Works?" Both the fact that it is an interregnum, and that it comes, *not* in 1910–11, but after that period, as she is beginning to work out her greatest theoretical work, *Accumulation of Capital* (*her* greatest work, not *the* greatest theoretical work; indeed, it would be a deviation from Marx's theory of accumulation of capital), mark a new stage in comprehension of the dialectic. Perhaps I should have said, instead of "comprehension," a great *inadequacy* in the comprehension of dialectic. It was comparatively easy for Rosa Luxemburg to defend Marx against a revisionist's demand for the "removal of the dialectic scaffolding." It is a very different thing when, in facing a new reality—imperialism— one feels no compulsion to dig into the "dialectic." The task is that of the reworking of the whole of Marx's deep-rootedness in the Hegelian

---

*It should be noted that during the process of the book chapters were changed and that the chapter numbers referred to in these letters do not necessarily correspond to the chapter numbers in the published work.

dialectic *and* Marxian creativity of transforming dialectical methodology into dialectics of liberation.

Therefore, whereas previously I had only hinted at it, in this Chapter I have developed the fact that Luxemburg always disagreed with Marx's concept of self-determination of nations in general and of Poland in particular. I want you to get a whiff of that from a magnificent letter Engels wrote to Kautsky about two weeks after he had co-authored with Marx that fantastically prophetic new Preface to the Russian edition of the *Communist Manifesto*, which had projected the possibility of Russia having a revolution in advance of the industrially developed nations. Here it is, dated February 7, 1882:

> Polish socialists who do not place the liberation of their country at the head of their program appear to me as would German socialists who do not demand first and foremost repeal of the socialist law, freedom of the press, association and assembly ... It is unimportant whether a reconstitution of Poland is possible *before* the next revolution. *We* have in no case the task to deter the Poles from their efforts to fight for the vital conditions of their future development, or to persuade them that national independence is a very secondary matter from the international point of view. On the contrary, independence is the basis of any common international action ... We, in particular, have no reason whatever to block their irrefutable striving for independence. In the first place, they have invented and applied in 1863 the method of fighting ... and secondly they were the only reliable and capable lieutenants in the Paris Commune.

I am using very little of the draft chapter on the *Ethnological Notebooks*, except for the first section, and even in that the paragraphs are considerably transposed. What I am now calling Excursus into why it took a century to publish all of Marx's works is not tied in Chapter III to the Man/Woman relationship, but to what resulted from Marx's delving into primitive societies insofar as it related to the Russian conditions. To put it differently, what has to be the pivotal point for this excursus is tied to the concreteness of the book and the specific subject of Rosa Luxemburg in the 1905 Revolution. No doubt I will later in the book return again to the rest of what I had written last year on the *Ethnological Notebooks*, except that I will definitely reduce Draper to a long footnote—but it is really more relevant to our age than to the manner in which male-chauvinism appeared in Luxemburg's period. Here, what we have to learn methodologically is that, no matter how comprehensively you think you have dealt with a subject, the aspect that makes it concrete in a *historic* period is the only proof.

Let me cite one other section of Chapter III, which relates to the question of dialectics in another new way. In 1903, Luxemburg had written an essay on "The Progress and Stagnation of Marxism." At first reading, that looks like the highest compliment to *Marx's* Marxism, since the essence of it is that not only has Marxism not stagnated, but we, the Marxists, haven't yet reached the totality of historical materialism. On second reading, you suddenly begin to realize what a very big gap there was in the thought of Marxists once Marx died, because far from regarding Marx's thought as a whole new continent, they regarded Marx as a revolutionary economist who taught them all about the class struggle. Just as Engels thought that he was following out a bequest of Marx when he wrote *The Origin of the Family*, so Luxemburg thought she was on the way to "extending" Marx's theory of Accumulation of Capital by concentrating on the new reality and sloughing off the dialectic as "rococo."

But that will be for Chapter IV. Here what is crucial—whether you consider it as an entirely new idea or as a further development of Chapters I and II—is that a transition period can be either a great leap forward or a fall backward—*not*, however, as retrogression, but as an illumination of what happens when the dialectic is kept only in the back of your mind. The very nearly subordinate point I am trying to make is that Luxemburg's "Progress and Stagnation of Marxism" is used as a transition point between her very wrong position on the National Question, dialectically as well as factually, and the move towards a new theory which deviates not from Kautsky but from Marx . . .

Yours,
Raya

March 19, 1980

On the Death of Erich Fromm

Dear Sisters:

The death of Erich Fromm naturally saddened me, the more so that when I looked into our lengthy correspondence I found that not only had it continued over two full decades, but that he was so magnificently objective a person that he would not be deterred by the fact that psychoanalysts were evidently not my favorite breed of people. The first time I heard from him—and it was upon his initiative—was with the publication of *Marxism and Freedom*, when he congratulated me on it and asked me to translate two more of Marx's 1844 Essays. I said no, because I had been translating from the Russian, and it would have been a double-translation. The point is that I had evidently made it clear that my admiration was for Marx, not Freud. He nevertheless sent me his essay, "Marx's Concept of Man"—and even accepted my criticism that it was abstract, writing to me: "As to the substance of the points you make about the concrete nature of Marx's humanism, I naturally entirely agree with you. Also about what you write of the role of the Plant psychoanalyst and Daniel Bell's position."

The reason I singled out the form of a Dear Sisters letter was that, in re-reading the correspondence, I found that he had quite a bit to say about the Man/Woman relationship; he even repeated the manner in which I write it, with both capitalized and a slash between. *And*, of all things, he referred back to Bachofen. It turns out he found reading of Bachofen congenial, *not* because he believed in any matriarchal society, but because it did give a vision of an alternate society to the patriarchal, authoritarian, capitalistic, alienating existing society. He even had a word for it: patricentric-acquisitive.

A few years back, I wrote to him about the American woman Hegelian, Susan E. Blow, and her experience with Dr. Putnam, the Freudian psychoanalyst whom she interested in Hegelian dialectics, and who, in turn, tried to get the anti-Hegelian Freud interested. Here is what Fromm wrote me: "I find it of considerable historical interest, and Freud's reaction to Putnam's philosophical remarks is also an interesting historical footnote to Freud and the history of the psychoanalytic movement. Why don't you write a note on this and publish it somewhere?" Whereupon he tried to get me to write for *Contemporary Psychoanalysis* or the Spanish psychoanalytic journal *Revista*.

What excited me most was his attitude to my work on Rosa Luxemburg: "I feel that the male Social Democrats never could understand Rosa Luxemburg, nor could she acquire the influence for which she had the potential because she was a woman; and the men could not become full revolutionaries because they did not emancipate themselves from their male, patriarchal, and hence dominating, character structure. After all, the original exploitation is that of women by men and there is no social liberation as long as there is no revolution in the sex war ending in full equality, which has never existed since prehistory. I believe she was one of the few fully developed human beings, one who showed what a human being can be in the future . . . Unfortunately I have known nobody who still remembers her personally. What a bad break between the generations."

    Yours,
    Raya

October 6, 1980

Dear Friends:

... Let me give you the new sequence of the chapters of the book, since there has been a change ... The first four chapters stand as is except that I definitely will rework the article on the *Ethnological Notebooks*, not as an Appendix or Afterword to Chapter III, but as an integral part of the final chapter. The fifth chapter now is "Prison, War, and Revolution"; Chapter VI is entitled "Women's Liberation—Then and Now"; Chapter VII is on "Spontaneity, Organization, and Philosophy." The final chapter is "Philosophy of Revolution: The Development of Marx from a Critic of Hegel to the Author of *Capital* and Theorist of Permanent Revolution."

This week, when I finished the Notes for Chapter V, I suddenly remembered that awful first sentence of Mary-Alice Waters' Introduction to her *Rosa Luxemburg Speaks*, which stressed that Luxemburg was born in the year of the Paris Commune and died "a little more than a year after the Bolsheviks came to power in the October Revolution." And I said to myself, Wasn't that the year of the German Revolution? Wasn't Luxemburg a leader of that revolution? Isn't that her greatest legacy? Where *is* the Geman Revolution?

I went to check, and by golly, it isn't. Not only does Mary-Alice Waters not mention it, as she first introduces Luxemburg, but when we finally come to the climax of the book, and we have Luxemburg's speech at the Congress held two weeks before her murder, it is: (1) the Party, "the founding convention of the German Communist Party"; (2) the only speech Luxemburg is permitted to make in Waters' collection from her last two and a half months, after her liberation from prison. Oh pardon me, there is a brief minor article, "Against Capital Punishment," which does creep in, but that only stresses the fact that if you want to know something about the German Revolution—the German, not the Russian—you have to depend on that miserable Trotskyist introduction to the last piece in the book, Luxemburg's speech at the Congress—and, believe it or not, the German Revolution doesn't enter Waters' introduction here until after her mention of Luxemburg's murder, and then only to stress, when the spontaneous revolution occurred in November, "the Spartakus leaders decided to remain within the USPD as long as possible." That, however, is *not* the Spartakus uprising; that is the overthrow of the Kaiser. In fact, I believe Waters never mentions the Spartakus uprising. We hear *her*, Mary-Alice Waters, *not Rosa Luxemburg*, and Mary-Alice Waters talks about "demonstrations," "hundreds of thousands of workers poured into the streets," "revolutionary ferment," but oh my dear there is no revolution, unless you take as a compliment that "it was much like the early months of 1917 in Russia, following the February Revolution." Don't be finished with your disgust yet. When I asked myself, Where *is* the German Revolution? it was because I suddenly realized that I was writing my chapter with no references to Waters' book at all, which is supposed to be the best because it has a few more pieces represented. The few more pieces just don't happen to be about the German Revolution. On *What the Spartakusbund Wants* I was quoting from a 1919 pamphlet I have had from way back when; "The Beginning" I quoted from the first issue of *Die Rote Fahne* that Robert Looker includes in his book; and the ending—one single day before she was murdered—is what she called "Order Reigns in Berlin," also included in Looker. Please listen to that great revolutionary's final words:

"Order reigns in Berlin!" You stupid lackeys! Your "order" is built on sand. Tomorrow the revolution will rear its head once again and, to your horror, will proclaim, with trumpets blazing: I was, I am, I will be!

Yours,
Raya

P.S. Do you think I forgot Women's Liberation? No, not I. Mary-Alice Waters forgot it. Here's all she has to say, every word of which is false: "Unfortunately, she rarely, if ever, wrote about the special problems of the struggle for women's liberation . . . and she dismissed the insults directed against her because she was a woman as simply part of the overhead of political battle." No wonder so many women shy away if male-chauvinism is dismissed as "overhead political battle." The truth, of course, is—and you will soon read it for yourself—that Luxemburg wrote from 1902 on, on the "Woman Question," and back in 1898 when she first met Plekhanov she wrote to Jogiches that he was the kind of a great man whose pomposity makes you want to thumb your nose at him.

There is no limit to Mary-Alice Waters' pomposity, as she warms up to the conclusion by claiming on the one hand that the selections from Rosa Luxemburg "tell more about her than any biography could," and on the other hand, regarding the early selections: "They seem stiffer and more self-conscious. Throughout, her style seems somewhat longwinded, at least to the modern ear, and one often wishes she could have found some more concise way to make her point and get on with it. But... she made her living as a journalist—sometimes simply turning out copy—and such training hardly provided great incentive to brevity"...

November 3, 1980

Dear Colleagues:

The individualism manifested by the correspondents in the letters written directly to me on Chapter VI ("Women's Liberation, Then and Now") has resulted in a sort of new category. That is to say, as against what I get from a "collective" discussion, this time I felt that, whatever contribution the letters will make to the final draft, there is a great deal that each one can learn from the others. Therefore, I would like to propose that a special bulletin be issued. It is true that I will need to abbreviate the collection of letters, but I will not otherwise edit. On the contrary, rather than expressing any view on them individually or collectively, I will actually not work on them further at this point, because I am no longer on that chapter at all. Here is what happened to me while "waiting" for your letters:

The so-called last chapter, the one on Karl Marx's philosophy of revolution, just wouldn't get written. It refused to be confined into a single chapter. The subject demanded more, and not alone because it has always been central to everything we do, but because specifically in relationship to Rosa Luxemburg, precisely because she was such a great revolutionary, the lacuna of philosophy in her concepts came to a very sharp near-breaking point on the question of the 1917 Russian Revolution and 1919 German Revolution. It extends to our period in this sense: Could Luxemburg's near tone-deafness on philosophy possibly have had an impact on 1919? It is not a matter of trying to have hindsight see what foresight could not have seen and thereby pat oneself on the back. No, the gnawing point is the working out of what it means to us, no matter what it meant to her age.

Thus the last chapter has become Part Two—"From a Critic of Hegel to Author of *Capital* and Theorist of Permanent Revolution"—and it will have three chapters:

Ch. I —Marx Discovers a New Continent of Thought and Revolution, 1841–1851

Ch. II —From the *Grundrisse* to *Capital* and the *Critique of the Gotha Program*

Ch. III—Marx's Unknown *Ethnological Notebooks*, Unread Drafts of *Letter to Zasulitch*, and Undigested 1882 *Preface* to the Russian Edition of the *Communist Manifesto*

Naturally I cannot tell you what these three chapters will contain whey they have only been conceived and not yet realized. However, I think that the surprise in the fact that the new continent of thought now seems to me to start in 1841, when Marx had still not broken with the bourgeoisie, can be answered—and this, indeed, touches on the whole question of originality, genuine originality in a revolutionary way—by showing you the subheadings of Chapter I of Part Two.

The chapter is introduced by "A Preliminary Note on the Dialectic, in Marx of the Early 1840s; in Luxemburg, 1902; and in Lenin, 1914." And it is this context, i.e., the 20th century, which makes one see (for the first time, I might add) that even before Marx had broken with the bourgeoisie, but when he was already working on his doctoral dissertation, (thoroughly dissatisfied with academia, with the Prussian state, with himself), that the dialectic of an ancient period—Ancient Greece— when looked at with eyes of "today" (i.e., 1839-1841, when he was a young Hegelian) showed Marx the significance of a crisis in thought. Or perhaps this should be turned around. It was the crisis in thought and in the life of Marx, a graduate student striving for a new world, that illuminated the ancient period he had to write about. In any case, there is a terrific drive and direction seen in that doctoral dissertation which was followed by the philosopher becoming a revolutionary journalist, and fighting, at one and the same time, with Prussian censorship, with the young Hegelians, and being drawn, instead, to the Mosel peasantry and the peasants charged with wood theft, deciding also to take on none less than Hegel.

The first subsection, *therefore*, is called "Prometheus Bound, 1841-1843." There will be two other sections—one dealing with 1844-1847 and the other dealing with 1847-1851 . . .

Yours,
Raya

December 16, 1980

Dear Friends:

Believe it or not, the draft of the book is actually finished—well, almost. The little "almost" is really little, since it refers to the third section of the final chapter which will be a reworking of the very first chapter you had, on the *Ethnological Notebooks* of Marx.

The final chapter of the entire book is entitled "Philosopher of Permanent Revolution and Organization Man." Section 1 of that chapter, "*Critique of the Gotha Program* (of a United Workers' Party of

Germany)," begins with: "The fetish of a vanguard party to lead is very nearly beyond comprehension when it affects as great a revolutionary as Rosa Luxemburg who had such overpowering confidence in the spontaneous action of workers that she was considered as simply a spontaneist."

The fact that such a great contradiction could pervade her thought—and that the passion of conviction of spontaneity, on the one hand, and the never-ending adherence to "the party," on the other hand, were just lying there side by side without ever being jammed up so they could be transcended—could never be resolved because there was a lack of philosophy.

In a certain sense, it also explains why I felt that the chapter on organization in Part One of the book was insufficient. What I mean is that the relationship of spontaneity and organization, when it is within the framework of her debates with Lenin, would not really answer the burning question of our day. That could only be worked out if we returned to Marx and especially if we returned on the ground that has never been considered an "organization" document—the *Critique of the Gotha Program*. Not only has that never been comprehensively worked out, but the one person, Lenin, who did use the *Critique of the Gotha Program* as the ground for his greatest work, *State and Revolution*, *did not apply it to the question of the party, even as he did not reorganize himself on that question with his philosophic reorganization* . . .

Please note that Section 2 on the question of Permanent Revolution has as part of its title "1843 to 1883"—in a word, its development throughout the whole mature life of Marx from the moment when he broke with bourgeois society until his death. To put it another way, whereas, at most, others use the 1850 Address to show that Marx wrote "something" on the Permanent Revolution, we show that it was integral to his philosophy whether it was one of his early essays on religion and the Jewish Question or the very last work on Ethnological Notebooks when, far from leaving it as a matter of "primitive society," he at once concretized it to show—in 1882, mind you!—that the revolution could come first in backward Russia.

I know that we are all so concrete that what we are now thinking about is Poland, but all you Irish revolutionaries please note that the quote that comes directly after the title of Section 2 is from a *workshop* talk by James Connolly: "Revolution is never practical until the hour of revolution strikes. *Then* it alone is practical, and all the efforts of the conservatives and compromisers become the most futile and visionary of human language."

Now you have to admit that that is a lovely way to begin the new year...

Yours,
Raya

January 30, 1981

Dear Colleagues:

One more new moment has arisen in relationship to the "Rosa Luxemburg book." Where, previously, I had insisted that Women's Liberation was not a separate part, but only a chapter (and I did so in order to stress that the book is a *totality*, rather than three different parts), I have now decided that the totality is best seen when there is a separate part. Here is what I mean: What was Chapter VI, "Women's Liberation, Then and Now," is not only a matter of "Then and Now"—i.e., different historic periods—but also and above all so totally different a concept that it transforms the whole question of "timing." Naturally, the different historic periods are important, but that can easily be seen by expanding the section "Yesterday, Today and Tomorrow." Indeed, that historic section will also be expanded, insofar as the Black dimension is concerned, to include Africa as well as the U.S. But we cannot limit the concept of Women's Liberation to a contrast of different historic periods, important as that subject is. Rather, Marx's concept of the Man/Woman relationship, which we quote so often, instead of being "taken for granted" must first be worked out for all periods.

We must roll the historic clock back, not just to questions of the women's movement, but back to the post-Marx Marxists, beginning with Engels himself. I now see that *Engels'* "philosophy," when it comes to Women's Liberation, is only a form of "*biologism.*" Otherwise, he couldn't possibly have come up with that fantastic phrase about "the world historic defeat of the female sex," with which to explain the change from matrilineal to patrilineal society. Contrast that to Marx's concept of a totally new human being, man and woman, and so total an uprooting of capitalist relations that the dialectic itself totally changes from an Hegelian self-development of thought to a revolutionary (Marxist) self-development of humanity.

Clearly, the new Part II that I am now proposing will not be just a critique of modern women's liberationist theorists but a critique of all post-Marx Marxists, beginning with Engels' *Origin of the Family*. It may be an exaggeration to say that Engels had moved away from Marx's philosophy of revolution, but it is a fact that if you do not have as profound a concept of it as did Marx, it affects your whole interpretation of humanity's development, and you have thereby already narrowed the battle for the uprooting of the old, the creation of a totally new society. If just the change from matrilineal to patrilineal society was the great determinant in humanity's development, what happened to the whole history of womankind since that time? Have we or have we not been in all revolutions and created the subject of women's liberation? Isn't it a fact that instead of digging into history, actual developing history, and tracing all the new developments, Engels concentrated so totally on "primitive communism" that it began to look as if all one needed to achieve liberation was modern technology? In any case, the residue of this view, accepted by the socialist women, even including the Marxists Clara Zetkin and Rosa Luxemburg, remains in the movement to this day.

Now let's go to our time. In this case, I mean the period since the Humanist Essays of Marx were published, first in the late 1920s in German and in post-WWII in French. We have two such absolutely opposite personalities and philosophies as Herbert Marcuse, a Marxist scholar, and Simone de Beauvoir, the Existentialist. No one has written more profoundly than Marcuse on the "Critique of the Hegelian Dialectic," and, indeed, the other Humanist Essays. And yet he did not at all see what Marx was saying on the Man/Woman relationship. Simone de Beauvoir, on the other hand, singled out that section, exalted it, but ended by twisting it to mean hardly more than the Existential "Other." What united these two opposites was that in each case it was left as *man's* task.

Now go over to Sheila Rowbotham, who extolls the primacy of Woman and certainly doesn't want to leave it as man's task. Yet she designates Women's Liberation as "an organizing idea," as if all the Women's Liberation Movement's task today consists of is to write its own *What Is To Be Done?*; as if the total opposition to elitism consists just of decentralization. What then happens to the new *human* relation? Doesn't that become a mere construct of a new Superwoman in place of a Superman? And with it, endowing that force with a Supertheory?

The new Part Two I'm proposing will probably be entitled, "The Women's Liberation Movement as Revolutionary Force and Reason." Having two chapters instead of one for this Part Two will affect also the section I called "Luxemburg's Activity in the Women's Movement." That is to say, the chapter will begin, not with Luxemburg's birth as a revolutionary, but with an historic, "geographic" background of where she was born, Poland, which is now in the headlines again.

Luxemburg's birthplace was where women were responsible for one of the first mass strikes, long before she was born. It was directed against the horrible, male-chauvinistic edict that women who worked in the factory must undergo the same sexual examination as prostitutes. No wonder that that type of patriarchal attitude caused Luxemburg, during her teens, to join the revolutionary movement and by age 16 to read Morgan's *Ancient Society*.

Finally, when it comes to the modern period, I do not know how much of the latest news I will include. For example, when I first learned about the new women dissidents in Russia I was quite excited; whereupon I found out about what Tatyana Mamonova herself has critiqued as the "Christianization" of that movement. Presently, I have noted that Mamonova, in her call for an International Feminist Union, did not include socialism and concentrated on opposition to "totalitarian" male chauvinism as if "democracy" was not as guilty.

The more I think of the disregard of Luxemburg by the whole movement, including Socialist Feminists, the more I realize that, once you leave out revolution as the only way to uproot the old society, you are not only reducing Women's Liberation to "a new sensibility," but leaving the whole of humanity right within the capitalist framework.

Yours,
Raya

P.S. Please change the titles of what will now be Chapter V to "Spontaneity, Organization, and Dialectics of Revolution," and what will now be Chapter VI to "War, Prison, Revolutions." What was Part Two on Marx now becomes Part Three. And I am now calling the last chapter in that Part Three, "The Philosopher of Permanent Revolution Relates Theory to Organization."

Presentation March 16, 1981, as Book Was Being Completed

Although I have discussed the book several times before, it has been as bits and pieces, even when they are as big as Part Two. That is not the same as the view you get when you see it as a totality. Even for myself, this is the first time seeing it as a whole. The different perspective affects every chapter, even one like Chapter I, which is virtually unchanged. Yet the order that follows gives it a completely different meaning. What had been Chapter III ("The Interregnum of Luxemburg, and an Excursus into Marx's New Continent of Thought") is no longer there. What is now Chapter III is *not* an excursus into Marx for the book, and *not* an interregnum for Luxemburg. Rather, Chapter III is now "Marx's and Luxemburg's Theories of Accumulation of Capital," and we see Rosa Luxemburg not in any interregnum, not taking on a Kautsky or Bernstein, but in a big clash with Marx at his highest point. Thus a whole new connotation is given to Chapters I and II which precede it.

What then becomes Chapter IV is very different. Half of the old Chapter III is thrown out, with only the part on Poland and the National Question retained. And the whole is combined with what had been Chapter V, on "Spontaneity, Organization, and the Dialectics of Revolution." Now the whole has a new title: "From the National Question to Dialectics of Revolution; the Relationship of Spontaneity and Organization, especially as regards Disputes with Lenin, 1904–1917." What it does dialectically, is that at the end of the section on the National Question, it moves right to spontaneity and organization, and the myth of the dispute between Lenin and Luxemburg. The need is to follow the actual articulation by Rosa Luxemburg of the question, and to see when she put organization subordinate to revolution, she was with Lenin. It goes into the differences with Lenin very specifically in each period. The contradiction on the National Question is exactly what keeps her from seeing philosophy. Her insistence is on listening to the masses—but not to Marx and not to his concept of organization.

The whole question of the relation of philosophy and revolution to organization was posed in Russia, but could not be solved there. The crisis could only be solved in the context of world revolution. That was what Luxemburg was great on; she was Russian, Polish, German revolutionist. The whole of Part One will have the title: "Rosa Luxemburg, Internationalist."

Chapter V is still titled "War, Prison and Revolutions," but the German Revolution of 1919 is seen very differently than we have ever seen it before. All of us have been a little brainwashed by the Communist Party on this period, where the whole question is presented to us: Lenin had a party; Luxemburg didn't; Lenin won; she didn't. I had to go to bourgeois sources, instead, to see the genuine mass revolutionary character of Spartakus Week, January 1919. First was the Kiel mutiny of sailors, which grew into workers, soldiers, sailors councils all over Germany. Ebert had appointed Noske as Defense Minister, but when the workers occupied the *Vorwarts* building, the counterrevolution didn't dare ask Berlin troops to take back the building. They had to bring in 6,000 troops from outside for the massacre. And what followed was a General Strike of no less than 200,000.

You also see that Luxemburg's years in prison were not just the "birds and flowers" that have been so much written about, but the *Junius* pamphlet and the *Anti-Critique*. Part One ends as the German Revolution has begun, with Luxemburg's speeches, "What does the Spartakus League want?" and the one to the "Founding conference of the Communist Party of Germany"...

The whole of Part Two is now called: "The Women's Liberation Movement as Reason and as Revolutionary Force." That Part will begin with quotes not only from Louise Michel, D.H. Lawrence ("A work is never beautiful, unless it in some way escapes its author"), and Luxemburg, but from Marx's 1844 Essays. The Marx quote here is the one that takes up each of the "human relations to the world—seeing, hearing, smell, taste, feeling, thought, perception, wishing, activity, loving..." Put in the context of the transcendence of private property, they shed a very different light on human *individuality*. It will be important to study the quotes in this context.

The very first chapter of Part Two is now called "Overview by Way of Introduction: Yesterday, Today, Tomorrow." Time now is shown not as time, but as Marx's concept of "space for human development." It is not just a question of "then and now." Rather, a form is created for a back and forth on all concepts. Thus, 1831 is where we begin, with Nat Turner's revolt in the same year as Maria Stewart became the first Black American woman to lecture publicly, calling on "O ye daughters of Africa" to awake and arise. But it does not stop there, does not limit itself either to the revolutionary Black dimension or to the U.S.A., when you see 1848 as a world historic moment. 1848 shows that *revolution* was actually present, and that intercommunication was real in the answer of American women's liberationists to the greetings sent them by French women in prison after the defeat of the 1848 revolutions in Europe. Then we can go from Marx 1844 on Man/Woman to how Marcuse in 1932 could not see that concept; from Sojourner Truth's story about Jesus (man had nothing to do with it) to Harriet Tubman as leader, organizer—and to many Black women.

The next section of Chapter VI takes up "Individualism and Masses in Motion," and it is at this point I bring in Luxemburg's letter where she speaks of Penthesilea, revealing how totally original a character was Luxemburg in the way she lived. Penthesilea isn't raised in relation to the "Woman Question," but in relation to the war and betrayal. It is important to see what instinct can force you to do. The chapter then ends with the "Aba Riots" as a "Women's War." This permits us to connect to the Polish 1863 "Women's War" and to Marx's *Ethnological Notebooks*. In the "Aba Riots," it was called "sitting on a man." In Marx's notebook on Morgan, the Indian women called it "removing the horns" of the chief.

Chapter VII is the least changed, but it is very important to note that the title is now: "Rosa Luxemburg as Revolutionary, as Feminist," NOT "Rosa Luxemburg as Revolutionary Feminist." What is expanded is both the section on the relationship of Luxemburg and Jogiches, and the attack on Nettl, who I have finally figured out, called 1906–09 "The Lost Years" for Rosa Luxemburg, because they were the years of the breakup with Jogiches!

"The Task that Remains to be Done: The Unique and Unfinished Contribution of Today's Women's Liberation Movement" is the title of Chapter VIII. It gives more credit to the current Women's Liberation Movement than ever before, actually breaking the style of writing to let those voices speak for themselves, yet showing that we are still nowhere. It brings in the Moslem women, and then, before we ever get to the concluding chapter, takes up some of the section on the *Ethnological Notebooks*. It brings in Draper on two points: on the "world historic defeat of the female sex"; and on the first division of labor, which Marx saw as a social division as well as a sexual one. The whole of Part Two ends, not with the *Ethnological Notebooks*, but on a very different note, coming back to today's movement. We see Portugal with do Carmo and Barreno; Rowbotham on women's liberation as "an organizing idea" (which concept I see as being a return to Lenin's *What Is To Be Done?*); and Iran's Women's Liberation Movement—all raising the question of form of organization. But it is a matter of posing the question, not answering it. By the end of this section, we go back to Ding Ling on "Noras who came home," like Jiang Qing, and forward to the trial of the "Gang of Four," 1981.

Part Three is titled "Karl Marx—from a Critic of Hegel to Author of *Capital* and Theorist of Permanent Revolution." That is the same title, but very little else is the same. Take the question of "style." In Parts One and Two, there are subheads in the chapters, but here each subhead is a *section*, almost chapters in themselves, and all the sections will be listed right in the Table of Contents.

Section 1 of Chapter IX thus extends into the 20th century: "A Preliminary Note on the Dialectic: in Marx of the Early 1840s; in Luxemburg 1902; in Lenin 1914." Now that we have seen Luxemburg's life, the crises at the turn of the century are seen as the beginning of the *downgrading* of Marx. Everyone from Mehring to Kautsky becomes more important than Marx, since they were the ones who supposedly "interpreted" Marx, enabled us to "understand" him. You never saw Marx, but only the popularization. Thus, there is no way to re-connect without going back to the dialectic in Marx himself.

The re-connection begins before what is considered the beginning, with the section "Prometheus Bound, 1841–43." This is entirely new on Marx. Marx as a student of Hegel wants to add "a few details" on Democritus and Epicurus to Hegel's analysis. The "details" turn out to be both opposite to Hegel's analysis, and the notes turn out to be 300 pages. Marx turns against Hegel's concept of totality, in which there is not really a unity of theory and practice; and he turns against the world that is, and into action. What is more astonishing yet is the way Epicurus reappears suddenly in 1867, in *Capital*, in the "Fetishism of Commodities." For years I have read that reference, and it did not mean what it means in this context. This precise paragraph (p. 172 in the Vintage edition) is one where Marx is accused of anti-Semitism. Far from that being the case, it is against all blinding fetishisms—against petty-bourgeois mercantilism, against religion.

The final section, "Prometheus Unbound, 1844–48" is more familiar. Yet here is where Marx first comes out with the formulation of permanent revolution in the essay on the Jewish Question.

Chapter X, "A Decade of Historic Transformation: From the *Grundrisse* to *Capital*," is a very different one than even a few weeks ago. Before, when I thought of the separate parts, all had to flow from Luxemburg. Now, after you see the book as a totality, the beginning of the chapter on Rosa Luxemburg is thrown out entirely, and we begin instead with the 1857 crisis. But even there, the first section title gives a hint that the economic crisis of 1857 isn't that alone: "'Economics': Only Class Struggles or 'Epochs of Social Revolution'?, 1857–58." Immediately the question is posed on what happened before the *Grundrisse*—the Taiping Rebellion. That is what concretely drove Marx to look at what forms preceded capitalism. When we move to the second section, on *Capital*, it becomes clear that we still don't have *Capital* as Marx wrote it. Fowkes followed Engels rather than Marx. Thus the Part 8 on "So-Called Primitive Accumulation" is placed as a separate Part, instead of placing it, as Marx did, under Part 7, "The Process of Accumulation of Capital." You miss entirely seeing that Marx meant it as one movement.

This brings us to the final chapter, "The Philosopher of Permanent Revolution Relates Theory to Organization." It begins with the section on the "*Critique of the Gotha Program* (of a United Workers' Party of Germany)." What is key here is the way this section is not a question of having to rid ourselves of Lassalleanism. Indeed, throughout the whole of the book, we are not arguing with reformists or counterrevolutionaries. All are revolutionaries, in theory and in fact. Yet they still did not make it without philosophy. This is crucial to see.

Again the book returns to Marx on permanent revolution, now over the whole period 1843–83, in Section 2. And it is here that I wish to stress the "Afterword" to that section. It is what we think we know from the Political-Philosophic Letter I had written, now called "Leon Trotsky's Theory of Permanent Revolution." It is very different in this context. Consider Trotsky on the peasantry in the context of Marx's letter to Engels that what the German Revolution needs is a "second edition of the Peasant War."

(I have just learned—through material in the Harvard University Trotsky Archives—that I *had* looked at the 1907 Congress all the way back when I was doing research for Trotsky. But since it was a very specific assignment to expose Stalin on something he supposedly wrote in 1907, I didn't look at the Congress as a whole.)

The very last section on the "Unknown *Ethnological Notebooks*, Unread Drafts of Letter to Zasulitch, as well as Undigested 1882 Preface to the Russian Edition of the *Communist Manifesto*," has now eliminated the pages relating directly to Rosa Luxemburg. This is not only because of Rosa Luxemburg, but because it is necessary to break down the biggest slander of all, and by the greatest of the Marxist archivists—Ryazanov. He is the one who fostered the concept of Marx's last years as a slow death and derided the *Ethnological Notebooks* as "indefensible pedantry." To unearth the problem fully, we then go directly back to, not Rosa Luxemburg, but Engels, the very first of Marx's "heirs," and with *The Origin of the Family*. But it isn't just *The Origin of the Family* that is the question. It is: what is your relationship to the new revolutionary force in the world?*

---

*Before the book was actually published, Chapter XI was expanded to become a whole new Chapter XII: "The Last Writings of Marx Point a Trail to the 1980s."

CHAPTER 26

On Rosa Luxemburg, Women's Liberation, and Marx's Philosophy of Revolution*

Yesterday, at midnight, the counterrevolution took its greatest step forward in Poland; so we must be conscious today that we are meeting under the whip of counterrevolution. It's sad, indeed, to think that 39 years ago it was precisely such a move—that time it was the fascists and the Stalinists both—that the world witnessed. I'm referring to the crushing of the Jewish Ghetto Uprising in Poland and the Warsaw Uprising when the Red Army stood outside the gates to make sure that the Nazis first destroyed it before the Russians moved in. What was opposite to that (and that's what dialectics means—that you always have to see the opposites as struggle) was that, at that time, we issued the slogan, "All roads lead to Warsaw," by which we did not mean the counterrevolution but the new beginnings, the new age that began with the national resistance movement. That fight has continued for 39 long years.

It is important to recognize that, precisely because we are meeting under the whip of counterrevolution, we must hold high the banner of revolution and see to it that it is not a confrontation in which the counterrevolution wins, but in which we will win. What becomes ever more imperative is the Absolute Method of the dialectic—how to overcome, how to see the dual rhythm of revolution, the overcoming of the old and the creation of the new. The adventurous journey that we're starting on here will permit us to see 150 years of confrontation, revolutions, forward moves, and unfortunately also backward moves. We will have a chance to meet great revolutionaries—Marx, Luxemburg, Lenin, Trotsky; and those not so great, like Plekhanov. And we will examine the great revolutions—from 1848, to 1905–07, to 1917–19, to those in our own day.

---

*Excerpts from a lecture presented in Detroit, Mich., Dec. 13, 1981, on the completed manuscript of the work.

In order to establish this intercommunication between the ages, in order to see that philosophy and revolution is not an abstraction, in order to grasp what is the task for today, let me begin first with the *purpose* and the *method* of *Rosa Luxemburg, Women's Liberation, and Marx's Philosophy of Revolution*: Why today? Why now? What is its significance?

First, we had in the early 1970s the transcription and publication of Karl Marx's *Ethnological Notebooks*. It's the raw transcription as to how Marx was thinking in the last years of his life. Now, we want to always have before us the phrase "at one and the same time," so that we always get the opposites together and see that it isn't a matter of development as just quantitative, but development through contradiction. Thus, with the publication of the *Ethnological Notebooks* came the realization, at the same time, that far from Marx and Engels being one person, they were *not*. It wasn't because Engels betrayed; it was that there is only one founder of a movement.

Engels published *The Origin of the Family* just a few months after Marx's death. He said he published it as a "bequest" of Marx and referred to those particular studies of Morgan's *Ancient Society* that Marx did not have a chance to write up. But we never saw Marx's Notebooks. When we did, we found out that, far from there being the three or four paragraphs that Engels quoted in his *Origin*, there were 250 pages worth of notes. They weren't only on the American study; they were also against the imperialists of Great Britain. And Marx's work, above all, was not at all a unilinear study; it was a multilinear study. Whereas it was very great to find out that, far from being backward, primitive society was a very high stage of development, it wasn't a question of adding a frigidaire to primitive communism to have the new society. Marx was using that study to show what the actual development of humanity was, but was not saying that's all the future society will be, much less that the move from matriarchal or matrilineal societies to patriarchy was the "world historic defeat of the female sex."

This does not mean that we forget that Engels was Marx's closest collaborator, without whom we would not have had Volumes II and III of *Capital*. But neither is it a matter of needing to delude oneself by considering that Engels said all there was to be said on the subject when he stated that Marx was a genius and all the rest, including himself, only talented. What *is* needed is to view their complex relationship in the context of our age. It is our age that is the first to have Marx's works *as a totality*. It is thus incumbent on us to draw a dividing line between what *Marx's* Marxism is and what Engels *interpreted* that to be. To do this we cannot consider the category "post-Marx Marxists" a mere chronological designation. Rather, the category must be seen as the essential *dividing line* between Marx's own works and those of any interpreter, and that includes Engels.

The second event in the 1970s we want to take up was the development of Women's Liberation from an Idea whose time has come into an actual movement. The interesting and exciting part about that is not only the uniqueness of today's Women's Liberation Movement and the fact that it did or didn't inspire the finding of the *Ethnological Notebooks*, but that suddenly there was an abrupt inter-merging with Rosa Luxemburg. Here was Luxemburg, the greatest woman revolutionary, whom the women weren't paying any attention to but who had been revived as a serious revolutionary with the rise of the new generation of revolutionaries in the 1960s. She was not revived as a feminist, but as a spontaneist.

Naturally, in the break from bureaucratism and totalitarianism—and the Vietnam War and everything we had to fight against—the concentration was on the fact that Luxemburg had recognized the spontaneity of the workers' movement as the greatest force forward. Therefore, they said, that's what we have to learn. Well, aside from the exaggeration (because she certainly didn't give up the Party), the point is that the totality of Luxemburg was not seen. She was a revolutionary; she was a feminist; she was a great literary person—she was multidimensional. So how does it happen that in all these years—whether one liked her as a spontaneist or didn't like her as a vanguardist, or whatever—the particular original character she was, both as a person and as a revolutionary, was not seen?

The third event of those 1970s was the most fundamental; in many respects it's old, but in other respects it's very new. It's the great economic crisis of 1974-75, the myriad crises all over the world. Heretofore we have stressed that it was so very deep that it influenced the very structure of the capitalist economy. But what I want to stress today—and that's why it's so important to remember the little phrase: "at one and the same time"—is something different. It is the new type of revolution.

Here is what I mean. For the first time, you couldn't answer the question: "Who/Whom?" Take the Portuguese Revolution; you had revolutions in Angola, Mozambique, Guinea-Bissau. Who exactly inspired whom? Did Portugal, the underbelly of the European and NATO forces come first? What about the fact that Portugal's imperialist army was stationed in Mozambique and Angola, "its" African colonies, and the Portuguese soldiers were inspired by the Blacks who were asking them: Why have you come to fight us? You have fascism in your own country—why not stay there and get rid of them? The Portuguese Revolution was made in Angola.

There was one other Portuguese colony we have to look at and ask ourselves: How does it happen we don't know anything about East Timor? Did it have to do with the fact that the revolution there was led by a woman, a Black woman? Rosa Muki Bonaparte. We keep talking about other struggles and completely forget that one. When we describe the horrors of this society—whether it's what's happening in El Salvador or in Africa or wherever—why don't we know that among the worst of all starvations was in East Timor? When the counterrevolution overtook that colony, the first person the Indonesian army shot was Rosa Muki Bonaparte...

...Let's move to Luxemburg. I was going to start with her favorite expression when the 1905 Revolution erupted: "The revolution is magnificent, all else is bilge." I didn't because it might be misunderstood by someone who would think she was just a fanatic; she was anything but. Instead I start with how she answered a letter from another woman whose husband had betrayed on the question of war credits to the Kaiser. Luxemburg was writing to her from prison and telling her off:

> I'm telling you that as soon as I can stick my nose out again I will hunt and harry your society of frogs with trumpet blasts, whip crackings, and bloodhounds—like Penthesilea I wanted to say, but by God, you people are not Achilles. Have you had enough of a New Year's greeting now? Then see to it that you stay *human*... Being human means joyfully throwing your whole life 'on the scales of destiny' when need be, but all the while rejoicing in every sunny day and every beautiful cloud. Ach, I know of no formula to write you for being human...

Now why was Penthesilea suddenly brought in? This is an anti-war letter, and Penthesilea is the Queen of the Amazons... It shows a very new development on a lot of levels, not all of which she herself was conscious of. The first had been in relationship to Jogiches. It is not true that the breakup of their relationship was over whether there was or wasn't a triangle involved. The question was that she suddenly said, "I am I only when I am free of Leo." What did that mean? They were both revolutionaries. And it is not the way the modern woman thinks—that you have to have a room of your own (which is absolutely true). In this case it was both the question of the organization and the spontaneity; and it was the attempt to *fly alone* in revolutionary events. It was the question of all her theories, which were much higher in the period after she broke than when she was with Jogiches.

But it wasn't even only that. It was the *relationship* between the Individual and the Universal. It's good to say: Oh yes, we are great revolutionaries and absolutely our Individualism lets nothing interfere with its Universalism. But what do you do when it comes down to the point of having your personal life involved?

Then there is the question of her relationship to women and the anti-war work. Again Luxemburg drew no conclusions, but she did magnificent work because the women were the greatest, the most massive, the most militant part of the anti-war movement. She fought also on the question of the vote for women, and not on the level of: We'll have the vote and be equal. That's nonsense. She said, "To a bourgeois woman, her house is the world, but to the proletarian woman the whole world is her house."

All of these activities, all the great mass movements were ongoing long before the revolution of 1919. In fact, Luxemburg was in prison even before the war because she dared to make a speech considered insulting to the Kaiser. And suddenly, from prison, comes this particular letter about Penthesilea. I've asked my German friends which legend Luxemburg was referring to. Was she talking about the Greek myth of the Queen of the Amazons who fought on the side of the Trojans and was killed by Achilles? Or was it the play a German dramatist had written in which it was Penthesilea who killed Achilles? I don't know which one Luxemburg meant and my friends tell me she was a very erudite woman and may have meant both of them. The question is why did she suddenly bring in this legend?

Marx also wrote about these magnificent goddesses, saying that the creation of these myths must mean one of two things. Either life at one time was so beautiful and free and great and women were not oppressed that they represent a remembering of what life really was; or life was so miserable that they were trying to show the exact opposite of what it could be. In either case, Marx felt, these myths tell us something historical and shouldn't be dismissed.

It's in that sense that—whether it's Luxemburg's reference to Penthesilea, or her break with Jogiches, or her saying she had no particular feeling for Women's Liberation but meanwhile being the most active with the women and the actual leader of the greatest anti-war movement—you have to ask: Why is it that the modern Women's

Liberation Movement hasn't paid attention to this great revolutionary? It's a question of grasping what is involved in "at one and the same time." Each part of the book has an "overview" because I'm trying to show how complex are the elements as they developed. In relationship to the Women's Liberation Movement of today, it is right to say: We are very unique, and it's not that we're trying to be just as good as a man—that's nonsense. We want a damn sight more than just being equal. And don't tell us how many thousands of women *Gleichheit* organized. They were a great mass movement but they let the male chauvinism continue right within the Party, and they kept quiet about it.

The women of today's generation are right on that. It's they and they only who have said: No! You're not going to make us into mimeographers, or whatever you consider to be the lesser work. We are going to be part of the decision-making process and we're not going to wait until the day after the revolution to expose the male-chauvinism...

In discussing the struggles of women I took up an entirely different period. I began in 1831, with what one of the great Black women, Maria Stewart, had said. I chose 1831 because that is the year of the greatest slave revolt, Nat Turner's revolt. We all know about that, but who knows that in the same period Maria Stewart was saying this: "O ye daughters of Africa, awake! awake! arise! no longer sleep nor slumber but distinguish yourselves. Show forth to the world that ye are endowed with noble and exalted faculties... How long shall the fair daughters of Africa be compelled to bury their minds and talents beneath a load of iron pots and kettles?... How long shall a mean set of men flatter us with their smiles, and enrich themselves with our hard earnings: their wives' fingers sparkling with rings and they themselves laughing at our folly?"

The Black dimension was always the vanguard dimension in American history. But even as Black, it was the Black man who was recognized. It was Nat Turner, but not Maria Stewart we learned about... Then I took the question through on several levels: the Iroquois women in America, the Igbo women in Nigeria in 1929, and the war in Poland in 1863. I chose them because Marx took up some of them and that synthesizes them into something new...

In relationship to the Absolute Method, we have to ask: How does it happen that we still have to return to Marx? Why didn't the women recognize the revolutionary, Rosa Luxemburg? What was it that was so great in Marx that we suddenly developed the expression of "post-

Marx Marxists" as a category that was a deviation from Marxism and wasn't the challenge to our age?

I will start way in advance first and then go directly to Marx's high point. By way in advance I mean when Marx was just a college student. Believe me, he was no Marxist yet. He hadn't found the class struggle. It was even before 1841; it was 1837. He was just choosing an occupation, and his father wanted him to be a lawyer. The greatest philosopher of law was Savigny, who was Marx's teacher, and Marx wrote 300 pages on that. Here is what he said afterwards about his own great work—the 300 pages he had just written on Roman law which he called the "unhappy document"—and about why he was giving up that work and turning to Hegel: "The whole thing is replete with tripartite divisions, with tedious prolixities. And the Roman constitutions are misused in the most barbaric fashion in order to force them into my system." (Talk about self-criticism!)

He then went to the Hegelian dialectic. He thought that, compared to Law, it was going to be really great and he wrote to his father how wonderful life was going to be now that he had discovered negativity. That was 1837; he was 19 years old. Four years later, in 1841, he was writing his Doctoral Dissertation on Epicurus and Democritus. Now if there is any strong part in Hegel it's thought, the history of thought. Whereupon, Marx decided to disagree with Hegel's interpretation of the history of Greek thought of 500 or 600 B.C. He said that of course Hegel was the greatest philosopher, but because he was so comprehensive and so total he couldn't pay attention to detail. And the detail Marx wanted to look at was Epicurus . . . What, however, was really happening? Marx was seeing in Hegel's Absolute a new beginning. What he was breaking with was that, in Hegel, Absolute meant some sort of God. What he was accepting was *self*-development, *self*-determination, *self*-transcendence, in the sense that it all comes from *inside*. The revolutionary nature—whether it's in you as an individual, or whether it's in the nations that will fight for freedom—is there.

I have to appeal to literature at this point, because I think that Melville had the greatest sense—not of Marx, I don't think he knew Marx—but of what he called "abrupt intermergings." Let me read you what Melville says happens to a writer who doesn't know where he's going, but who is going somewhere great: "The profounder emanations of the human mind intended to illustrate all that could humanly be known of life. These never unravel their own intricacies, and have no proper annex but, in imperfect, unanticipated, disappointing sequels as mutilated stumps hurry to abrupt intermergings with eternal ties of time and space."*

We see these abrupt inter-mergings in the 1840s when the question Marx posed to himself in challenging his master, Hegel, was: Is it possible to continue something as great as Hegel's dialectical philosohpy after he has gone? What are the new beginnings? How do you begin anew? Marx said that the totality Hegel had achieved was very great but that there are really *two* totalities: the totality of thought as it self-develops to the Absolute Idea; and the objective world. Here are the Moselle peasants, Marx said, and they are stealing wood. He counted all the laws against wood theft and proved there were more laws against that than against all other crimes including murder—without anyone bothering to ask why the peasants had to steal wood to stay warm. He concluded there were really two worlds—the world of thought and the objective world. He wasn't saying the world of thought was no good, because he was going to take a lot from Hegel. But, he said, we need to oppose the philosopher for being abstract; and we need to oppose the actual reality for all the misery we have—whether that's the Moselle peasants, or press censorship, or whatever. And now Marx had a new Subject—the proletariat . . . Declaring the proletariat to be the "universal" class did not mean that Marx abandoned either all other forces of revolution, like the peasantry, or other lands than the industrialized ones. That is seen most clearly in his last decade. *The universal that Marx never abandoned was revolution*—whether that was in relation to the proletariat or the peasantry or the Arabs in Algeria or the "intelligent black", i.e., the Aborigines in Australia . . .

Look at what Marx was writing at the end of his life, *after* he had finished *Capital*. Think of it—he spends 25 years working out *Capital*, his greatest theoretical work; and its greatest part is "The Historical Tendency of Capitalist Accumulation." (The idea he developed there was that capitalism develops to this point and then finally collapses; and that since the capitalist lands are the technologically advanced world, they will show the backward world its path.) Now he says that was true only of West Europe. It is *not* a universal. The Russians could escape that horror of capitalism *if* they had a revolution and saw to it that it was related to the other revolutions.

The question always was: What is the relationship of revolution in your own life, in the life of your country, in your international life, and

*Herman Melville, *Pierre* (Evanston: Harcourt Brace, 1971), p. 199.

in the world revolution. And what is the relationship of your activity to a particular thought—whether that be against capitalism, or against feudalism, whether it be against the old relationship, or the new relationship, of Man to Woman.

What he had laid as a trail for us, therefore, was that the question of permanent revolution was not something that happened only in 1848 or 1850, or even in 1871 with the greatest revolution of his lifetime, the Paris Commune; it was also in the 1880s when there was nothing like that happening. What he was saying was that there might *be* something happening if the Russians really had a revolution. The so-called backward countries, instead of being the ones that would be "shown the light" by the advanced, would themselves show the light to the world.

The post-Marx Marxists have not only kept hidden the various writings of Marx so that each generation has had to discover a new work that hadn't been known before, whether that be the 1844 Humanist Essays, or the 1857 *Grundrisse*, or the full 1872 French edition of *Capital* that all reveal Marx's return to Hegel. But what do we find Marx doing in 1882–83? He is returning to what he had done from the very beginning—when he said that even if you forget the class struggle you still would have to see what a miserable society we have when man can treat woman, the one he loves, so miserably. Something is so wrong we have to get rid of it not only by overthrowing it but by transforming it into totally new human relations.

It is that new moment, that return to the questions he raised in 1844, that return also to what is the historical tendency of capitalist accumulation, where we pick up *Marx's* Marxism and show that it wasn't only the betrayers who deviated. That's easy to expose. But it was also those who *weren't* betraying, but who were separating the philosophy of revolution from the actual revolution.

Let's conclude today, therefore, with where the book ends—with "A 1980s View." And that has to start with where I started today—with Poland. It is actually East Europe in the 1950s where a new movement from practice was born that was itself a form of theory and therefore demanded very different answers—not only for how to attain a new unity of theory and practice, but a new *relationship* in that unity. The East Europeans in the 1950s were asking about what Marx meant by a "new Humanism." They said that can't be an abstraction; it has to be very concrete. And the concrete is that the Communism which claims to be Marxism is the exact oppressor; and you have to fight against that which exists. That's the very first thing. Marx began with when he called for the "ruthless critique" of that which is . . .

The absolute challenge to our age is precisely the 1880s trail Marx left for us to realize. But we have to work very hard to realize it. What we have developed out of what we saw in the 1950s with new forms of workers' revolts, and in the 1970s with the new types of revolutions, is what we have documented in the Marxist-Humanist Archives.* By now, 1981, the Archives of Marxist-Humanism in the United States number 7000 pages alongside the basic theoretical works of *Marxism and Freedom, Philosophy and Revolution,* and the new work on *Rosa Luxemburg, Women's Liberation, and Marx's Philosophy of Revolution.*

The challenge is to catch the continuous link to Marx's revolution in permanence. As I put it in the new book: "Every moment of Marx's development, as well as the totality of his works, spells out the need for 'revolution in permanence.' This is the absolute challenge to our age."

---

*I turned over my entire collection of documents from 1941 to the Wayne State University Archives of Labor and Urban Affairs in 1969. A new donation expanded the collection back to 1937 and forward to 1981 as this new work was being completed. The collection is available on microfilm from Wayne State University, Detroit, Mich. 48202.

CHAPTER 27

Answers to Questions Raised During the Marx Centenary Lecture Tour on the Book

1. On the relationship of philosophy to reality, as discussed in the Introduction to *Rosa Luxemburg, Women's Liberation, and Marx's Philosophy of Revolution* on p. xi*:

That seems to have been the first point so misunderstood by post-Marx Marxists, beginning with Frederick Engels, who, without having known all of the massive *Ethnological Notebooks* Marx had left behind, undertook to write his own version of Morgan's work—his *Origin of the Family*—as a "bequest" of Marx. When Ryazanov discovered these notebooks, he rushed—before he ever had a chance to decipher them, to characterize them as "inexcusable pedantry." If an Engels, who was a close collaborator of Marx and without whom we would not have had Volumes II and III of *Capital*, could nevertheless suddenly have gotten so overconfident about his own prowess of interpreting Marx as to assume he was speaking for Marx; if an archivist-scholar like Ryazanov could, at a time when he was actually publishing those magnificent early essays of Marx (the 1844 Economic-Philosophic Manuscripts), spend a good deal of his first report on the Archives of Marx in asking for 20 to 30 people to help him sort these manuscripts out, and yet pass judgment before he dug into them—it says a great deal about literary heirs but nothing whatsoever about so great an historic phenomenon as *Marx's* Marxism.

2. Further questions were raised also on the difference between Marx and Engels on the whole question of transition period taken up on p. 180; that is, what happens during the transition from one stage to

---

*All page references in the following pages are to the 1982 Humanities Press edition of *Rosa Luxemburg, Women's Liberation, and Marx's Philosophy of Revolution.*

another, both as it relates to Women's Liberation and to the Asiatic Mode of Production, which Engels somehow omitted from his *Origin of the Family*. I had, indeed, considered that question crucial as Marx always related it to new revolutionary upsurges:

In the 1850s, for example, what inspired Marx to return to the study of pre-capitalist formations and gave him a new appreciation of ancient society and its craftsmen was the Taiping Revolution. It opened so many doors to "history and its process" that Marx now concluded that, *historically-materialistically* speaking, a new stage of production, far from being a mere change in *property-form*, be it "West" or "East," was such a change in *production-relations* that it disclosed, in embryo, the dialectics of actual revolution.

What Marx, in the *Grundrisse*. had defined as "the absolute movement of becoming" had matured in the last decade of his life as new moments—a multilinear view of human development as well as a *dialectic duality within each* formation. From within each formation evolved *both* the end of the old *and* the beginning of the new. Whether Marx was studying the communal or the despotic form of property, it was the human resistance of the Subject that revealed the direction of resolving the contradictions. Marx transformed what, to Hegel, was the synthesis of the "Self-Thinking Idea" and the "Self-Bringing Forth of Liberty" as the emergence of a new society. The many paths to get there were left open.

As against Marx's multilinear view which kept Marx from attempting any blueprint for future generations, Engels' unilinear view led him to mechanical positivism. By no accident whatever, such one-dimensionality kept him from seeing either the communal form under "Oriental despotism" or the duality in "primitive communism" in Morgan's *Ancient Society*. No wonder, although Engels had accepted Marx's view of the Asiatic mode of production as fundamental enough to constitute a fourth form of human development, he had left it out altogether from *his* analysis of primitive communism in the first book he wrote as a "bequest" of Marx—*Origin of the Family*. By then Engels had confined Marx's revolutionary dialectics and historical materialism to hardly more than Morgan's "materialism."

3. On the question of the Black dimension as it flows from the view (p. 194) of how Marx was returning to his first discovery of a new continent of thought, on the one hand, and on the other was developing anew his concept of "revolution in permanence":

With this dialectical circle of circles, Marx's reference in the *Ethnological Notebooks* to the Australian aborigine* as "the intelligent black" brought to a conclusion the dialectic he had unchained when he first broke from bourgeois society in the 1840s and objected to the use of the word, "Negro," as if it were synonymous with the word, "slave." By the 1850s, in the *Grundrisse*, he extended that sensitivity to the whole pre-capitalist world. By the 1860s, the Black dimension became, at one and the same time, not only pivotal to the abolition of slavery and victory of the North in the Civil War, but also to the restructuring of *Capital*, itself. In a word, the often quoted sentence: "Labor cannot emancipate itself in the white skin where in the black skin it is branded," far from being rhetoric, was the actual reality *and* the perspective for overcoming that reality. Marx reached, at every historic turning point, for a concluding point, *not* as an end but as a new jumping off point, a new beginning, a new vision.

4. The persistence of the questions on philosophy ran throughout the whole book. Indeed, I felt that the question that was asked regarding p. 45, on Marx's and Luxemburg's theories of Accumulation, had less to do with that subject than with the question of methodology, specifically the difference between Hegel's *Phenomenology* and his *Philosophy of Mind*:

While it is true that in the *Phenomenology* we speak not just of appearance, much less of mere show, but of a *philosophy* of appearance, it is not true that the methodology, as we follow the movement of the dialectic in *Philosophy of Mind*, is either the philosophy of phenomena or even of essence. Rather, the dialectic in the Notion is that the Absolute there opens so many new doors in both the objective and subjective spheres as to reveal totality itself as new beginning.

Thus, as against the phenomenology of imperialism being merely a reflection of new surfacings of oppression, new appearances surface as so profound a philosophy of revolution as to disclose that what inheres in it is a living Subject that will resolve the great contradiction of its absolute opposites, imperialism and national oppression. It is this which Marxist-Humanists call the new revolutionary forces as Reason. Therein is the nub of the Great Divide between *Phenomenology* and *Philoso-*

---

*A new book on the aborigines, edited by a woman and concentrating on the aboriginal women, has just appeared. See Fay Gale, *We Are Bosses Ourselves, The Status and Role of Aboriginal Women Today—Borroloola Women Speak* (Canberra: Australian Institute of Aboriginal Studies, 1983), distributed by Humanities Press.

phy—and because it is no abstraction, but a live Subject, it unites rather than divides theory and reality.

5. Finally, my main point—the challenge to non-Marxists as well as post-Marx Marxists about the missing link of philosophy in the theories of revolution, Women's Liberation, new forms of organization—raised a question about p. 195. I rearticulated that it wasn't a question of who was "smarter":

This generation can see so much further because: 1) While previous generations rested on a truncated Marxism, ours can see Marxism *as a totality*. No doubt there will continue to be other finds to dispute whether we really have Marxism "as a totality" even now. Witness the publication of *The Mathematical Manuscripts of Karl Marx* in 1983 (London: New Park Publications).* Nevertheless, we do have, in essence, the new moments of Marx's last decade.

And, 2) The maturity of our age and the totality of its crises produced new forces of revolution—woman, Black, peasant, youth, indeed the emergence of a whole Third World. This is what has led non-Marxists as well as Marxists to dig into the relationship of philosophy to reality in general, and to new forms of organization in particular. No other generation could have had the problematic of our age or solve our problems. Only live human beings can recreate the revolutionary dialectic forever anew. It is our generation that experienced the need for measuring up to "revolution in permanence." It is our generation that has suffered through so many transformations into opposite and new tyrannies even after the old was overthrown and power won. It is to our generation that what happens "the day after" became so urgent. It is not a question of asking for a blueprint. It is the imperativeness for a philosophy that has as its goal not only the overthrow of the old system, but creation of the new that would be truly a classless, non-racist, non-sexist society of new human relations.

The search for new forms of organization flowed from rejecting the "party-to-lead" but finding that the committee form which replaced that elitist concept was not the whole answer. It was true that the committee form and the "party-to-lead" were opposites; however, they were not absolute opposites. A new relationship of practice to theory

---

*For a discussion of "Marx's Mathematical Manuscripts vs. 'Computer Consciousness,'" see "The Fetish of High Tech" by Ron Brokmeyer, including the discussion by Franklin Dmitryev, myself and others around it (Chicago: News & Letters, 1984).

demanded also that no single force of revolution tower above the others; all new forces of revolution had to be synthesized on the day after as well as the day of revolution.

It is true that new paths to freedom are not easy to work out; each generation has to do it for itself. Doing it cannot be achieved without a philosophy of revolution as well as the actuality of the revolution itself. That little phrase of Marx—"revolution in permanence"—points to the only philosophy which can assure that the revolution will not stop when power is won, but will continue into the kind of self-development in which the individual freedom and the universal freedom are one; indeed, will continue until the division between mental and manual labor is once and for all abolished. It is this Promethean vision of Marx that transformed Hegel's abstract category of "the self-thinking Idea" into the concrete masses in motion who were "making" the revolution not only as force but as Reason. It is this and this alone which paves the way for the development of an "Individualism that lets nothing interfere with its universalism, i.e. freedom." This is the reason why Marx, instead of isolating organization in a separate realm, created that philosophy of revolution as ground also for organization. It is this challenge which post-Marx Marxists have not met.

Selected Bibliography of Works Cited

Albers, Patricia and Beatrice Medicine, eds., *The Hidden Half: Studies of Plains Indian Women* (Washington, D.C.: University Press of America, 1983).

Althusser, Louis, *Reading Capital* (London: New Left Books, 1970).

Anderson, Kevin, "The 'Unknown' Marx's *Capital*, Volume I: The French Edition of 1872–75, 100 Years Later," *Review of Radical Political Economics*, 15:4 (1983).

Barreno, Maria Isabel, "Maria Barreno Speaks for Herself," *News & Letters*, April 1975.

─────, Maria Teresa Horta, and Maria Velho da Costa, *The Three Marias: New Portuguese Letters* (New York: Doubleday, 1975).

Blackstock, Paul W. and Bert F. Hoselitz, eds., *The Russian Menace to Europe* (Glencoe, Illinois: Free Press, 1952).

Brokmeyer, Ron, Franklin Dmitryev, Raya Dunayevskaya et al., *The Fetish of High Tech and Karl Marx's Unknown Mathematical Manuscripts* (Chicago: News & Letters, 1985).

Bukharin, Nikolai, *Economics of the Transition Period* (New York: Bergman, 1971).

Cabral, Amilcar, *Return to the Source: Selected Speeches of Amilcar Cabral* (New York: Monthly Review Press, 1973).

Cade, Toni, ed., *The Black Woman* (New York: New American Library, 1970).

Chaliand, Gérard, *Revolution in the Third World: Myths and Prospects* (New York: Viking Press, 1977).

Davis, Angela Y., *If They Come in the Morning* (New York: Joseph Okpaku, 1971).

de Beauvoir, Simone, *The Second Sex* (New York: Alfred A. Knopf, 1953).

Denby, Charles, ed., *Workers Battle Automation* (Detroit: News & Letters, 1960).

Domanski, Olga, "Women's Liberation in Search of a Theory," *News & Letters*, June 1980.

Draper, Hal, *Karl Marx's Theory of Revolution* (New York: Monthly Review Press, 1977).

Dunayevskaya, Raya, *American Civilization on Trial: Black Masses as Vanguard*, with Appendix by Charles Denby, 4th edition (Detroit: News & Letters, 1983).

_____, "Ghana: Out of Colonization, into the Fire," *Africa Today*, December 1962.

_____, "Hegel's Absolute Idea as New Beginning," in *Art and Logic in Hegel's Philosophy*, Warren Steinkraus and Kenneth Schmitz, eds. (New Jersey: Humanities Press, 1980).

_____, "In the Gambia during elections ... It's a long, hard road to independence," *Africa Today*, July 1962.

_____, *Iran: Revolution and Counter-Revolution (A Collection of Political-Philosophic Letters)* (Detroit: News & Letters, 1981). Translated by Iranian revolutionaries and published in Persian (Farsi), 1982.

_____, *Marxism and Freedom ... from 1776 to Today* (New York: Bookman, 1958). Contains first English translation of Marx's early essays and of Lenin's *Abstract of Hegel's Science of Logic*; 2nd edition (New York: Twayne, 1964) contains new chapter, "The Challenge of Mao Tse-tung"; 3rd edition (London: Pluto Press, 1971) has new chapter, "Cultural Revolution or Maoist Reaction?"; 5th edition (Humanities Press and Harvester Press, 1982) contains new Introduction by author. International editions: Italian (Florence: La Nuova Italia, 1962); Japanese (Tokyo: Modern Thought, 1964); French (Paris: Champ Libre, 1971); Spanish (Mexico, D.F: Juan Pablos, 1976).

_____, *Marx's Capital and Today's Global Crisis*, (Detroit: News & Letters, 1978).

_____, "Marx's 'New Humanism' and the Dialectics of Women's Liberation in Primitive and Modern Societies," *Praxis International*, January 1984.

_____, *Nationalism, Communism, Marxist-Humanism and the Afro-Asian Revolutions* (London: Cambridge University Labour Club, Left Group, 1961); expanded edition (Chicago: News & Letters, 1984).

_____, *New Essays* (Detroit: News & Letters, 1977). Includes "Post-Mao China: What Now?"; "Dialectics of Liberation in Thought and in Activity"; "Leon Trotsky as Man and as Theoretician."

_____, "A New Revision of Marxian Economics," *American Economic Review*, September 1944.

_____, *Philosophy and Revolution: from Hegel to Sartre and from Marx to*

Mao (New York: Dell, 1973); 2nd edition (Humanities Press and Harvester Press, 1982), contains new Introduction by author. International editions: Spanish (Mexico, D.F.: Siglo Veintiuno, 1977); Italian (Milan: Feltrinelli, 1977); German (Vienna: Europa Verlag, 1981).

_____, "Poland: Counter-revolution drives the revolution underground; the resistance continues," *News & Letters*, January-February 1982.

_____, *The Political-Philosophic Letters of Raya Dunayevskaya*, 2 vols. (Detroit: News & Letters, 1977, vol. 1; 1980, vol. 2).

_____, *The Raya Dunayevskaya Collection: Marxist-Humanism, Its Origin and Development in the U.S., 1941 to Today* (Detroit: Wayne State University Archives of Labor History and Urban Affairs, 1981. Available on microfilm. New vol., 1981–1985, forthcoming.

_____, *Rosa Luxemburg, Women's Liberation, and Marx's Philosophy of Revolution* (New Jersey: Humanities Press and Sussex: Harvester Press, 1982).

_____, *Sexism, Politics and Revolution in Mao's China* (Detroit: Women's Liberation-News & Letters, 1977).

_____, "Socialismes africains et problèmes nègres," *Présence Africaine*, #48, Paris, 1963.

Engels, Frederick, *Herr Eugen Dühring's Revolution in Science (Anti-Dühring)* (Chicago: Charles H. Kerr, 1935; New York: International Publishers, 1966).

_____, *The Origin of the Family, Private Property and the State* (New York: International Publishers, 1942); published in 1972, 1975 with a new Introduction by Eleanor Burke Leacock.

Firth, Raymond, "The Sceptical Anthropologist? Social Anthropology and Marxist Views on Society," in *Marxist Analyses and Social Anthropology* (London: Malaby Press, 1975).

Gale, Fay, ed., *We Are Bosses Ourselves: The Status and Role of Aboriginal Women Today* (Canberra: Australian Institute of Aboriginal Studies, 1983).

Gould, Carol C. and Marx W. Wartofsky, eds., *Women and Philosophy: Toward a Theory of Liberation* (New York: Putnam, 1976).

Gramsci, Antonio, *Selections from the Prison Notebooks* (New York: International Publishers, 1971).

Halliday, Fred, *Arabia Without Sultans* (Middlesex, England: Penguin Books, 1974).

_____, *Iran: Dictatorship and Development* (Middlesex, England: Penguin Books, 1979).

Hamilton, Mary, Louise Inghram et al., *Freedom Riders Speak for Themselves* (Detroit: News & Letters, 1961).

Harding, Timothy F., "Dependency Theory and Dimensions of Imperialism," *Latin American Perspectives*, Fall 1976.

Hegel, G.W.F., *Phenomenology of Spirit*, trans. by A.V. Miller (Oxford: Oxford University Press, 1977); trans. by J.B. Baillie (London and New York: Macmillan, 1931).

—————, *Philosophy of Mind*, trans. by William Wallace; *Zusatze* trans. by A.V. Miller (Oxford: Clarendon Press, 1971).

—————, *Science of Logic*, 2 vols., trans. by W.H. Johnston and L.G. Struthers (New York: Macmillan, 1951). See also new translation by A.V. Miller (London: Allen and Unwin, 1969; New York: Humanities Press, 1969).

Lenin, V.I., *Collected Works*, vols. 1–45 (Moscow: Foreign Languages Publishing House, 1960, vol. 1; 1970, vol. 45).

Luxemburg, Rosa, *Accumulation of Capital* (London: Routledge & Kegan Paul, Ltd., 1951; New York: Monthly Review Press, 1968).

—————, *Reform or Revolution* (New York: Three Arrows Press, 1937; New York: Pathfinder Press, 1973).

—————, *Rosa Luxemburg Speaks*, ed. by Mary-Alice Waters (New York: Pathfinder Press, 1970).

—————, *Selected Political Writings of Rosa Luxemburg*, ed. by Dick Howard (New York: Monthly Review Press, 1971).

Lerner, Gerda, *The Majority Finds Its Past* (Oxford: Oxford University Press, 1979).

Leys, Simon, "China's Fallen Empress," *New Republic*, June 25, 1977.

Mamonova, Tatyana, ed., *Women and Russia* (Boston: Beacon Press, 1984).

Mao Tse-tung, *Miscellany of Mao Tse-tung Thought* (1949–1968), Part I (Springfield, Virginia: NTIS, U.S. Dept. of Commerce, 1974).

Marcuse, Herbert, *Studies in Critical Philosophy* (London: New Left Books, 1972).

Marx, Karl, *Karl Marx—Frederick Engels, Collected Works*, vols. 1–14, 16–19, 38–40, incomplete (New York: International Publishers, 1975–).

—————, *Karl Marx and Frederick Engels, Selected Works*, 3 vols. (Moscow: Progress Publishers, 1978).

—————, *The American Journalism of Marx and Engels*, ed. by Henry Christman (New York: New American Library, 1966).

—————, *Capital*, 3 vols., Moore-Aveling trans. vol. 1; Untermann, vols. 2, 3 (Chicago: Charles H. Kerr, 1909). New translation of vol.

1 by Ben Fowkes, which re-established Marx's philosophic language was published in 1976 (Middlesex: Penguin Books, and New York: Vintage Books, 1977); vols. 2, 3 trans. by David Fernbach published by Penguin in 1978, 1981.

_____, *A Contribution to the Critique of Political Economy*, trans. by N.I. Stone (Chicago: Charles H. Kerr, 1904).

_____, and Friedrich Engels, *Correspondence*, 1846–1895 (New York: International Publishers, 1934). New revised edition (Moscow: Progress Publishers, 1975).

_____, *Critique of the Gotha Program* (New York: International Publishers, 1966).

_____, *Economic-Philosophic Manuscripts, 1844*, trans. and ed. by Raya Dunayevskaya as Appendix to *Marxism and Freedom* (New York: Bookman, 1958). See also trans. by Martin Milligan (London: Lawrence and Wishart, 1959); trans. by T.B. Bottomore in *Marx's Concept of Man* by Erich Fromm, 2nd ed. (New York: Frederick Ungar, 1963); and the Easton and Guddat trans. in *The Writings of the Young Marx on Philosophy and Society* (New York: Doubleday, 1967).

_____, *The Ethnological Notebooks of Karl Marx*, transcribed and with an Introduction by Lawrence Krader (Assen: Van Gorcum, 1972).

_____, and Friedrich Engels, *The German Ideology* (Moscow: Progress Publishers, 1964; New York: International Publishers, 1972).

_____, *Grundrisse*, trans. with Foreword by Martin Nicolaus (London: Penguin Books, 1973; New York: Vintage Books, 1973).

_____, and Friedrich Engels, *The Holy Family* (Moscow: Foreign Languages Publishing House, 1956).

_____, "Imprisonment of Lady Bulwer-Lytton," in *The Karl Marx Library, Vol. VI: On Education, Women, and Children*, ed. by Saul K. Padover (New York: McGraw-Hill, 1975).

_____, *The Mathematical Manuscripts of Karl Marx* (London: New Park Publications, 1983). For the first American discussion of these manuscripts see *The Fetish of High Tech and Karl Marx's Unknown Mathematical Manuscripts* by Brokmeyer et al. (Chicago: News & Letters, 1984), above.

_____, "Notebooks on Kovalevsky," Appendix to Lawrence Krader's *The Asiatic Mode of Production* (Assen: Van Gorcum, 1975).

_____, *Pre-Capitalist Economic Formations* (excerpted from *Grundrisse*), ed. by Eric Hobsbawm, trans. by Jack Cohen (London: Lawrence and Wishart, 1964).

_____, *Theories of Surplus-Value*, 3 vols. (Moscow: Progress Publishers, 1963, vol. 1; 1968, vol. 2; 1971, vol. 3).

_____, and Friedrich Engels, *Writings on the Paris Commune*, ed. by Hal Draper (New York: Monthly Review Press, 1971).

Maupin, Joyce, *Labor Heroines* (Berkeley: Union Wage, 1974).

_____, *Working Women and Their Organizations* (Berkeley: Union Wage, 1974).

Melville, Herman, *Pierre* (Evanston: Harcourt Brace, 1971).

Mondlane, Eduardo, *The Struggle for Mozambique* (Baltimore: Penguin Books, 1969).

Moon, Terry, "Eleanor Marx in Chicago", *News & Letters*, March 1984.

Morgan, Lewis Henry, *Ancient Society* (Chicago: Charles H. Kerr, 1907).

Moriarty, Claire, "On Women's Liberation," *New Politics*, Spring 1970.

News & Letters, a Marxist-Humanist journal, available in 4 bound volumes (June 1955-July 1962; January 1962-July 1970; August 1970-July 1977; August 1977-May 1984) from News & Letters, 59 E. Van Buren, Chicago, Illinois 60605. Available on microfilm from University Microfilms International, Ann Arbor, Michigan 48106.

Notes on Women's Liberation: We Speak in Many Voices (Detroit: News & Letters, 1970).

Padover, Saul K., *Karl Marx: An Intimate Biography* (New York: McGraw-Hill, 1978).

Phillips, Andy and Raya Dunayevskaya, *A 1980s View: The Coal Miners' General Strike of 1949-50 and the Birth of Marxist-Humanism* (Chicago: News & Letters, 1984).

Portugal: A Blaze of Freedom, Birmingham, England: Big Flame Publications, 1975.

Portugal: Key Documents of the Revolutionary Process, Berkeley: People's Translation Service, 1975.

Reed, Evelyn, *Woman's Evolution* (New York: Pathfinder Press, 1975).

Rowbotham, Sheila, *Women, Resistance and Revolution* (New York: Vintage Books, 1974).

_____, *Women's Liberation and Revolution* (Bristol, England: Falling Wall Press, 1972; expanded ed. 1973).

Sartre, Jean-Paul, *What Is Literature?*, trans. Bernard Frechtman (New York: Washington Square, 1966).

The 70s, ed., *The Revolution Is Dead, Long Live the Revolution: Readings on*

the Great Proletarian Cultural Revolution from an Ultra-Left Perspective (Hong Kong: The 70s, 1976).
The 70s Front, ed., *Peking Spring* (Hong Kong: The 70s Front, 1979).
Shuster, W. Morgan, *The Strangling of Persia (A Personal Narrative)* (1912: reprint ed., New York: Greenwood Press, 1968).
Spector, Ivar, *The First Russian Revolution: Its Impact on Asia* (Englewood Cliffs, N.J.: Prentice-Hall, 1962).
Terrano, Angela, Marie Dignan and Mary Holmes, *Working Women for Freedom* (Detroit: Women's Liberation – News & Letters, 1976).
Thomas, Edith, *The Women Incendiaries* (New York: George Braziller, 1966).
Ting Ling, "Thoughts on the Eighth of March," in *Ting Ling, Purged Feminist* (Tokyo: Femintern Press, 1974).
Trotsky, Natalia, "Natalia Trotsky Denounces Khrushchev, Mao Tse-tung" (letter), *News & Letters*, January 1962.
Vitkin, Mikhail, "The Asiatic Mode of Production," *Philosophy and Social Criticism*, 8 (1) 1981.
_____, "Marx Between West and East," *Studies in Soviet Thought*, 23 (1982).
_____, "The Problem of the Universality of Social Relations in Classical Marxism," *Studies in Soviet Thought*, 20 (1979).
Weaver, Fredrick S., "Capitalist Development, Empire and Latin American Underdevelopment: An Interpretive Essay On Historical Change," *Latin American Perspectives*, Fall 1976.
Wislanka, Urszula, ed. and trans., *Today's Polish Fight for Freedom* (Detroit: News & Letters, 1980).
Witke, Roxane, *Comrade Chiang Ch'ing* (Boston: Little, Brown, 1977).
_____, "Report from China," *China Quarterly*, December 1975.

Addendum

Note: Since Raya Dunayevskaya's death in 1987 all the works of her "trilogy of revolution" have been published in new, expanded editions, and several new translations of her major works have appeared, as have a number of her writings never before published. These include:

Marxism and Freedom . . . from 1776 until Today (New York: Columbia University Press, 1988). Includes new material by the author.

Philosophy and Revolution: from Hegel to Sartre and from Marx to Mao (New York: Columbia University Press, 1989). Includes new material by the author and Prefaces by Erich Fromm and Louis Dupré. A Russian translation of the work was published in Samara, 1993; a Slovak translation was published in Bratislava in 1996.

Rosa Luxemburg, Women's Liberation, and Marx's Philosophy of Revolution (Urbana: University of Illinois Press, 1991). Includes Foreword by Adrienne Rich and new material by the author.

All of the trilogy as well as *Women's Liberation and the Dialectics of Revolution* are now in print in Spanish translation and are available from their Mexican publishers through the Raya Dunayevskaya Memorial Fund, 59 E. Van Buren, Chicago, IL 60605.

The Philosophic Moment of Marxist-Humanism—two historic-philosophic writings by Raya Dunayevskaya (Chicago: News and Letters, 1989).

The Marxist-Humanist Theory of State-Capitalism—Selected Writings by Raya Dunayevskaya (Chicago: News and Letters, 1992).

Among recent works which include significant discussions of Dunayevskaya's work are:

Alexander, Robert, *International Trotskyism* (Durham: Duke University Press, 1991).

Anderson, Kevin, *Lenin, Hegel, and Western Marxism* (Urbana: University of Illinois Press, 1995).

Beilharz, Peter, *Trotsky, Trotskyism and the Transition to Socialism* (London: Croom Helm, 1987).

Easton, Susan, "Raya Dunayevskaya, 1910–1987," *Bulletin of the Hegel Society of Great Britain*, No. 16, Autumn-Winter 1987.

Haug, Frigga, *Beyond Female Masochism: Memory-Work and Politics* (New York: Verso, 1992).

Historical Encyclopedia of Chicago Women (Indiana University Press, forthcoming in 1997).

Ito, Narihiko, "Raya Dunayevskaya on Rosa Luxemburg," *Gekkan Forum*, May 1992. In Japanese.

Johnson, Patricia Altenbernd, "Women's Liberation: Following Dunayevskaya in Practicing Dialectics," *Quarterly Journal of Ideology*, 1989.

Kellner, Douglas, "Raya Dunayevskaya," *Encyclopedia of the American Left* (Urbana: University of Illinois Press, 1992).

Linden, Marcel van der, *Von der Oktoberrevolution zur Perestroika: Der westliche Marxismus und die Sowjetunion* (From the October Revolution to Perestroike: Western Marxism and the Soviet Union), Frankfurt, dipa-Verlag, 1992.

Portales, Gonzalo, "Raya Dunayevskaya: A Humanist Tradition of Marxism in America," *Hegel-Studien*, Bonn, 1990. In German.

Randall, Margaret, *Gathering Rage: The Failure of 20th Century Revolutions to Develop a Feminist Agenda* (New York: Monthly Review Press, 1992).

Rich, Adrienne, *What is Found There, Notebooks on Poetry and Politics* (New York: W. W. Norton & Co., 1993).

Index

A

Abolitionism see Anti-slavery
Absolute(s) (see also Dialectic; Hegel; Marx), 186, 263, 269–270
  Idea, 263–264
  Idea as new beginning, 263, 269
  Method, 6, 15, 257, 262–263
  movement of becoming, 10, 28, 54, 116, 182–186, 192, 199, 203, 221, 268
  Substance, 184
Abstract see Concrete
Accumulation of capital see Marx
Afghanistan, 238
Africa (see also Algeria; Angola; Dunayevskaya; Egypt; Eritrea; Ethiopia; Gambia; Guinea-Bissau; Liberia; Morocco; Mozambique; Namibia; Revolution; Self-determination; South Africa; Women), 2, 86, 145, 165
  Portuguese Revolution, and, 8, 86, 89 (n. 9), 127–129, 259
  Black America, "two-way road" to, 36, 43, 166, 248
  African National Congress see South Africa
African students in China, 145
Agriculture (see also Peasantry), 129–130, 190, 199, 210, 213, 218, 220
Albers, Patricia, 202
Alienation (see also Marx), 141, 191, 232
ALIMUPER (Peruvian Feminists), 163, 173–174
Algeria, 59, 61, 202, 264
Althusser, Louis, 96, 187
Amazons, 50, 57, 260–261
Anarchism, 82
Ancient Society see Morgan
Anderson, Judith, 20
Anderson, Kevin, 204 (n. 9)
Angola, 86, 89 (n. 9), 127, 132 (n. 1), 152, 259–260
Anjumans (Iranian soviets), 56, 65, 67, 235

Anthony, Susan B., 16 (n. 2), 22, 46, 161
Anthropology (see also Marx (works) *Ethnological Notebooks*), 58–59, 190, 193, 199, 202–203, 208, 214–215, 219, 220–222, 223 (n. 6), 225 (n. 31), 231–233
Anti-imperialist movements see Imperialism
Anti-slavery movement (see also slavery; women), 2, 21–22, 31, 33, 35–38, 45, 93, 105, 107, 185, 269
  Britain, in, 21, 37
Anti-war movements (see also Women; Youth), 56–57, 84, 89 (n. 9), 122–123, 260
  Vietnam War, 3, 47–48, 87, 121, 259
Apartidarismo see Organization
Aptheker, Herbert, 94
Arafat, Yasir, 65, 69 (n. 1)
Archives see Marx; Wayne State University
Argentina, 163, 165–166, 167 (n. 8), 167–172
Aristotle, 214
Asia (see also Afghanistan; Bangladesh; Burma; Cambodia; China; Hong Kong; India; Indonesia; Japan; Marx; Pakistan; Philippines; Revolution, Iran; Vietnam; Women, Iran), 184, 193
Asiatic mode of production see Marx
Australia (see also Black Dimension), 61, 264
Automation (see also Miners, coal), 1, 92, 104, 123, 124, 169, 197
  "Computer consciousness", 270
  Robotics, 197
Autoworkers, 124–125
  support of miners' strike, 30

B

Bachofen, Johann, 233, 242
"Backward lands", relation to "advanced" countries (see also Marx,

Backward Lands (*continued*)
"revolution in permanence"), 1, 12, 14, 59, 89 (n. 9), 96, 184–185, 190, 221, 240, 247, 264–265
Bangladesh, 155
Barreno, Maria Isabel, 89 (n. 8), 97, 132, (n. 4), 253
Bates, Daisy, 94, 106
Bazargan, Mehdi, 65–66, 69, 69 (n. 3)
Bebel, August, 4, 216
Beethoven, Ludwig von, 100
Bell, Daniel, 242
Bernstein, Eduard, 83, 99, 251
Black Dimension (see also Africa; Antislavery; Marx; Reason; Third World; Women), 2, 26, 46, 87, 121, 169, 174, 187, 248, 262, 270
  Australia, in, 61, 264, 269
  Civil Rights Movement (USA), 3, 47, 51, 87, 121
  Freedom Rides, 3–4, 16 (n. 3), 44, 169
  Harlem Renaissance, 98
  Marxism in U.S., in, 35, 46–47,
  Montgomery, Ala. Bus Boycott (1955–56), 2, 46–47, 51
  Niagara movement, 94
  white workers, relation to, 24–25, 32, 93, 269
Black women, 3–4, 24–25, 37, 49–51, 60, 80, 93–95, 97, 98, 105–106, 111, 113, 161, 185–186, 252, 260, 262
  Australia, in, 269
  Black male leaders, critique of, 3, 47, 50, 93–94, 106, 114
  "Woman Power Unlimited", 3–4
Blake, William, 97
Blow, Susan E., 242
Bolsheviks (see also Lenin; Organization; Trotsky; Zhenotdel), 5, 35, 76, 82–83, 85, 89 (n. 9), 99, 170
Bonaparte, Rosa Muki, 55, 260
Bortnowska, Halina, 135
Bottomore, T.B., 192
Brazil, 167 (n.8)
Britain (see also Anti-slavery; Imperialism), 92, 216
Brokmeyer, Ron, 270
Bronte, Emily, 97
Brooks, Gwendolyn, 98
Brown, John, 38, 194
Browne, Edward G., 69 (n. 4)
Bukharin, Nikolai, 133 (n. 9), 170
Bulwer-Lytton, Lady Rosina, 194
Burma, 113

C

Cabral, Amilcar, 89 (n. 9), 128, 172 (n. 1)
Cade, Toni, 106, 117 (n. 6)
Caetano, Marcello, 87, 130
Cambodia, 155
Capital (see also Automation; Labor; Marx, accumulation; Marx (works) *Capital*)
  concentration and centralization of, 200
  constant (dead labor, machinery), 59, 186, 198, 201
  preponderance of constant over variable, 59, 198
  variable (living labor), 186
Carmichael, Stokely, 47, 114
Carter, Rosalynn, 160
Caste (see also Gens), 214
Castro, Fidel, 111–113, 117 (n. 4), 164, 167, (n. 1, 6)
Chaliand, Gérard, 164–165
Chartists, 194
Chen Boda (Chen Po-ta), 157 (n. 1)
Chiang Kai-shek, 72, 151
Chiefs and ranks (see also Gens), 50, 58–59, 80, 94, 213–215, 219, 225 (n. 27), 253
Children see Labor; Women
Chile, 127, 167 (n. 8)
China (see also Dunayevskaya; Mao Zedong; Marx, Asiatic mode; Peasantry; Revolution; Women; Youth), 2, 9, 72, 166, 185, 218, 238
  Communist Party of, 142, 144, 152–153, 154 (n. 5)
  "Cultural Revolution" in, 8, 16, (n. 8), 134 (n. 5), 150–152, 155–156, 157, (n. 1, 4), 166
  "Gang of Four", 149, 153, 154–157, 253
  Great Leap Forward, 142–145
  Hundred Flowers campaign, 142–144, 154 (n. 4)
  May 4 (1919) Movement, 141
  People's Liberation Army, 151–152, 157 (n. 1)
  Sino-Soviet conflict, 145–146, 150, 152, 156, 164
  state-capitalist society, as, 111, 146, 153
  U.S. imperialism, and, 151–152, 155–156
Chou En-lai (Zhou Enlai), 152, 155–157
Chou Yang (Zhou Yang), 151
Chudaszek, Andrzej, 135
Churchill, Winston, 157
Civil Rights Movement see Black Dimension

Index

Civil War (USA), 38, 45, 49, 81, 93, 116, 170, 195, 203, 269
Class struggles see Labor; Women
Classical political economy see Marx
Coalition of Labor Union Women (CLUW), 92, 102
Cohn-Bendit, Daniel, 48
Collins, Margery, 108 (n. 3)
Colonialism see Imperialism; Marx
Commodity (see also Marx, fetishism), 186–187, 195–196, 218
Communism see Marx, vulgar communism; State-capitalism
Communist Manifesto see Marx
Communist Party of China see China
Communist Party of Japan see Japan
Communist Party of Russia see Russia
Communist Party of Germany (KPD), 85, 243, 252
Concrete, abstract and, 199, 224 (n. 23), 264, 271
Congress of Industrial Organizations (CIO), 96, 124
Connolly, James, 247
Connor, Eugene "Bull", 47
Consciousness see Dialectic
Contradiction see Dialectic
Counter-revolution, 89, 92, 96, 101–102, 127, 131, 139 (n. 1), 160–161, 217–218, 235, 237, 257, 260
Country and city, historic division between, 211
Critique see Marx
Cuba (see also Revolution; Women), 9
  Africa, relationship to, 164–166, 167 (n. 2)
  Russia, relationship to, 164–165
"Cultural Revolution" see China
Czechoslovakia, 111

D

da Costa, Maria Velho, 89 (n. 8)
Darwin, Charles, 214
Davenport, Katherine, 9, 179,
Davidson, Basil, 132 (n. 1)
Davis, Angela, 111
de Beauvoir, Simone, 26, 95–97, 99, 101, 103–104, 108, 108 (n. 1, 3), 186, 191–192, 223 (n. 15), 249
Debray, Régis, 112–113, 117 (n. 4), 167 (n. 6)
Democritus, 254, 263

Denby, Charles, 123
Deng Xiaoping (Teng Hsiao-ping), 152–153, 156–157
Dependency theory see Latin America
Depression (1929), 11, 80
Deroin, Jeanne, 107
Dewey, John, 75
Dialectic (see also Absolute; Hegel; Marx; Philosophy), 6, 14–15, 27, 116, 270
  appearance, 186, 269
  Cognition, Idea of, 14
  consciousness, 6, 14, 27, 98
  contradiction, 6, 14, 258, 268
  Essence, 13, 186, 269
  Engels, in, 215, 219, 225 (n. 33), 267–268
  Hegel, in, 14, 27, 170, 183–184, 237, 239, 242, 264, 268–269
  Lenin, in, 14, 132, 170, 246–247, 253
  Life, 13–14
  Luxemburg, in, 83, 239–241, 245–246, 253
  Marx, in, 14–15, 116, 170, 183–185, 195, 200, 214–215, 219, 239, 246, 248, 253, 263, 267–269
  mediation, 6, 25
  "negation of the negation", 10, 51, 81, 100, 116
  Notion, 14, 269
  revolution/liberation, of, 6, 13, 15, 45, 48, 116, 166, 184, 240, 251, 268, 271
  subjectivity/objectivity, 6, 20, 264, 269
  totality, 258, 264, 269–270
  transcendence in, 25, 232, 263
  transformation into opposite, 57, 132, 270
  unchained, 14–15
Diamond, Stanley, 202
Diefenbach, Hans, 227
Ding Ling (Ting Ling), 149, 151, 154 (n. 4), 235, 253
Dixon, Marlene, 125
Dmitrieva, Elizabeth, 82, 95, 199, 217
do Carmo, Isabel, 8, 15, 87, 194, 253
Domanski, Olga, 5, 91–109
Douglass, Frederick, 21, 33, 38, 49–50, 81, 93, 106
Draper, Hal, 209, 211–213, 215–217, 222, 223 (n. 9, 10), 224 (n. 16, 17, 20, 26), 231–233, 240, 253
DuBois, W.E.B., 93–94
Duda-Gwiazda, Joanna, 135–136
Dunayevskaya, Raya, 19, 27, 31, 107–108, 109 (n. 7), 232, 262

Dunayevskaya, Raya (*continued*)
  Africa, trip to, 43–44, 168
  Chinese refugees, discussions with, 141–147
  Frondizi, Silvio, correspondence with, 8, 166–172
  Japan, trip to, 7, 121–126, 126 (n. 2)
  law of value, analysis of revision of, 75, 77 (n. 4), 123
  Marx centenary lecture tour, 13, 15, 53, 267–271
  Mexico, trip to, 172–173
  miners' general strike, work with, 16 (n. 1), 29–30
  process of writing a book, on, 13, 91–92, 169–170, 172, 207, 227–271
  translation of Marx's *Humanist Essays*, 28 (n. 3), 192, 241–242
  Trotsky, work with, 72–75, 255
Dunbar, Ethel, 24

E

East German workers' revolt (1953), 1, 166, 169
East European revolts (see also Czechoslovakia; East Germany; Poland; Revolution, Hungary), 2, 57, 61, 86, 166, 265
Easton, Loyd, 192
East Timor, 55, 260
Ebert, Friedrich, 251
Economic crisis (1857), 203, 254
Economic crisis (1929) see Depression
Economic crisis (1974–75), 88, 129, 259
Education, 3, 9, 61, 194, 263
  bureaucracy in, 193
  "flying university" (Poland), 137
  Freedom schools (U.S. Civil Rights Movement), 3, 47
  Free Speech Movement (1964), 3, 47, 121, 123
Egypt, 69 (n. 2)
Einstein, Albert, 180
Eisenhower, Dwight, 125
Engels, Friedrich (see also Dialectic), 11, 186, 203 (n. 1), 210, 224 (n. 24), 240, 258, 267
  editor of *Capital*, as, 57, 199–201, 204 (n. 10), 254, 258, 267
  human development, view of, 12, 15, 58–59, 201, 215, 249, 268
  primitive communism, on, 28 (n. 1), 58, 189, 199–200, 202, 214–215, 217–219, 229, 249, 268
  women, on, 11, 28, (n. 1), 58, 189, 200–201, 212–213, 215–220, 223 (n. 6), 224 (n. 20), 229–231, 233, 248, 258, 268
Engels, Friedrich (works)
  Anti-Dühring, 211
  Origin of Family, Private Property and the State, 11–12, 57–60, 189, 200–201, 208–209, 213–215, 218–219, 221–222, 223 (n. 5), 224 (n. 20), 229, 231, 241, 248, 255, 258, 268
Epicurus, 254, 263
Equal Rights Amendment (ERA) see Women
Eritrea, 9, 163–164
Essence see Dialectic
Ethiopia, 164, 166, 167 (n. 2)
Ethnological Notebooks see Marx (works)
Eufemia, Caterina, 86, 130
Eurocommunism, 163
Evolution/human development see Engels; Marx
Existentialism (see also deBeauvoir; Sartre), 79, 95–96, 101, 103–104, 108 (n. 3), 122, 191, 249

F

Family see Marx; Women
Fanon, Frantz, 93, 163
Fascism, 8, 11, 86–87, 100, 128, 166, 167 (n. 8), 257, 260
Fedayeen (Iran), 65, 69 (n. 3)
Feminism see Luxemburg; Marx; Women
Fetishism of commodities see Marx
Feudalism (see also Serfdom), 10, 59, 193, 208, 264
Feuerbach, Ludwig, 116, 169–170
Firth, Raymond, 202–203, 204 (n. 12), 225 (n. 31), 232
Ford, Gerald, 127
Forest, F. see Dunayevskaya
Fourier, Charles, 211–212, 223 (n. 15, 16), 224 (n. 20)
Fowkes, Ben, 254
France (see also Revolution; Women; Paris Commune), 129, 179
  revolt of 1968, 47–48, 165
Freedom, 44, 65, 80, 92, 114, 116, 170, 234
Freedom Rides see Black Dimension
Freedom schools see Education
Freud, Sigmund, 87, 96, 104, 187, 242
Friedan, Betty, 3, 95, 160
Fromm, Erich, 192, 241–242
Frondizi, Silvio (see also Dunayevskaya),

Index

8, 163, 165–166, 167 (n. 8), 167–172
Fuller, Margaret, 98

G

Gafoor, Miriam, 55
Gale, Fay, 269
Gambia, 43–44
Gapon, Father, 68
Garrison, William Lloyd, 21, 35–38
Garvey, Amy Jacques, 50, 94
Garvey, Marcus, 50, 93–94
Gay liberation, 180
General strikes (see also Luxemburg (works); Miners), 48, 83–84, 135, 236, 252
Gdansk, Poland (1980), 136, 139
Gens (see also Engels, primitive communism; Marx, primitive communism), 214–215, 218–219, 225 (n. 27)
German Social Democratic Party (see also *Gleichheit*; Women), 4, 84, 236, 242
  World War I, support of, 57, 260
Germany (see also Communist Party; East Germany; Imperialism; Revolution), 59, 81, 129, 236, 255
Gleichheit (German working women's newspaper edited by Zetkin), 4, 85, 216, 262
Godwin, William, 97
Gorszczyk-Kecik, Marzena, 137
Gramsci, Antonio, 6, 163
Greece, Ancient, 198, 246
  literature, 20–21, 97, 231, 261
  philosophy, 170, 246, 263
  women in mythology, 20–21, 201, 261
Grundrisse see Marx (works)
Guatemala, 55
Guddat, Kurt, 192
Gueyras, Jean, 69 (n. 3)
Guerrilla war, 112–113, 117 (n. 4), 151, 164–165
Guettel, Charnie, 208, 223 (n. 6), 233
Guevara, Ché, 113, 167 (n. 6)
Guillermaz, Jacques, 154 (n. 5)
Guinea-Bissau, 86, 89 (n. 9), 132 (n. 1), 259

H

Halliday, Fred, 69 (n. 4)
Hamer, Fannie Lou, 106
Harding, Timothy F., 167 (n. 3)
Harlem Renaissance see Black Dimension
Hegel, Georg Wilhelm Friedrich (see also Absolute; Dialectic; Lenin (works) *Abstract of Hegel's Science of Logic*; Marx (works) *Economic-Philosophic Mss*; Subject), 6, 14, 20, 23, 27, 92, 98, 100, 116, 122, 170, 173, 238, 246
  Marx, relationship to, 10, 14, 53, 183, 186, 192, 195, 211, 239, 246, 248, 254, 263–265, 268, 271
  Self-determination of the Idea, 61, 263, 271
  "Self-Thinking Idea", 268, 271
Hegel, G.W.F. (works)
  Phenomenology of Mind, 100, 269
  Philosophy of Mind, 269
  Science of Logic, 10, 14
Hill, Robert, 50
History see Marx
Hobsbawm, Eric, 208, 222 (n. 4)
Hong Kong, 2, 8, 141–142, 144, 146, 158 (n. 4)
Horta, Maria Theresa, 89 (n. 8)
Howard, Dick, 89 (n. 6)
Hua Guofeng (Hua Kuo-feng), 149, 152–153, 155, 157 (n. 3)
Humanism (see also Marx; Marxist-Humanism), 164, 169–171
Humanist Essays see Marx (works) *Economic-Philosophic Mss*.
Hungary see Revolution

I

Ibsen, Henrik, 154 (n. 4)
Idealism/materialism, 27, 116, 170, 199, 211, 224 (n. 23), 268
Igbo Women's War see Women
Imperialism (see also Luxemburg; Marx, colonialism), 56, 122, 269
  anti-imperialist movements, 56, 66–67, 83, 218, 229
  British, 61, 68, 80, 94, 185, 201, 218–219, 258
  German, 56, 84, 236, 238
  Japanese, 123
  Portuguese, 55, 86, 128, 259–260
  Russian, 68, 86, 164, 166
  South African, 127
  United States, 66, 69, 112, 126, 164, 166, 167 (n. 8), 185
India, 185, 218
Individual(ism)/Universal(ism), 13–14, 19, 23, 28, 96, 101, 114, 116, 173, 184, 191, 214–215, 230, 252, 261, 264, 271
Indonesia, 55, 260
Internationals see International Working-

Internationals (*continued*)
men's Association; Second International
International Women's Day, 5, 9, 16 (n. 4), 19, 65, 82, 99, 135, 154 (n. 4), 179, 216, 234–235
International Women's Year, 91, 101, 161
International Women's Year Conference (1977), 8, 102, 159–161
International Workingmen's Association (First International), 82, 107, 170, 195, 198–199, 212, 215, 217, 224 (n. 19, 25)
Internationalism see Women
Iran see Revolution; Women
Ireland, 61, 196, 201, 219
Iroquois (see also Women), 12, 222
Islam see Women
Israel, 69 (n. 2)

J

Jackson, Anne Molly, 174
James, C.L.R., 31
Japan (see also Dunayevskaya; Imperialism; Women; Youth), 2, 7, 113
anti-war demonstrations (1960), 121, 125–126
Communist Party of, 7, 122, 125–126
Hiroshima, 122–123
New Left in, 7, 113, 121–126
Toyota, 124–125
Waseda University, 122
Jews, 216, 254
Jiang Qing (Chiang Ch'ing), 8, 149–157, 154 (n. 3), 157 (n. 2), 253
Jogiches, Leo, 85, 244, 253, 260–261
Johnson, Lyndon B., 47

K

Kanba, Michiko, 125
Kaplan, Marcos, 168–169
Kautsky, Karl, 4, 56, 83–84, 99, 213, 235–238, 240–241, 251, 254
Khomeini, Ayatollah Ruhollah, 65–66, 69, 69 (n. 3), 234–236
Khrushchev, Nikita, 73, 76, 77 (n. 1)
King, Coretta Scott, 159
King, Jr., Martin Luther, 51
Kissinger, Henry, 127, 155
Knights of Labor, 93
Komisar, Lucy, 161
Korean War, 75

Kowalewska, Krystyna, 138
Kovalevsky, Maxim, 189
Krader, Lawrence, 58, 189, 208, 222 (n. 1), 223 (n. 13), 224 (n. 22), 232
Kugelmann, Ludwig, 198, 211–212, 215
Ku Klux Klan, 93, 160
Kurdistan, 69

L

Labor (see also Black Dimension; Capital; General strike; Marx, alienated labor; Reason; Women workers)
child, 9, 25, 81, 194
class consciousness, 83–84, 96
class struggles (see also Women), 48, 81–82, 86–87, 92, 96, 107, 116, 121, 124, 157, 165, 191, 207
forced, 142–143
hierarchic structure of control over, 198
intellectuals and workers, 91, 122, 137, 169
machinery, domination by, 26, 194, 197–198
mental and manual, 1, 6–7, 25, 81, 87, 95–96, 102, 114, 116, 144, 183, 198, 201, 203, 217, 271
sexual division of, 211, 213, 217–218, 253
skilled and unskilled, 216
slavery, in, 35
social division of, 213, 217–218, 253
unemployed, 129
Lafargue, Paul, 202
Lamas, Marta, 163, 172–173
Landes, Joan, 109 (n. 6)
Lassalle, Ferdinand (and Lassaleans), 15, 255
Latin America (see also Argentina; Brazil; Chile; Cuba; Guatemala; Mexico; Peru; Uruguay; Women), 8, 163–174
dependency theory, and, 164–165, 167 (n. 3)
Law, Harriet, 82, 198, 212, 215
Lawrence, D.H., 87, 252
Leacock, Eleanor Burke, 208, 223 (n. 5, 6), 233
Lebanon, 69 (n. 1)
Lefebvre, Henri, 171
Lemlich, Clara, 93
Lenin, V.I. (see also Dialectic; Luxemburg), 13, 72, 83, 84, 99, 113, 116, 165, 169–170, 224 (n. 25), 228-229, 235, 238, 257

Index

organization, on, 96, 113, 132, 133 (n. 8), 247
self-determination of nations, on, 165
Lenin, V.I. (works)
Abstract of Hegel's Science of Logic, 14, 133 (n. 9), 167
Imperialism, 144
State and Revolution, 132, 144, 247
"Theses on the National and Colonial Question", 165
What is to be Done, 96, 113, 132, 249, 253
Lerner, Gerda, 104–106, 108
Lesbian and gay rights see Women
Lewis, Augusta, 93, 224 (n. 19)
Lewis, Flora, 156–157
Leys, Simon, 153, 154 (n. 6)
Liberation see Dialectic; Revolution; Self-determination; Women
Liberia, 36
Liebknecht, Karl, 57, 85, 99, 103
Lin Biao (Lin Piao), 151–152, 154–157
Lin Hsi-ling (Lin Xiling), 142
Literature see Greece, Ancient; Women
Little, Joan, 94
Locke, John, 169
Looker, Robert, 244
Lorde, Audre, 98
Lubbock, John, 12, 58, 61, 189, 221–222, 225 (n. 35), 231
Luczywo, Helena, 136
Luthuli, Chief Albert, 41
Luxemburg, Rosa (see also Dialectic; Women), 4, 26, 55–57, 71, 82–88, 95–96, 99, 173, 227, 234, 238, 242, 254–255, 257
  feminist dimension of, 56–57, 84–86, 88, 89 (n. 6), 173–174, 179, 227–230, 235–236, 238, 242, 244, 249, 252–253, 259–261
  German Revolution (1919), in, 56, 85, 103, 243–244, 251–252, 261
  imperialism, on, 56–57, 83–85, 89 (n. 5), 99, 236–238
  Lenin, and, 237, 247, 251
  Russian Revolution (1905), in, 56, 83–84, 99, 228–229, 234, 240, 260
  spontaneity and organization, on, 11, 56, 83–84, 96, 99, 230, 235–237, 247, 251, 259–261
Luxemburg, Rosa (works)
  Accumulation of Capital 83, 85, 89 (n. 5), 237–238, 239, 251, 269
  Crisis of the Social Democracy (Junius pamphlet), 252
  Mass Strike, the Party and the Trade Unions, 84, 236
  Reform or Revolution, 83
Lysistrata, 98

M

McDaniel, Robert A., 69 (n. 4)
Machinery see Labor
McKay, Claude, 93–94
McShane, Harry, 123
Mailer, Norman, 87
Maine, Sir Henry, 12, 58, 189, 219, 222, 225 (n. 27, 35), 231
Malaya, 113
Male-chauvinism, 1, 4, 6, 24, 28, 60, 87, 114, 150–151, 172–173, 236, 240, 244, 250, 262
Mamonova, Tatyana, 16 (n. 7), 250
Mandel, Ernest, 222 (n. 2)
Mandinkas, 43–44
Maoism, 69 (n. 3), 132, 154 (n. 4), 164, 172
Mao Zedong (Mao Tse-tung), 72, 76, 77 (n. 1), 112, 141, 144–147, 149–157, 154 (n. 2, 3, 4), 157 (n. 1, 3), 165, 235
Mao Zedong (works)
  "How to Handle Contradictions Among the People", 145–146
  "On Contradiction", 145–146
  "On the Ten Major Relationships", 149, 153, 154 (n. 2)
Marcuse, Herbert, 27, 191–192, 204 (n. 5), 249, 252
Martov, Yurii, 72
Marx, Eleanor, 216
Marx, Karl (see also Dialectic; Hegel; Reason; Subject; Women), 12, 98, 107, 113, 144, 203 (n. 1), 257
  accumulation of capital, on, 12, 59, 190, 199–201, 210, 239, 241, 251, 254, 264–265, 269
  alienated labor, on, 7, 10, 25, 28, 194
  archives of, 2, 16 (n. 9), 58–60, 191, 200, 207–210, 222, 222 (n. 1, 2, 3), 223 (n. 11, 13), 224 (n. 29, 30), 229, 239–240, 249, 255, 258, 265, 267, 270
  Asiatic mode of production, on, 10, 55, 59, 184–185, 193, 196, 203 (n. 2), 215, 218, 220–221, 223 (n. 13), 268
  Black Dimension, and, 61, 194–195, 202–203, 264, 268–269
  classical political economy, and, 170, 195–196

Marx, Karl (*continued*)
  colonialism, on, 201–202, 218
  critique, concept of, 10, 181, 193, 195–196, 265
  family, critique of, 9, 179–180, 192, 197, 210, 212–215, 218–220, 230
  fetishism of commodities, on, 25, 98, 187, 196, 254
  "history and its process", on, 23, 28, 28 (n. 1), 54, 59, 190, 194, 207, 215, 219–220, 224 (n. 23), 225 (n. 31, 33), 268
  human development, view of, 10, 12, 15, 58–60, 193, 196, 201, 202, 214–215, 218–219, 249, 258, 268
  humanism of (see also Marxist-Humanism), 2, 7, 10, 23–28, 53–54, 61, 81–82, 115, 122, 125, 147, 166, 169–170, 183–184, 190–192, 221, 242, 265
  last decade, "new moments" in, 13–14, 53–55, 57–61, 189–192, 200–203, 255, 270
  man/woman concept in, 7, 10–11, 23–26, 28 (n. 1), 53–55, 58, 81–82, 100, 104, 107–108, 126, 179–181, 183, 189–203, 204 (n. 6), 207–222, 223 (n. 14, 15), 224 (n. 16), 229–232, 240, 248–249, 252, 261, 265, 268
  organization and philosophy, on, 14–15, 16 (n. 5), 247, 251
  peasantry, on, 202, 246, 255, 264
  primitive communism, on, 28 (n. 1), 55, 57–59, 181, 189–190, 196–205, 213–215, 217–222, 225 (n. 33), 229, 231, 258, 268
  "revolution in permanence", on, (see also Organization), 6, 10, 54, 61, 181–182, 192–193, 203, 203 (n. 3), 221, 238, 247, 254–255, 265–266, 268, 270–271
  Russia, on, 12, 60, 190, 193, 199, 207, 220–221, 231, 240, 247, 264–265
  science, on, 15, 180, 194, 198–199, 215, 224 (n. 23)
  state, on the, 181, 193, 198, 213, 215, 218
  theory, break in the concept of, 170, 195–196, 224 (n. 18)
  "vulgar communism", on, 2, 24, 53–54, 183, 191, 265
  women workers, and, 81, 107, 194–195, 197–199, 212, 224 (n. 19)
Marx, Karl (works)
  Address to the Communist League (1850), 221, 238–239, 247
  Capital, Vol. I, 25, 59–60, 81, 95, 107, 115, 170, 187, 190, 192, 195–201, 202, 204 (n. 9), 207, 212, 221, 222 (n. 2), 224 (n. 23), 254, 264–265, 269
  Capital, Vols. II and III, 57, 195–196, 200, 213, 217, 225 (n. 29, 31)
  Civil War in France, 108 (n. 2)
  Communist Manifesto, 9, 59, 179, 184, 192, 212
  *Communist Manifesto, Introduction to the Russian Edition*₀(1882), 12, 59–60, 190, 221, 225 (n. 33), 238, 240, 255
  Contribution to the Critique of Political Economy, 10, 170, 195, 197
  Critique of the Gotha Program, 6, 14–15, 16 (n. 5), 181–182, 246, 255
  "Difference between the Democritean and Epicurean Philosophy of Nature" (Doctoral Thesis, 1841), 246, 254, 263
  Economic-Philosophic Mss. (1884 Essays), 2, 7, 10–12, 14–15, 25, 28 (n. 3), 61, 100, 104, 107, 115, 166–167, 170, 180, 183–184, 191–192, 202, 204 (n. 5), 207–208, 211–212, 220, 229, 241, 249, 252, 265, 267
  Ethnological Notebooks (1880–1882), 11–12, 58, 61, 189, 191–193, 196, 200–203, 208–210, 213–220, 222, 222 (n. 1, 4), 223 (n. 6, 14), 225 (n. 27, 35), 231–233, 239, 240, 243, 246–247, 253, 255, 258–259, 267–269
  German Ideology, 107, 166, 212, 218
  Grundrisse ("Economics"), 10–11, 16 (n. 9), 25, 28, 28 (n. 1), 59, 183–187, 192–193, 195–197, 200–201, 208, 221, 222 (n. 3, 4), 224 (n. 24), 231, 254, 265, 268–269
  Holy Family, The, 166, 224 (n. 16)
  Introduction to the Critique of Hegel's Philosophy of Right, 166
  Jewish Question, On the, 166, 247, 254
  "Kovalevsky, Notebooks on", 58, 189, 200, 223 (n. 13)
  Mathematical Manuscripts, 270
  "Mihailovsky, Answer to", 12, 59, 190, 199, 204 (n. 4)
  Theories of Surplus Value (*Capital*, Vol. IV), 195, 197
  "Theses on Feuerbach", 212
  "Zasulitch, Draft Letters to", 12, 58, 60, 71, 190, 207, 219–221, 225 (n. 29, 30, 32), 231, 255
Marx Centenary Year (1983), (see also Dunayevskaya), 2, 13, 53, 189, 201–202

Marxist-Humanism, development in the U.S. (see also Dunayevskaya; *News & Letters*; Wayne State University Archives; Women's Liberation-News and Letters Committees), 16 (n. 1), 24, 31, 89 (n. 5), 115, 123, 146–147, 167–171, 172–174, 186, 266, 269
Materialism see Idealism/materialism
Matriarchy, 34, 213, 216, 218, 223 (n. 6), 225 (n. 28), 233, 242, 258
Maupin, Joyce, 224 (n. 19)
Maxwell, Kenneth, 132 (n. 3)
Medecine, Beatrice, 202
Mehring, Franz, 253
Melville, Herman, 98, 173, 263–264
Mengistu, Haile Mariam, 164
Merleau-Ponty, Maurice, 126, 171
Mexico (see also Dunayevskaya; Women), 9, 163, 172–173
Michel, Louise, 82, 95, 103, 217, 252
Middle East War (1973), 128
Mihailovsky, N.K., 12, 199–200
Milewicz, Ewa, 139 (n. 3)
Millett, Kate, 67, 69 (n. 3), 96, 115
Milligan, Martin, 192
Miners (see also Dunayevskaya; Women), coal general strike (1949–1950), 1–2, 16 (n. 1), 29–30, 104, 169, 197
Poland, in, 135, 139 (n. 1)
South Africa, in, 39–40
Mir (Russian agricultural commune), 71
Mitchell, Juliet, 96–97, 187
Mondlane, Eduardo, 89 (n. 9), 132 (n. 1)
Mondolfo, Rudolfo, 170
Montgomery, Alabama Bus Boycott see Black Dimension
Moon, Terry, 139 (n. 2), 216
Morgan, Lewis Henry, 12, 55, 58, 189, 200–201, 207, 209–210, 214, 219–222, 223 (n. 6, 14), 225 (n. 29, 33, 35), 229, 231, 250, 258, 267–268
Moriarity, Claire, 26–27, 28 (n. 2)
Morocco, 56, 85, 235–236, 238
Moscow frame-up trials, 74–76
Mott, Lucretia, 22
Mozambique, 86, 89 (n. 9), 132 (n. 1), 259
Mullaney, Kate, 224 (n. 19)

N

Namibia, 56, 237
Narodniki (Russian populists), 220
National Black Feminist Organization, 60, 102
National Labor Union, 93, 224 (n. 19)
National liberation see Self-determination of nations
National Organization for Women (NOW), 24
Native Americans ("Indians") (see also Iroquois), 55, 61, 201–202, 253
"Negation of the negation" see Dialectic
Neto, Agostinho, 132 (n. 1)
Nettl, Peter, 99, 253
New Left see Japan; Women
News & Letters, 123, 139 (n. 4), 169
News and Letters Committees, 168–171, 172
Nigeria (see also Women, Igbo), 50, 80
Nixon, Richard, 152, 155
Norway, 74
Noske, Gustav, 251
Notion see Dialectic
Nuclear power, 180
Nuclear war, threat of, 9, 11, 15, 88, 122–123, 193

O

Object see Dialectic; Women
O'Neill, Eugene, 21
Oreseia, 20–21, 97
Origin of the Family see Engels (works)
Organization (see also International Workingmen's Association; Lenin; Luxemburg; Marx; Soviets), 3, 108, 136, 253
apartidarismo ("non-partyism"), 8, 15, 131
autonomous organizations of women, 3–4, 6–7, 88, 107, 114, 129, 216
committee-form of, 270–271
decentralized forms of, 6, 114–115, 249
"horizontal solidarity" (Poland), 136
leadership in, 112, 237
military foco form of, 112–113, 116, 165, 167 (n. 6)
"organizing Idea", 6, 249, 253
philosophy, and, 6, 9, 11, 169, 237, 270–271
"revolution in permanence" as ground for, 6–7, 16 (n. 5), 250, 254–255, 271
spontaneity, and, (see also Luxemburg), 11, 56, 67, 88, 91, 128, 131, 133 (n. 8), 230, 236, 247, 251, 259, 261
"vanguard party" form of, 4, 56, 88, 96–97, 112, 115, 123, 126, 132, 133 (n. 8), 247, 259, 270
"Other" see Women

P

Padover, Saul, 204 (n. 6, 11)
Paine, Tom, 97
Pakistan, 155
Palestine Liberation Organization (PLO), 65, 69 (n. 1)
Palestinian resistance, 165
P'an Tzu-nien (Pan Zinian), 145
Pan-Africanist Congress see South Africa
Paris Commune see Revolution, France; Women
Parks, Rosa, 51, 92, 94, 106
Patriarchy, 87, 151, 210, 213, 218–219, 242, 258
Peasantry (see also Agriculture; Marx), 67, 85, 112, 117 (n. 4), 157, 202, 203 (n. 3), 216, 246, 264, 270
 China, in, 157, 185
 Poland, in, 137
 Portuguese Revolution, in, 87, 128–131
 proletariat, relationship to, 128, 165, 255, 264
 women in, 129–130, 137
Pelikan, Jiri, 111
Pelz, William, 89 (n. 7)
Penthesilea, 57, 229, 252, 260–261
Pereira, Carmen, 132 (n. 1)
Permanent Revolution see Marx, "revolution in permanence"; Trotsky
Peron, Isabel, 167 (n. 8)
Peron, Juan, 166, 167 (n. 8)
Peru, 9, 163, 173–174
Phear, John, 58, 189, 222, 225 (n. 35), 231
Philippines, 113
Phillips, Andy, 16 (n. 1), 27
Phillips, Wendell, 35–38
Philosophy (see also Absolute; Dialectic; Marx; Organization; Theory),
 revolution, relation to, 6, 89, 100–101, 116–117, 126, 147, 165–166, 187, 228, 237, 258, 265, 270
Pienkowska, Alina, 135–136, 139
Pierce, Christine, 108 (n. 3)
Plekhanov, Georg, 7, 72, 190, 244, 257
Plutarch, 214
Poland (see also Peasantry; Women), 8, 55–56, 240, 249–251, 257, 265
 KOR (Committee to Defend Workers), 136–137, 139 (n. 3)
 rebellion (1956), 2
 Solidarnosc, 8, 55, 135–139
 Warsaw uprisings (1943, 1944), 257
 uprising of 1863, 195, 253, 262
Portugal (see also Africa; Imperialism; Peasantry; Revolution; Women), 8, 86
Post-Marx Marxism (see also Marx, archives), 7, 9, 11–12, 57, 61, 190, 195, 203, 248–249, 259, 262, 267, 270–271
Practice, movement from as form of theory (see also Theory), 1–2, 60, 80, 91, 100, 104, 116, 265
Preston (England) strike, 194
Primitive communism see Engels; Marx
Production see Automation; Capital; Marx, accumulation
Proletariat see Autoworkers; Labor; Miners; Peasantry; Reason; Shipyard workers; Women workers
Property, "career of", 210, 214
 communal, 196, 207, 210, 214–215, 220–221, 268
 form of, 23, 53–54, 196, 268
 private, 10, 23–24, 53–54, 183, 192, 207, 210–211, 213–215, 220–221, 252
 state, 116, 207, 210, 215
Pushkin, Alexander, 19
Putnam, James J., 242

R

Reason, Black masses as, 26, 80, 262
 forces of revolution as, 3, 53, 60, 221, 269–271
 Marx, in, 106, 196, 221
 women as, 5, 8, 15, 45, 80, 82, 108, 136, 139 (n. 2), 161, 172–174, 186–187, 217, 249
 workers as, 92, 136, 171, 264
Reed, Evelyn, 223 (n. 6), 233–234
Reformism (revisionism), 83, 112, 145, 238, 255
Religion and revolution, 68, 138, 237, 254
 women, and, 66, 130, 137–138, 160–161, 179, 185, 235
Retrogressionism, 122, 146–147, 154
Reuther, Walter, 124
Revolution (see also Dialectics; Marx, "revolution in permanence"; Philosophy; Women),
 African, 39–44, 132 (n. 1), 167 (n. 5)
 Afro-Asian, 2, 80, 164, 167–168
 China (see also Women), Taiping Revolution (1850s), 93, 185, 193, 203, 215, 221, 224 (n. 24), 254, 268

Index

China (1949), 22, 117 (n. 4), 141–147, 208
Cuba (1959) (see also Women), 4, 22, 111–113, 164–165
France (1789), 97, 100, 170
France (1848) (see also Women), 81, 92, 116, 170, 184, 221, 238, 252
France (Paris Commune of 1871) (see also Women), 25, 58, 79, 82, 95, 116, 170, 193, 203, 216, 221, 240, 243, 265
Germany (1919) (see also Luxemburg; Women), 56–57, 79, 82, 85, 99, 243–245, 251–252
Hungary (1956), 2, 47, 76, 122, 142, 171, 208
Iran (1906–11) (see also Women), 4–5, 56, 67–69, 69 (n. 4), 238
Iran (1979) (see also Women), 4, 65–70, 234–236
Portugal (1974) (see also Africa; Women), 8, 79, 86–88, 89 (n. 9), 99–100, 127–134, 259–260
Russia (1905) (see also Luxemburg), 4, 7, 56, 67–68, 69 (n. 4), 228–229, 234, 238
Russia (1917) (see also Women), 5, 7, 22, 71, 79, 82–83, 85, 99, 113, 191, 208, 235, 243–245
Spain (1936–39), 96
United States (1776), 92, 97, 170
world, 22, 113, 221, 251, 265
"Revolution in permanence" see Marx; Organization
Richardson, Gloria, 94, 106
Robotics see Automation
Roman law, 263
Rousseau, Jean-Jacques, 170
Rowbotham, Sheila, 82, 87–88, 96–97, 106–108, 208–209, 223 (n. 7), 249, 253
Russia (see also China; Imperialism; Marx; Revolution; Women), 71, 164
Communist Party of, 142
Decembrist revolt (1825), 19
de-Stalinization, 73, 76
state-capitalist society, as, 1, 7, 31, 57, 72, 75–76, 111, 113, 146, 208, 210
Vorkuta labor camp revolt (1953), 19
Russian Social Democratic Labor Party (RSDLP), Congress of 1907, 234, 255
Russo-Japanese War, 7
Ryazanov, David, 191, 200, 209, 223 (n. 11), 255, 267

S

Saquic, Manuela, 55
Sartre, Jean-Paul, 13, 21, 95, 101, 108 (n. 3), 122, 171
Savio, Mario, 48
Schneiderman, Rose, 93
Schram, Stuart, 154 (n. 3)
Schumpeter, Joseph, 196, 202
Science see Marx
Scotland, 123
Second International, 7, 84, 170, 191, 208, 235
World War I, support of, 14, 170
Sedoff, Leon, 73–74, 77 (n. 3)
Segal, Robert M., 41
Self-determination of the Idea see Hegel
Self-determination of nations, struggle for (see also Lenin; Marx, colonialism), 2, 129, 240–241, 251, 257, 263, 269
Sen Katayama, 7
Self-thinking Idea see Hegel
Serfdom, 213, 218, 230
Sexism see Male chauvinism
Shah of Iran (Reza Pahlavi), 65–66, 68–69
Shakespeare, William, 21, 98, 227–228
Shipyard workers, 123
Shuster, W. Morgan, 67–68, 69 (n. 4)
Sino-Soviet conflict see China
Slavery (see also Anti-slavery), 10, 25, 35–38, 44, 54, 59, 193, 213, 218, 230, 269
Sobukwe, Robert Mangaliso, 41
Socialist-feminism see Women
Socialist Workers Party (U.S.), 34–35, 75, 77 (n. 1)
Social Revolutionary Party (Russia), 5, 82
Soldiers councils, 85, 127–128, 131, 251–252
Solidarnosc see Poland; Women
South Africa (Azania) (see also Imperialism; Women), 2, 39–41, 55, 127, 152, 166
African National Congress, 41
anti-apartheid movement in, 39–41, 55, 166
bus boycotts in, 40
Pan Africanist Congress, 41
workers' actions, 39–41
Soviets/Workers' councils (see also Anjumans), 85, 99, 131–132, 251–252
Hungary, in, 47
Russian Revolution (1905), in, 7, 67

Soviets/Worker's Councils (*continued*)
women, of, 15, 56, 235
Spain see Revolution
Spartacists (Germany, 1919), 56–57, 85, 243–244, 251–252
Spector, Ivar, 69 (n. 4)
Spinola, Gen. Antonio de, 87, 128
Spontaneity and organization see Luxemburg; Organization
Stalin, Josef, 57, 73–76, 83, 144–145, 149, 165, 180–181, 235, 255
Stanton, Elizabeth Cady, 16 (n. 2)
State see Lenin (works), *State and Revolution*; Marx
State-capitalism (see also China; Marx, "vulgar communism"; Marxist-Humanism; Russia), 2, 47, 72, 88, 123, 166, 169–170, 210
State-capitalist tendency, 31
Stewart, Maria, 252, 262
Stone, Lucy, 46
Stowe, Harriet Beecher, 38
Strauss, Franz Joseph, 152, 156
Structuralism, 96–97
Students for a Democratic Society (SDS), 48
Subject, in Hegel, 6, 14, 184, 269
Marx, in, 184–185, 215, 264, 268–269
Subjectivity/objectivity see Dialectic
Suffrage movements see Women
Sue, Eugène, 224 (n. 16)

T

Taiping Rebellion see Revolution, China
Terrano, Angela, 92
Theory (see also Marx; Philosophy; Practice; Women),
philosophy, relation to, 13, 60–61, 95, 169, 228, 230, 269–270
practice, relation to, 5–6, 13, 60, 91, 95, 100, 102, 113, 117, 131, 185–186, 254, 265, 270
Theseus, 214
Thiers, M., 79
Third World (see also "Backward lands"; Women), 2, 61, 104, 191, 270
USA, within, 8, 157, 163
"Third World-ism", 164–165
Third World Women's Conference (1983), 2, 53, 201
Thomas, Edith, 89 (n. 1), 108 (n. 2), 199, 216–217, 224 (n. 26)
Three Marias, The (New Portuguese Letters), 8, 86, 89 (n. 8), 98, 100, 130, 132 (n. 4)
Time, 93, 252, 264
Tito, Marshall, 75
Toguchi, Masahi, 124
Totality see Dialectic
Transcendence see Dialectic
Triangle Shirtwaist, 93, 235
Tribe/tribalism, 51, 80, 218
Tristan, Flora, 81, 92, 95, 103, 107, 224 (n. 16)
Trotha, Gen. von, 56
Trotsky, Leon (see also Dunayevskaya), 5, 72–75, 84, 171, 228–229, 238, 257
permanent revolution, theory of, 7, 181, 203 (n. 3), 238, 255
Trotsky, Natalia, 5, 71–77, 77 (n. 1, 2)
Trotskyism, 126 (n. 1), 131, 132 (n. 2), 133 (n. 6), 165, 168, 171–172, 243
U.S., in, 31–35, 73, 75, 77 (n. 1)
Truth, Sojourner, 21, 45, 49–50, 54, 80–81, 93–94, 105–106, 185, 252
Tsarism, 5, 19, 68, 71–73, 83, 88, 195, 234
Tubman, Harriet, 21, 49, 80, 93–94, 105, 252
Turner, Lou, 50
Turner, Nat, 93, 252, 262

U

Underground Railroad, 21, 49, 93
Unemployed see Labor
Union des femmes pour la défense de Paris, 82, 95, 103, 199
United States see Anti-slavery; Black Dimension; Imperialism; Marxist-Humanism; Revolution; Women
Universal see Individual/Universal
Uruguay, 167 (n. 8)

V

Value, law of (see also Dunayevskaya), 75, 77 (n. 4), 186
Value, surplus, 214
"Vanguard party" see Organization
Verwoerd, Henrik, 40
Vietnam War (see also Anti-war movements), 112, 117 (n. 4)
Vitkin, Mikhail, 203 (n. 2)

W

Walentynowicz, Anna, 55, 135–136, 139 (n. 2)

Index

Washington, Booker T., 94
Waters, Mary-Alice, 89 (n. 4), 243–245
Wayne State University Archives of Labor and Urban Affairs (Raya Dunayevskaya Collection), 31, 266
Weaver, Frederick, 167 (n. 3)
Welfare rights see Women
Wells, Ida B., 94
Werden, Eugenio, 168
Wilde, Oscar, 180
Wislanka, Urszula, 135–139
Witke, Roxane, 8, 149–154, 154 (n. 8), 158 (n. 3)
Wollstonecraft, Mary, 92, 97, 100
Women/Women's liberation (see also Black women; Engels; Greece; International Women's Day; Marx; Organization; Peasantry; Reason; Religion),
  abortion rights, 23, 102, 114, 128, 138, 160–161, 234
  African Revolutions, in, 43–44, 50, 80, 132 (n. 1)
  anti-slavery movement, in, 21–23, 33, 37–38, 45, 93, 105, 185
  anti-war movements, in, 7, 56, 98, 216, 229, 252, 260–261
  Black Dimension and women's liberation, 2–4, 21–22, 33, 37–38, 45–47, 49–51, 60, 80, 93–95, 105–106, 185–187
  children, and, 33, 37, 40, 81, 180–181, 204 (n. 6), 212, 214
  Chinese Revolution, and, 8, 141–147, 149–157, 181
  class struggle, relation to, 3–4, 82–83, 115, 128–129, 138, 265
  Cuban Revolution, and, 4, 51, 95, 111
  Equal Rights Amendment (ERA), and, 102, 161, 230
  family, critique of (see also Marx), 32, 113, 130, 154 (n. 4), 179–182
  French Revolution (1848), in, 81
  German Revolution (1919), in, 85, 89 (n. 7), 99
  German Social Democratic Party, in, 4, 85
  Igbo Women's War (1929), 50–51, 79–80, 94, 253, 262
  internationalism of, 8, 67, 69 (n. 3), 130, 132 (n. 4), 252
  Iranian Revolution (1906–11), in, 5, 15, 56, 67–69, 69 (n. 4), 235
  Iranian Revolution (1979), in, 19, 66–67, 69, 69 (n. 3), 102, 161, 234–236, 253
  Iroquois, 1, 55, 190, 201–202, 209, 214, 223 (n. 14), 229, 262
  Islamic world, in, 66–67, 235, 253
  Japanese New Left, in, 7, 125–126
  Latin America, in, 9, 19, 102, 172–174
  Left, and the, 1, 26, 31–35, 69 (n. 3), 71–77, 100, 128–130, 151, 154 (n. 4), 262
  lesbian and gay rights, 160, 180
  literature, and, 20–21, 97–98, 103, 130, 227–228
  Luxemburg, Rosa, attitude to, 11, 85–86, 88, 99, 173–174, 227, 234, 244, 250, 259, 260–261
  Marx, Karl, attitude to, 12, 60, 82, 105–108, 109 (n. 6), 174, 209, 223 (n. 6), 233–234
  miners' wives, 1–2, 29–30
  minority women in U.S., 102, 114, 159–160
  New Left, origins of Women's liberation in, and critique of, 3, 11, 26, 47–48, 60, 102, 106, 108, 114–115, 172–173, 185–186, 262
  newspapers and journals, 1, 4, 81, 85, 102, 138,
  objects, as, 20, 103, 113
  "Other", as, 103–105, 249
  Paris Commune (1871), in, 5, 58, 79, 82, 89 (n. 1), 95, 103–104, 107, 108 (n. 2), 199, 216–217, 224 (n. 26), 234
  personal/political questions, and, 4, 6, 23, 31–32, 34, 86, 97, 114, 138, 154, 172–173
  Portuguese Revolution, in, 8, 15, 86–87, 89 (n. 8), 99–100, 102, 128–130, 132 (n. 2)
  post-World War II world, in, 1, 31–35, 95, 104, 186
  pre-capitalist society, in, 1, 25, 190, 201–202, 209, 213–215, 217–219, 221, 223 (n. 6), 224 (n. 20), 233–234, 249, 261
  social revolution, women's liberation's relation to, 3, 5, 8, 15, 83, 85–87, 115, 166, 172, 227–230, 250
  Russia today, in, 16 (n. 7), 102, 250
  Russian Revolution (1917), in, 5, 15, 71, 82–83, 95–96, 99, 180–181, 234
  socialist-feminism, 102, 107, 109 (n. 6), 151, 173, 222, 250
  Solidarnosc (Poland), in, 8, 55, 135–139
  South African resistance, in, 2, 41, 55
  suffrage movements, 1, 21, 45–46, 49–50, 81, 101, 228–229, 261

Women/Women's Liberation (*continued*)
theorists, today's Women's liberation, 46, 86–88, 95–97, 99–108, 186–187, 208–209, 223 (n. 6), 226, 249
Third World, in, 4, 53, 202
today's Women's liberation movement, 1, 3–5, 7, 19, 22–24, 101, 159, 173–174, 191, 208–209, 211, 216, 253, 259, 262
welfare rights groups, 102, 115
Women's Liberation — News and Letters Committees, 24, 141, 161, 174, 245
Women's Rights Conventions, 21, 54, 79–82, 92, 107
Women's Studies, 102
Women workers (see also International Women's Day; Marx), 2–5, 23–24, 31–35, 46, 81–82, 85–88, 89 (n. 7), 92–93, 104, 106–107, 115, 129, 181, 186, 194–195, 197–198, 212, 216, 224 (n. 19), 250, 261
health/hospital, 24, 130, 136
telephone, 32, 102
textile/garment, 82–83, 86, 92, 99, 102, 128–130, 136, 138, 153, 235
tobacco, 94
World War II, during, 31–33
Woolf, Virginia, 97
Workers see Labor
Workers Party (U.S.), 33–34
Working day, struggles to shorten, 86, 95, 170, 196, 212, 224 (n. 18)
World War I, 82, 99, 216, 224 (n. 25)
World War II, 31–32, 198

Woyicka, Irena, 136
WRAP (Women's Radical Action Project), 7, 19, 24, 125
Wright, Doris, 51, 94–95
Wujec, Ludwika, 136
Wu Kuei-hsien (Wu Gueixian), 153
Wurm, Mathilde, 57, 229

Y

Youth, 2–3, 46–48, 55, 61, 86, 111, 128–129, 130, 143, 263, 270
anti-draft resistance of, 86, 129
China, in 143–145, 147, 157
Japan, in, 121–126
Yugoslavia, 189
Yu Shuet, 16 (n. 8)

Z

Zasulitch, Vera, 58, 71–72, 190, 220, 225 (n. 32)
Zengakuren, 7, 125–126
Zeng Hangzhou (Teng Hang-chou), 155
Zenshin, 121, 123, 126 (n. 1)
Zetkin, Clara, 4, 85, 215–216, 229, 235, 249
Zhang Linzhi (Chang Lin-chih), 156
Zhenotdel (Working and Peasant Women's Department of Bolshevik Party), 180–181